OUTDOOR ADVENTURE PURSUITS:

FOUNDATIONS, MODELS, AND THEORIES

OUTDOOR ADVENTURE PURSUITS:

FOUNDATIONS, MODELS, AND THEORIES

ALAN W. EWERT
Research Social Scientist
USDA FOREST SERVICE

Publishing Horizons, Inc.
Scottsdale, Arizona

An affiliate of Gorsuch Scarisbrick, Publishers
8233 Via Paseo del Norte, Suite F-400
Scottsdale, Arizona 85258

Printed in the United States

3 4 8 7 6 5

LIBRARY OF CONGRESS
Library of Congress Cataloging-in-Publication Data

Ewert, Alan W., 1949–
Outdoor adventure pursuits: foundations, models, and theories/
Alan W. Ewert.
p. cm.
Bibliography: p.
Includes index.
ISBN 0-942280-50-4
1. Outdoor recreation. 2. Outward bound schools. I. Title.
GV191.6.E85 1989 88-23651
370.11'07'11–dc19 CIP

CONTENTS

PREFACE

This book is an outgrowth of three classes I have taught at Ohio State University and my experience as an Outward Bound instructor since 1977. The three classes taught were the "Foundations of Outdoor Adventure," "Models and Theories in Outdoor Pursuits," and "Research Methods and Findings in Outdoor Pursuits." My practical experience, coupled with the academic orientation of the university setting, seemed well suited to more formally describe the processes and foundations of the outdoor adventure pursuits profession. The profession has grown from one of school camps and Boy Scouts to one of a multifaceted industry with offerings in adventure travel, personal growth, and group development.

The goal of this book is to provide a source of information that can be used by a variety of people with differing levels of expertise in the outdoor adventure pursuits field, from both academic and practitioner communities. This book is designed to provide a more scholarly approach to a field in which, heretofore, there has been relatively little formalized writing. Consequently, its orientation is highly theoretical and research-based. Numerous references and citations have been included, presenting a thorough scholarship of information and conceptual thought. It is hoped that the researcher, practitioner, and academic person in outdoor adventure pursuits will find this book a useful asset in his or her present endeavors. It is also expected that the readers will use the concepts and theories presented as a basis to further expand their own beliefs and ideas based on their personal experiences and training. Moreover, the book will have served its purpose if the researcher or graduate student gains new ideas for future research or conduct from its contents.

The time has come for the profession of outdoor adventure pursuits to assume a more formal and clearly delineated role in the education and recreation of our society. Outdoor adventure pursuits are not activities solely for the daredevil but, rather, they are legitimate educational and leisure pursuits in which a broad spectrum of people can participate. While not just an end in themselves, outdoor adventure pursuits can be powerful agents of individual and social change. It is toward this end that the book, *Outdoor Adventure Pursuits: Foundations, Models, and Theories,* has been written in order to better understand the outdoor adventure pursuits phenomenon.

Alan Ewert, Ph.D
1988

ACKNOWLEDGMENTS

Writing a book on any subject is both a privilege and a great challenge. This is particularly true with a topic such as outdoor adventure pursuits. This is true, in part, because of the "newness" of the field and the relative lack of other literary guidelines. On the other hand, this lack of precedent has also led to a sense of greater freedom and liberty. Rather oddly, I wish to first acknowledge my appreciation at having this relative freedom and feel it reflects the openess and lack of dogmatism that this field has avoided so far.

Two institutional settings have contributed to the conceptualization and formation of this book. First, the Ohio State University has provided the resources, time, and encouragement to follow through with this project. Second, Outward Bound has afforded me the opportunity to observe, learn, and experience the unique world of the outdoor adventure instructor. Both the academic and experiential settings have greatly contributed to my sense of having something to say.

From a personal perspective there have been many people "involved" in the writing of this book. For their professional help and encouragement, my thanks to Dr. Charles Mand (Ohio State University), Victor Walsh (Pacific Crest Outward Bound), and Nils Anderson (Publishing Horizons).

In addition, I would like to thank Dr. Dan Dustin (San Diego State University) and Dr. Steve Hollenhorst (West Virginia University), both of whom kindly consented to review the initial drafts of the manuscript. In addition, Steve helped me keep a semblance of sanity by continuing to lead the crux pitches while I belayed the rope during our climbing adventures.

I am especially grateful to my wife, Alison, for she not only acted as editor and reviewer but also was one I could turn to for bouncing ideas off of and providing the personal encouragement that only a person you love can.

DEDICATION

This book is about outdoor adventure pursuits. It would seem fitting that it should be dedicated to individuals who in some way are or have been involved in the promotion of those peculiar types of activities. With this in mind I've dedicated the book to three groups.

First, to my parents, Walter and Florence, for providing an upbringing that led to a love of the outdoor environment. This love was translated into hunting and fishing trips and adventurous expeditions up the Eau Claire river in a rowboat.

Second, I would like to dedicate this book to my friend and fellow adventurer, Dr. James Black. Jim lived his life as an adventure and shared his vision of adventure and its meaning in contemporary life to many of us—his past friends and students. Jim was killed in September of 1986 and I lost a good friend and outdoor adventure pursuits lost an articulate doer and supporter of adventure-based living. Here's to you, Jim!

Finally, no book on outdoor adventuring would be complete without an acknowledgment of the wondrous work done by the outdoor instructor. So, I'd also like to dedicate this book to all the outdoor instructors who, despite rain, cold, loneliness, and irate students, manage to pull off high-quality and safe courses that provide our society with powerful and positive learning experiences.

Alan W. Ewert
April 1988

FOREWORD

What is it that best describes a civilized society? In the United States, a concern for the health and safety of the citizenry is certainly near the top of the list. Since the Great Depression of the 1930's, good government has been equated with the protection of individuals from a whole host of catastrophic events. This "insurance mentality," as author George Leonard describes it, has contributed to numerous laws and lawsuits designed to immunize the American public from the sting of life's hard blows. Accordingly, the good life has come to be interpreted more and more as the safe life, the comfortable life, the predictable life.

How strange, then, that in the midst of this cultural climate there should appear a heightened interest in the deliberate pursuit of danger, discomfort, and unpredictability in the form of outdoor adventure pursuits. What is it about outdoor adventurers that accounts for their "swimming against the tide" of our societal preoccupation with safety? What is it about their psychological makeup that doesn't set well with the trend toward a more stable and secure way of living? What needs of theirs are going unmet? What motivates them? What are the rewards of their involvement?

In this book, Alan Ewert draws on his wealth of personal and professional experience in the field of outdoor adventure pursuits, his research on the topic, and his interpretation of others' research, to give us a better understanding of the outdoor adventurer. Such understanding is critical not only for those who are responsible for planning outdoor recreation opportunities, but also for those who desire to know what it is about the larger culture that outdoor adventurers find so unappealing.

In the novel *Nineteen Eighty-Four,* George Orwell predicted the failure of a society characterized by warmth, comfort, and the absence of strain. That society would fail because however appetizing on the surface, once bitten into it would be inherently distasteful to a human being. Could it be that the increasing popularity of outdoor adventure pursuits is evidence of Orwell's contention? Could it be that sanctioning opportunities for risk-taking and adventure is also the mark of a civilized society?

Daniel L. Dustin, Professor
Department of Recreation
San Diego State University

ABOUT THE AUTHOR

Alan Ewert currently holds a position with the U.S. Forest Service as a Supervisory Research Social Scientist. He is also an Adjunct Professor at Ohio State University where he teaches courses in Models and Theories in Outdoor Pursuits, Research and Evaluation in Outdoor Pursuits, and Outdoor Pursuits: Issues and Foundations. Dr. Ewert received his Ph.D. from the University of Oregon and has worked as a mountaineering ranger and resource management specialist for the U.S. Park Service. Most recently, he was the Director of Professional Development for Pacific Crest Outward Bound where he still acts as a staff trainer and course facilitator.

In addition to his professional interests in outdoor pursuits and outdoor recreation issues, Dr. Ewert is involved in mountaineering, rock climbing, spelunking, backcountry skiing, SCUBA, ice climbing, and sea-kayaking. These interests have included both personal involvement and instructing. He has been fortunate to participate in outdoor adventures in North America, Canada, Alaska, Mexico, South America, Nepal, and Tibet.

He has published in a number of journals including the journals of *Leisure Research, Environmental Education, Experiential Education, Response, Camping Magazine, Forestry, Underseas Journal, Adventure Journal,* and *Leisure Sciences.* He is also a member of the American Alpine Club, American Mountain Guides Association, Sierra Club, and International Wilderness Institute.

1

OUTDOOR ADVENTURE PURSUITS: AN INTRODUCTION

In 1906, an advertisement appeared in the London Times:

> Men wanted for hazardous journey. Small wages, bitter cold, long months of complete darkness, constant danger, safe return doubtful. Honor and recognition in case of success.

What is extraordinary about this announcement is not that it reads like an assumption of risk form, but rather that over 5,000 people applied for the 30 positions available. Seventy-eight years later, in 1984, another ad appeared in the Los Angeles Times announcing the search for one woman to learn and participate in a SCUBA diving expedition. The advertisement read:

> **WANTED: A YEAR OF YOUR LIFE FOR THE ADVENTURE OF YOUR LIFE

Once again thousands of people applied. Honor and recognition not withstanding, the underlying thread linking these two seemingly unrelated incidents is the quest for ADVENTURE. This search has carried over into educational and recreational delivery systems. Adventure activities such as backpacking, mountain-climbing, white-water rafting, and SCUBA are becoming increasingly popular forms of human endeavor. Support systems, such as adventure centers, training programs, and certification schemes, have developed around these activities. This chapter discusses outdoor adventure from the perspective of definitions, the nature of the adventure experience, and how it relates to other areas and disciplines.

SCUBA has become an increasingly popular outdoor adventure pursuit for millions of people.

OUTDOOR ADVENTURE

In contemporary society, the term *outdoor adventure* generally implies an educational or recreational activity that is exciting and physically challenging. It was the Chinese, however, who first successfully encapsulated the true essence of adventuring by their term "**wei-jan**." Translated as opportunity through danger, wei-jan incorporates many of the reasons for participating in the outdoor adventure. Outdoor adventure affords the participant the opportunity to experience the excitement and personal involvement in an outdoor setting which is often lacking in our traditional recreational or educational systems.

Various terms have been used to describe the outdoor adventure experience. These terms include: adventure recreation, high adventure, natural challenge activities, outdoor pursuits, and risk recreation. Several definitions have evolved to describe this form of activity:

- Any number of leisure pursuits which provide exposure to physical danger. (Meier, 1978, p. 33)
- All pursuits that provide an inherently meaningful human experience that relates directly to a particular outdoor environment—air, water, hills, mountains, . . . (Darst and Armstrong, 1980, p. 3)
- Activities which involve human participation as a response to the challenge offered primarily by the physical, natural world such as

hills, air currents, and waves. (Progen, 1979, p. 237)

- Outdoor activities involving the natural environment where the outcome perceived by the participants is unknown. (Yerkes, 1985)

In defining outdoor adventure pursuits, a number of components must be considered. First and most obvious, outdoor adventure pursuits involve an interaction with the natural environment. Second, this interaction requires an element of risk to which the participant is exposed by engaging in the activity. This risk can be physical, emotional, or material, but is usually associated with the possibility of being injured or even killed. This deliberate inclusion of risk in a recreational or educational framework helps distinguish outdoor adventure pursuits from more traditional outdoor recreation and/or outdoor education activities.

ADVENTURE AND RISK TAKING

Although some may view the deliberate seeking of risk as dangerous and foolhardy, risk taking is the sine qua non of the adventure experience. As Miles (1978) suggests, one cannot enjoy the view without the risk of passage. Past studies have indicated that climbers actively maintain a level of uncertainty by changing the "rules of engagement" (how a particular mountain or rock can be climbed) or the level of difficulty and danger (Emerson, 1966). For example, an experienced climber may climb in the winter or alone in order to increase the difficulty and danger to desired levels.

This is not, however, risk dictated solely by chance or fate. The outcome, while uncertain and not completely controllable, can be influenced by the participant. Risk, or the threat of physical and/or emotional harm, emerges when there is a loss of control or predictability. Control becomes an important factor in distinguishing between something that is difficult and something that is foolhardy.

> No true mountaineer ever courted danger for its own sake. The whole point of any sport is that it demands the acquisition of a special skill which cancels the danger. It was the mountaineer's justification that he climb by routes where his skill in mountaincraft, supported by courage and resolution of no mean order, made him competent to ascend and descend safely. (Stowell, 1967, p. 12)

This factor of control was more recently supported in a study by Ewert (1985) on climbers at Mt. Rainier. The climbers indicated that opportunity to express control over their lives and their immediate situation was an important motivation for climbing. This sense of control became even more important as the individual climber gained experience and expertise. Houston (1968) states that "experienced climbers understand, enjoy, and seek risk because it presents a difficulty to overcome

Mountaineering, like most outdoor adventure pursuits, demands both physical and technical skills.

and can be estimated and controlled. He equally abhors danger because it is beyond his control" (p. 56).

A permutation on this theme of danger is the differentiation between real and apparent risk. Mortlock (1983), an early advocate of this distinction, posits that, while real risk is common to the recreational outcome of outdoor adventure pursuits, apparent risk is more often used in educational or structured classes of outdoor adventuring activities. *Real risk* is that which actually exposes the participant to the possibility, even probability, of being hurt or having a close call. *Apparent risk* refers to the "illusion" of danger or the possibility of being injured. Outdoor instructors are usually encouraged to promote activities, such as top-roped rock climbing, that have a substantial degree of apparent risk but a low degree of real risk.

As previously stated, risk, or the threat of physical and emotional harm, emerges when there is a loss of control over the outcome of a particular activity. Within the outdoor environment, this loss of control can be aggravated by personal weakness, poor or incorrect decision making, and unforeseen circumstances. Conversely, personal abilities, correct decision making, and technology can serve to create a heightened sense of control. Figure 1.1 illustrates the interaction of these and other components in the outcome of an adventure experience.

For educational purposes this [adventure] is the most important stage

FIGURE 1.1
Influencing Factors on the Outcome of a Risk Activity

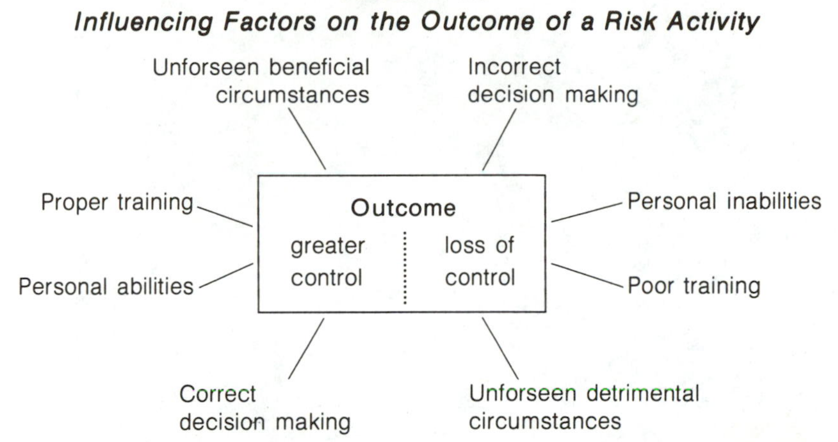

in the activity. Its validity is acceptable only if there is virtually no real danger for most pupils. As adventure is a state of mind it is possible for a pupil to experience adventure in an environment of apparent rather than real danger. As long as he feels the situation is dangerous, in the sense that a mistake or lack of effort on his part could lead to some sort of physical harm or unpleasant situation, then he may experience adventure in the fullest sense of the word (Mortlock, 1978).

Supporting the concept of real versus apparent danger can be demonstrated by the ropes course. A ropes course usually consists of a series of obstacles constructed from ropes, wooden beams, and cables suspended in trees and poles. Participants seek to negotiate the obstacles by themselves or in pairs. The participants are usually belayed from the ground or attached to a safety cable to prevent falling to the ground. Many ropes courses combine these high rope obstacles with initiative tasks such as the "wall" (scaling a 12 to 15 foot wall), or "electric fence" (crossing over an invisible wire four to six feet off the ground). While one could argue that the ropes course does not offer a true adventure experience, it does offer an excellent example of how apparent danger can be used to achieve certain outcomes.

DEFINING OUTDOOR ADVENTURE PURSUITS

It would appear that the outdoor adventure experience is made up of a number of components, including an interaction with the natural environment, the perception of risk or danger, and a concommitant sense of uncertainty of the outcome. Given these factors, outdoor adventure pursuits may be defined as:

The zip-line has provided a physically challenging experience for thousands of ropes course participants.

> A variety of self-initiated activities utilizing an interaction with the natural environment, that contain elements of real or apparent danger, in which the outcome, while uncertain, can be influenced by the participant and circumstance.

Outdoor adventure pursuits may be sought in terms of *structured experiences,* such as formal classes and programs, or *nonstructured* experiences, that is, activities done on an individual basis, with friends and/or family, whenever one chooses. Within the framework of structured outdoor adventure pursuits, any program that focuses on education through the activity or uses adventure in an educational context is termed *outdoor adventure education.* This might involve classes to learn a specific skill, such as rock climbing or adventure camping, or possibly enrolling in a course through an organization that sponsors outdoor

Belayed high-line activities are a common component in many ropes courses.

adventure education (e.g., Project Adventure or Outward Bound). *Outdoor adventure recreation* implies using adventure activities such as mountain climbing, river rafting, or hang gliding, and so on to achieve recreational outcomes. These outcomes could be excitement, socialization, enjoyment, and/or interaction with a natural environment.

Clearly, there can be a substantial amount of overlap. A person, for example, might seek outdoor adventure recreation in the form of white-water canoeing as a nonstructured experience, for the thrill and enjoyment of being active and outdoors in the water. White-water canoeing may also be considered as outdoor adventure education if one is learning the skill in a structured class or program. The specific context of an outdoor adventure pursuits activity will vary according to the goal and desired outcomes on behalf of the participant and/or program.

COMPARISON AND CONTRAST

Outdoor adventure pursuits can be subsumed under the broader category of *outdoor recreation.* The more traditional forms of outdoor recreation activities include fishing, hunting, boating, and so on. While these two areas may appear to be similar (i.e., activities usually done in an outdoor setting), there are definitive differences between outdoor adventure pursuits and outdoor recreation. More specifically, there are at least twenty distinctly different endeavors that fall under the classification of outdoor adventure pursuits. These activities include:

Backpacking	Bicycle touring	Hang-gliding
White-water canoeing	Cross-country skiing	Mountaineering
Hot-air ballooning	Rappelling	Kayaking
Rafting	Orienteering	Rock climbing
Ropes courses	SCUBA	Sailing
Backcountry snowshoeing	Spelunking	Wilderness camping
Wilderness trekking	Sky diving	Sea kayaking

What distinguishes these activities from those more commonly associated with outdoor recreation is a deliberate seeking of risk and uncertainty of outcome often referred to as *adventure.* While both forms of recreation involve elements of skill in specific settings, only in outdoor adventure pursuits is there a deliberate inclusion of activities that may contain threats to an individual's health or life. Figure 1.2 illustrates how a participant in outdoor adventure pursuits moves along a continuum based on developing skill and experience.

Outdoor recreation and outdoor adventure pursuits often serve different participants with different needs, expectations, and motivations. Knopf and Schreyer (1985) report that motives for participation may be activity-related. Following this line of reasoning, reported motives for participation in outdoor recreation generally consist of a desire for achievement, affiliation, control, escape, and self-awareness (Manning, 1986). In a more conceptual fashion, Iso-Ahola (1980) theorizes that the reasons why people engage in outdoor recreation are based on two dimensions: an attempt to achieve something and an attempt to avoid something. Findings from Davis (1973) and Bowley (1979) support this contention. In the case of outdoor adventure pursuits, this conceptualization is extended to include a third dimension: risk taking. Moreover, the concept of risk taking is central to outdoor adventure activities as the absence of risk may result in a decrease in satisfaction as well as a decrease in the desire to participate. In addition, the phenomenon of risk taking appears to become increasingly important as the participant gains experience and skill in the adventure activities (Schreyer and Roggenbuck, 1978; Ewert, 1985) (See Figure 1.2).

FIGURE 1.2
Outdoor Adventure Recreation: A Conceptual Model

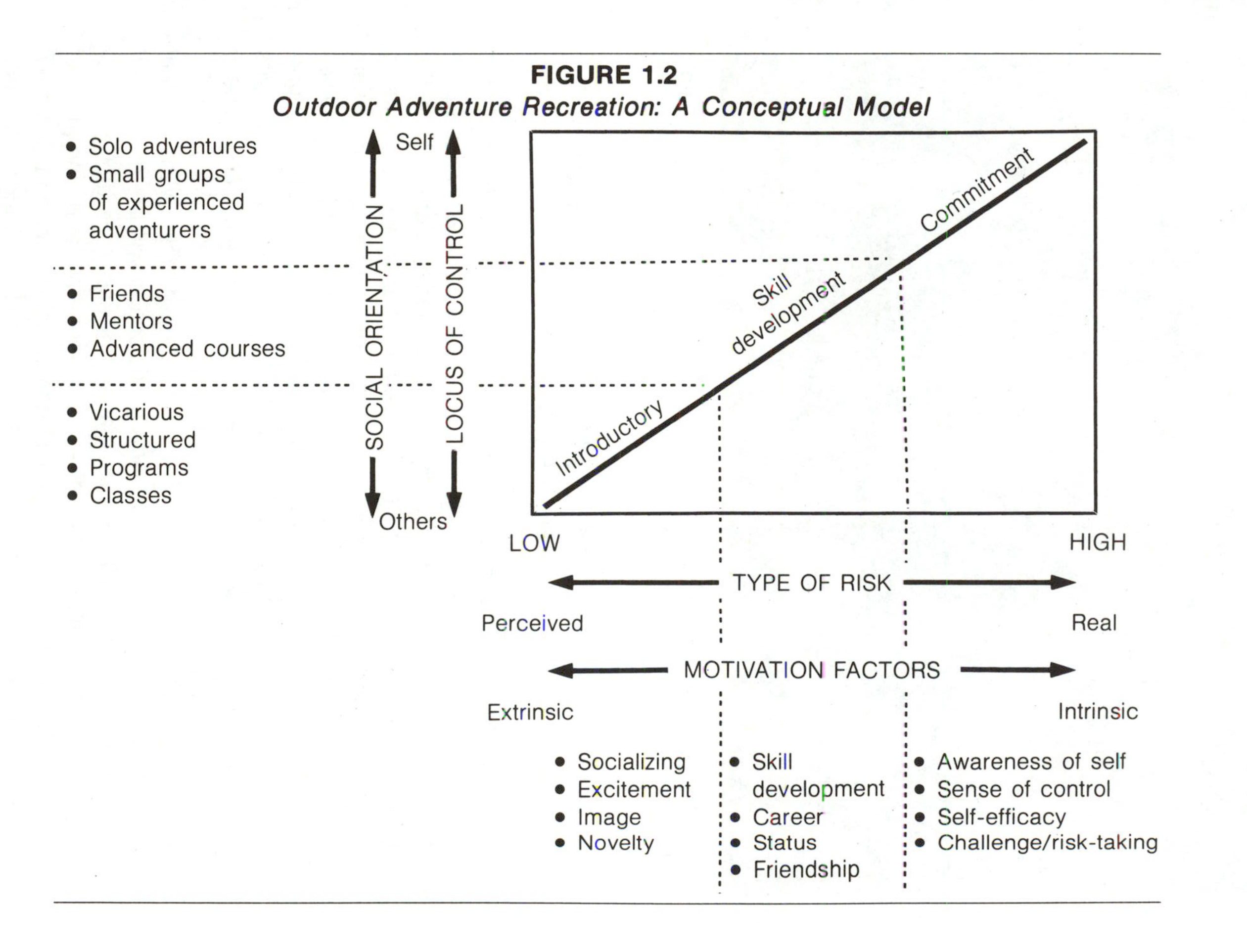

Aerial activities, such as hot-air ballooning, have become popular on many public lands.

MANAGEMENT OF OUTDOOR ACTIVITIES AND AREAS

The above suggestions and findings have implications for both the management of outdoor resources and the provision of activities in the outdoors. In part, the type of experiences engaged in depends on the opportunities provided. Manning (1986) suggests that, when choosing management objectives, the expectations and desires of potential users should be considered. While both classifications involve outdoor activities and settings, the risk-seeking recreationalist will also require opportunities for risk taking and adventure seeking. Although these factors may be present in the outdoor recreation context, they are usually peripheral to the primary motives for participation.

As suggested by Driver and Brown (1984), people with different motives and expectations for recreation participation will prefer different environmental settings. It follows that managing resources along strictly outdoor recreational lines invites a displacement and inequity of resource allocation for the adventure recreationalist (Knopf and Schreyer, 1985). Any attempt to reduce or interfere with the challenge and risk-taking potential of an area may severely inhibit the potential for satisfaction for this outdoor adventure user. Sax (1980) posits that there will be an "erosion" of risk and spontaneity in the outdoor resources that ultimately will attract those users seeking a risk-free environment.

PROGRAMMING FOR RISK VERSUS NONRISK ACTIVITIES

With respect to programming, these differences in the classification of activities can also lead to a bias in the opportunities provided to the user. Assuming that one goal of programming is to provide a sense of satisfaction for participants, the following questions are presented in an effort to better identify the most appropriate outdoor activity within a wide range of recreational opportunities:

- Is the participant seeking adventure and risk or are these factors peripheral to the experience? Identify the essence of the activity.
- What is the skill and experience level of the participants? Individuals with more skill and experience will usually demand a more self-determined, less leader-led program.
- Will the recreation experience be facilitated or diminished through development of the resource? While site modification and development may facilitate and enhance outdoor recreation use, it may detract from or even eliminate the opportunities for outdoor adventure recreation. For example, constructing boardwalks and fences can provide a sense of security for the sightseer but effectively reduce the sense of wilderness and adventure for the risk seeker.
- Will outdoor adventure programs require an element of real or perceived risk while outdoor recreation-oriented programs necessitate a down-playing of any real or perceived danger?

Outdoor recreation and outdoor adventure pursuits experiences will often require different approaches to both programming and the management of resources. For instance, those participants who are seeking risk will want less-developed natural resources to challenge themselves and surpass personal limits. Regulations regarding personal safety should be kept to a minimum. On the other hand, those individuals who would like to participate in outdoor recreation experiences without the deliberate seeking of risk may welcome a more regulated outdoor area. "Danger—Keep Out" signs can prove both a hindrance or a signal of sought-after hazard, depending on the goals of the outdoor participant. Toward this end, the resource manager may effectively meet the needs of the outdoor recreation/adventure seeker by better interpreting whether the participant is seeking an outdoor recreation or an outdoor adventure experience. With the increasing popularity of outdoor adventure activities, merely assuming that most people are interested in traditional activities such as walking, swimming, or bicycling might overlook the needs of a changing clientele.

NATURE OF THE OUTDOOR ADVENTURE EXPERIENCE

The outdoor adventure experience has been conceptualized in many ways. Schreyer et al. (1978) described the experience as a complex arousal system which goes beyond immediate turn-ons. Hollenhorst (1986) states that an outdoor adventure experience consists of three elements: uncertainty, freedom of choice, and intrinsic motivation. Phipps (1985) suggests that the adventure experience is essentially a psychological happening attained through physical activities. Figure 1.3 illustrates one conceptualization of the outdoor adventure experience.

Two other concepts have provided a conceptual foundation through which the adventure experience is characterized. This includes the "peak experience" described by Maslow (1962) and the "flow" theory first proposed by Csikszentmihalyi (1975). Both concepts continue to play a pivotal role in the way in which the adventure experience is currently described.

FIGURE 1.3
The Nature of the Outdoor Adventure Experience

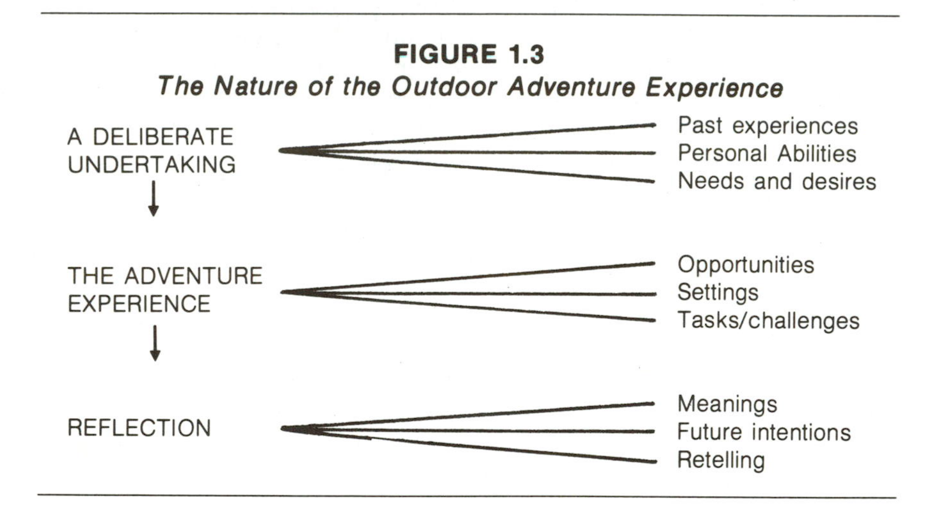

THE PEAK EXPERIENCE

Integral to Maslow's concept of the "peak experience" is the inexorable striving by the individual for self-actualization. First conceptualized by Goldstein (1939), self-actualization generally refers to an ongoing achievement of an individual's potentials, capacities, and talents. Maslow suggested that people who were self-actualized displayed a number of characteristics, including greater creativeness, changes in their value systems, an increase in spontaneity and problem centering, and a higher frequency of peak experiences.

According to Maslow (1962), a peak experience can be considered a cognitive happening in which an individual feels fulfillment, immense satisfaction, or a highest degree of happiness. The peak experience is characterized by reports of focused concentration on the tasks at hand, a transcendence of reality, an event which contains a substantial amount of intrinsic value, a disorientation of time and space, a special flavor of wonder and humility, and a sense of playfulness. Moreover, the peak experience has been termed an acute identity experience with individuals reporting feelings of integration with the environment, optimal levels of functioning (Rogers, 1961), a heightened sense of self-confidence with more control over their lives, and a sense of being concerned with the present rather than with the past or future.

The similarity between what happens in a peak experience and an outdoor adventure experience is striking. Indeed, many if not most, outdoor adventure education programs strive for their students to experience the same items as described by Maslow. The following section further illuminates the value of the peak experience and its inherent qualities of perceived freedom, positive emotions, and internal rewards.

PERCEIVED FREEDOM AND THE PEAK EXPERIENCE[1]

The positive influences resulting from outdoor adventure experiences seem to have a transcending application. What may have previously been a basic and routine life-style, void of any pattern of wholesome and challenging leisure pursuits, can become one of personal betterment via challenging and rewarding outdoor recreational activities. John C. Miles (1978), in his insightful summary entitled *The Value of High Adventure Activities,* stated:

> In the end, the ultimate value of high adventure risk recreation may be that one person confronts existentially the decision as to whether or not to venture forth into the unknown. Choice is exercised, the mind and body committed, and the consequences accepted. No one is drafted into the activity, but chooses to face the test. There are unlimited opportunities to exercise personal freedom so dramatically in the world today (p. 2).

The phrase ". . . to exercise personal freedom" is particularly significant in that it has advanced Miles' essential idea of self-development through the mediums of confidence and compassion. Moreover, the most universally agreed upon condition, which is characteristic of optimal leisure functioning, is the concept of freedom. The profound and intimate relationship between freedom and leisure is recognized by leading researchers and conceptual thinkers in the leisure services field. Based on two studies involving the relationship of freedom to leisure, Iso-Ahola (1980) concluded that ". . . the quality of leisure experience during non-working hours can be ameliorated by enhancing a person's perceived freedom and the intrinsic motivation in his leisure activities" (p. 9). But how is perceived freedom associated with the pursuit of

[1]Portions of this section are excerpts written by the late Dr. Jim Black.

excellence and enhanced self-concept, and where does one have the opportunities to explore personal outer limits, with the premium being placed not on success, ability to perform, or accomplishment, but on the willingness to try?

In the context of promoting the idea of "peak experiences," the needs and values of risk recreation (or outdoor adventure pursuits) again become the central theme. Is risk recreation really relevant to everyday life? What kind of positive influences can be appreciated from experiences steeped with risk of life and limb? When are you going to rappel off an overhang on a vertical wall, or white-water raft the Colorado River, or traverse Death Valley? What possible transcendent values are there? One might pose an additional question: How well do your experiences in nature enable you to cope more effectively with the problems of mankind when you come back to the city? In answer to these questions, it could be said that because of the opportunities to trade risk for the illusion of routine, an individual may gain the reassurance and reality that the world makes sense. A person "goes to nature for a metaphysical fix and returns with excess of confidence, of reassurance that there's something behind it all and it's good."

INTERNAL REWARDS

Peak experiences, risk recreation, challenge, adventure, and outdoor adventure education are all terms that can be related to outdoor adventure pursuits. We must be prepared to face risk as human beings in this world and face the stress and challenges it offers. But what are the measurable benefits of stress and risk and what are the prerequisites to gleaning the inherent rewards in adequate leisure functioning?

In recent years, increased attention has been given to the leisure portion of people's lives and to the numerous personal benefits derived from the attainment of a leisure state. According to Costilow (1982), "Leisure is the opportunity for personal growth and advancement; it is the seed bed of cultural development; it is the opportunity for coming close to the purpose and meaning of life . . . [it is]the feeling one gets when in the process of learning, or expressing, or creating" (p. 1). It is also important to recognize, however, that deficiencies in leisure functioning may not only preclude the development or occurrence of these benefits, but may in themselves create such undesirable consequences as drug abuse, vandalism, depression, and feelings of isolation. This need is responsible for our ultimate motivation. For, regardless of our immediate objective, everything we do is to achieve a sense of total well-being. To limit one's self to the "coincidental associations that one makes in daily living" seems pernicious, to say the least. As stated earlier, we must be prepared to risk as human beings in this world. The late William O. Douglas stated, "We cannot become self-reliant if our dominant aspiration is to be safe and secure." De Grazia (1962) stated,

Whitewater rafting demands teamwork, skill, and good communication between the rafters.

"Work, we know, may make a man stoop-shouldered or rich. It may even ennoble him. Leisure perfects him. In this lies his future" (p. 437).

CONCLUSIONS

While originally thought of as activities suited only for explorers or daredevils, outdoor adventures are now sought out by millions of people throughout North America and the world. Even though there are numerous definitions of outdoor adventure pursuits, there is now a consensus that these activities involve a deliberate seeking of risk and danger through recreational and/or educational endeavors. Moreover, the outcomes of these activities can be influenced by the actions of the participant and circumstances.

From a program perspective, a number of issues arise, such as the centrality of risk in the activity. That is, is risk peripheral or central in the activity? What are the skill and experience levels of the participants? Finally, will development of the resource diminish or facilitate the experience?

Other factors that are part of the outdoor adventure experience are the peak experience (Maslow, 1962) and the "flow experience" (Csikszentmihalyi, 1975; Mitchell, 1983). Together, these two conceptualizations are useful in describing the adventure experience from a motivational and perceptual perspective.

It appears that outdoor adventure pursuits have become a widely accepted set of activities that, for many, have enhanced and revitalized the use of leisure for personal growth and satisfaction. It will continue to be a challenge for the recreation provider and outdoor educator to provide high-quality opportunities for outdoor adventure pursuits.

MAIN POINTS

1. Outdoor adventure pursuits have been defined in a number of ways. A number of terms have been used to describe adventure pursuit activities, including risk recreation, challenge activities, or stress-challenge activities.
2. Despite the variety of terms used to describe outdoor adventure pursuits, there is a commonality of uncertainty of outcome and elements of risk and danger.
3. While often uncertain, the outcomes of an adventure pursuits activity can be influenced the the actions of the participant and circumstances.
4. The concepts of the "peak experience" and "flow" are related to the adventure experience. In addition, the nature of the adventure experience is dependent on the skills and experience level of the participant.
5. While similar, outdoor adventure pursuits and outdoor recreation are not the same, for the activities often serve different types of users with different expectations and motivations for engaging in the activity.
6. In the final analysis, the adventure experience is a highly personal experience entirely understandable only to the individual.

REFERENCES

Bowley, C. (1979). Motives, management, preferences of crowding of back-country hiking trail users in the Allegheny National Forest of Pennsylvania. Unpublished Master's thesis. The Pennsylvania State University.

Costilow, A. (1982). *The Leisure Diagnostic Battery: Background, Conceptualization, and Structure, and Theoretical and Empirical Structure, Remediation Guide and User's Guide.* Denton, TX: Division of Recreation and Leisure Studies, North Texas State University, Office of Special Education, Grant No. G008902257.

Csikszentmihalyi, M. (1975). *Beyond Boredom and Anxiety.* San Francisco, CA: Jossey-Bass.

Darst, P. and Armstrong, G. (1980). *Outdoor Adventure Activities for School and Recreation Programs.* Minneapolis, MN: Burgess.

Davis, R. (1973). Selected Motivational Determinants of Recreational Use of Belle Isle in Detroit. Unpublished Master's thesis. University of Michigan.

de Grazia, S. (1962). *Of Time, Work, and Leisure.* New York: The Twentieth Century Fund.

Driver, B. and Brown, P. (1984). Contributions of Behavioral Scientists to Recreation Resource Management. In I. Altman and R. Wohlwill (eds.). *Behavior and the Natural Environment,* pp. 307-339. New York: Plenum.

Emerson, R. (1966). Mount Everest: A Case Study in Communication Feedback and Sustained Group Goal Striving. *Sociometry,* 29(3): p. 213.

Ewert, A. (1985). Why People Climb: The Relationship of Participant Motives and Experience Level to Mountaineering. *Journal of Leisure Research,* 17(3): pp. 241-250.

Goldstein, K. (1939). *The Organism.* New York: American Book Company.

Hollenhorst, S. (1986). Towards an understanding of adventure and adventure education. Unpublished manuscript.

Houston, C. (1968). The Last Blue Mountain. In S. Klausner (ed.). *Why Men Take Chances,* pp. 49-58. New York: Doubleday.

Iso-Ahola, S. (1980). *The Social Psychology of Leisure and Recreation.* Dubuque, IA: William C. Brown.

Knopf, R. and Schreyer, R. (1985). The Problem of Bias in Recreation Resource Decision-Making. In D. Dustin (ed.). *The Management of Human Behavior in Outdoor Recreation Settings,* pp. 23-27. San Diego, CA: San Diego State University's Institute for Leisure Behavior.

Manning, R. (1986). *Studies in Outdoor Recreation.* Corvallis, OR: Oregon State University Press.

Maslow, A. (1962). *Toward a Psychology of Being.* Princeton, NJ: D. Van Nostrand.

Meier, J. (1978). Is the Risk Worth Taking? *Leisure Today,* 49(4): pp. 7-9.

Miles, J. (1978). The Value of High Adventure Activities. *Journal of Physical Education and Recreation,* April, pp. 27-28.

Mitchell, R. (1983). *Mountain Experience: The Psychology and Sociology of Adventure.* Chicago: University of Chicago Press.

Mortlock, C. (1983). *Adventure Education and Outdoor Pursuits.* Keswick, England: Ferguson.

Mortlock, C. (1978). *Adventure Education.* Keswick, England: Ferguson.

Phipps, M. (1985). Adventure—An Inner Journey to the Self: The Psychology of Adventure Expressed in Jungian Terms. *Adventure Education Journal,* 2(4/5): pp. 11-17.

Progen, J. (1979). Man, Nature, and Sport. In E. Gerber and M. Nillian (eds.). *Sports and the Body: A Philosophical Symposium,* pp. 237-242. Philadelphia: Lea and Febiger.

Rogers, C. (1961). *On Becoming a Person.* New York: Houghton-Mifflin.

Sax, J. (1980). *Mountains Without Handrails: Reflections on the National Parks.* Ann Arbor, MI: The University of Michigan Press.

Schreyer, R. and Roggenbuck, J. (1978). The Influence of Experience Expectations on Crowding Perceptions and Socio-Psychological Carrying Capacities. *Leisure Sciences,* 4. pp. 373-394.

Schreyer, R., White, R., and McCool, S. (1978). Common Attributes Uncommonly Exercised. In J. Meier, T. Morash, and G. Welton (eds.). *High Adventure Outdoor Pursuits,* pp. 24-29. Columbus, OH: Publishing Horizons, Inc.

Stowell, S. (1967). *On Top of the World.* New York: MacMillan.

Yerkes, R. (1985). High Adventure Recreation in Organized Camping. *Trends,* 22(3): pp. 10-11.

2

THE HISTORY OF OUTDOOR ADVENTURE PROGRAMMING

ANCIENT EXPLORERS

The quest for adventure has always played an important role in man's exploration of and relationship with the earth. While often ascribed to as a search for land or wealth, adventure was often the covert reason for exploring faraway lands. For, while adventuring is often a perilous task, who can deny the magical "pull" of the midnight watch, the next "lead," or the rapids around the bend?

The first written documentation of adventuring tells of a four-year expedition from Egypt to a mysterious land of Punt in 2500 B.C., presumably in search of incense, gold, and dwarfs (Lacey, 1978). So adventurous and thirsty for exploration were the early Phoenicians that, by 600 B.C., they had sailed around the continent of Africa from east to west. Chiefly interested in adventure and exploration for the wealth that could be accrued, the Phoenicians used one of the components of the adventure sequence—retelling the experience—to frighten away rival explorers with tales of boiling seas and other perils.

One such account of adventure and exploration is that of the Phoenician admiral Hanno. While the original document describing his voyage, *The Periplus,* has been lost, the story of man's first great expedition proceeds as follows:

> Originating from Carthage around the fifth century B.C., Hanno's fleet sailed through the pillars of Hercules at the Straits of

> Gibraltar and headed south along the great bulge of Africa, sailing past the dry coastline of Africa down to a site which was probably Herne Island. It was at this point, having completed his explicit purpose of establishing colonies, that Hanno's quest for adventure came to the forefront and the journey continued to a length of the Senegal River ["Great and wide, and swarming with crocodiles and hippopotamuses"]. The journey continued down the coast of Africa to a point close to Sherbo Sound or possibly even the Gulf of Guinea. (Lacey, 1978, pp. 5–6)

It was in the great Phoenician city, Carthage, on the coast of present-day Tunis, that the next set of players entered the remarkable saga of human adventure—the ancient Greeks. It was from the ancient Greeks that the first great adventure novel appeared: the myth of Odysseus in Homer's *Odyssey* (Fitzgerald, 1963). While most are vaguely familiar with the exploits of Odysseus in his search for his homeland, Zweig, author of *The Adventurer: The Fate of Adventure in the Western World* (1974), suggests that Odysseus was the first adventurer/hero in Western literature.

Ancient Greece, however, was not just a place for storytelling. It was here, at the close of the sixth century, B.C., that mountain climbing, hunting, and horseback riding became an integral part of the lives of many of the city-state youth, particularly those of Sparta, the ancient city-state of Greece (Hackensmith, 1966, pp. 27–37). Once again, adventure activities became a means to an end. In particular, it was a way in which to physically and emotionally strengthen youth for their eventual roles as citizens and soldiers. It is an ironic parallel to the "new development" in pedagogy today, where adventure-based education is used for the similar purposes of strengthening youth in preparation as future members of society.

CONCEPT OF LEISURE EMERGES

It is interesting to note that the concept of leisure emerged during this Athenian time period as a "cultivation of self" (Murphy, 1981, pp. 22–23). Athenian philosophers, such as Socrates and Aristotle, believed strongly in the unity of mind and body and in the importance of leisure for the proper, holistic development of an individual.

> Our children from their earliest years must take part in all the more lawful forms of play, for if they are not surrounded with such an atmosphere they can never grow up to be well-conducted and virtuous citizens. (Shorey, 1953, p. 335)

It is curious to compare this fifth-century statement with the philosophy of the National Outdoor Leadership School (N.O.L.S.) in Lander, Wyoming.

> We believe that youth demand excitement and adventure. And if society does not provide opportunities for these needs, youth will seek them out in often illegal or unsocial forms.

The term leisure was derived from the Latin word "licere" which literally means "to be permitted to abstain from occupation or service" (Murphy, 1981, p. 24). In addition, the Greek term "schole," from which we derived the word school, became aligned with leisure in the classical Greek sense as a place immune from occupational requirements and devoted to scholarly pursuits, individual freedom, and self-determination (Murphy, 1975, p. 5).

It was from these developments that the concepts of leisure and recreation emerged in the Western world. Leisure became a period of personal "space" free of the necessity to work or toil. It was, however, not unproductive, in that, while an individual was free of work, he or she was not free of activity, either physical or mental. "Schole" for the Greeks or "licere" for the Romans represented a serious way of life.

Here, then, is the beginning of a strange paradox surrounding the use of leisure and recreation—a paradox which suggests that, while these terms represent periods of unobligated time or activity, they are not to be confused with simply passing time. Even contemplation was considered a productive period. Adventure programs today have continued along these lines with the offering of seemingly "unproductive" activities such as mountain climbing or white-water canoeing. However, their intent has been to achieve very substantial goals such as changing the way people think about themselves or work together as a group.

EXPLORATION AND THE QUEST FOR ADVENTURE

From about 1800 until about 700 B.C., a warlike tribe of people called the Etruscans settled about the Tiber and Arno rivers in Italy. Horseback riding and hunting were favorite sports of these forerunners of the ancient Romans (Hackensmith, 1966, pp. 57–58). A precursor of the modern-day "Survival Game" emerged, with captives given arms and loosed on each other at a burial or other selected sites. The only real difference between then and now is that in the seventh century B.C. the combatants used swords and in 1987 the combatants use air-powered pellet guns loaded with relatively harmless red-dye gelatin pellets.

Similar to the Greeks, adventure activities such as hunting, horseback riding, and backcountry travel were important avenues of training for Roman youth, particularly boys. Roman explorations served to enlarge and unify vast parts of the then-known world. It was during this era (ca. the third century B.C.) that a sailor named Pytheas completed an amazing journey to ultima Thule (ultimate land)—the Arctic circle. During this adventure, Pytheas may have sailed as far north as Iceland or Norway. Upon returning, Pytheas retold the tale of a midnight sun, ever-shining fire (volcanoes of Iceland), and water as thick as jelly (another adventurer, Fridtjof Nansen, later rediscovered and related the phenomenon of ice sludge and ice fog, in a book succinctly entitled, *The Ocean*). The Pytheas adventure, which was not repeated for several hundred years, is truly one of the most adventurous in what has developed into a long list of "firsts."

The incredible voyage of Pytheas was repeated, only from the other direction, by the Vikings of A.D. 1000. Indeed, not only were the straits of Gibraltar revisited, but also Iceland, Greenland, and perhaps even North America (Jones, 1964).

Eclipsing even these daring adventures was the Brendan voyage (ca. A.D. 489/583). An Irish monk, Brendan, reportedly sailed a leather boat from Ireland to North America and back (Severin, 1978). The purpose of the journey was to explore the mythical "holy" land he believed was across the North Atlantic.

Two hundred years later, on the other side of the known world, a singularly intrepid adventurer, Marco Polo, was engaging in one of the most widely known and remarkable of all journeys. Chronicled in a book entitled, *A Description of the World,* the twenty-four-year expedition (1271-1295) described countless sagas of adventure and exploration.

By this time, improvements in agriculture and transportation (in addition to the general lessening of constant invasion and warfare) began to have a major effect which ultimately impacted man's search for adventure. This effect was greater urbanization of the people which eventually led to a greater affinity for commerce and travel (Burke, 1985). Nold (1978) in his elegant work, "Profiles in Adventure" calls this the age of the Merchant Ventures. Adventurers, like many before, traveled beyond familiar surroundings for the promise of wealth and fame. But once these goals were obtained, they continued their struggles in search of that elusive elixir—adventure.

In a sense, adventure became *the* motivating force, or as Wilfred Noyce sums it up, "Adventure: a novel enterprise undertaken for its own sake" (Noyce, 1958, 16). In 1336 Francesco Petrarch and his brother Gerado made the first recorded mountain climb (Mont Ventoux) for no other reason than to reach the top (Scott, 1974). For this feat, Petrarch is known as the "spiritual" father of Alpinism.

As Europe began to look cautiously beyond its immediate borders there emerged one of the first training facilities explicitly designed for exploration and its covert companion—adventure. In 1419, the celebrated Henry "The Navigator" established a school of navigation near Sagres, Cape St. Vincent, the westernmost point of Europe (Stromberg, 1969, pp. 214-215).

It was during this Great Age of Exploration that exploration and adventure became nationalistic exploits rather than purely individual endeavors. Bartolomeu Pias, a Portuguese explorer, reached the southernmost tip of Africa, the Cape of Good Hope, in 1488. Upon his return to Lisbon, one of the people greeting and admiring the triumphant explorer was Christopher Columbus (Newton, 1968).

The year 1492 was momentous for several reasons. Not only did Columbus reach the North American island of San Salvador, but it was also the year in which Antoine de Ville was ordered by King Charles VIII of France to climb the difficult Mount Aiguille (ca. 6500 feet) and to erect a cross on the summit. De Ville said the journey was the most terrifying and dangerous of his life (Scott, 1974, p. 3).

The rate of exploration and travel began to assume dizzying proportions as this era of change swept over the European continent. Indeed, this rate of change surely equalled that of our own society, a society in which change is considered the only stable condition.

In 1498, six years after the Columbus expedition, Vasco de Gama finally achieved the all-consuming quest of finding a sea route to India and beyond. Spanish exploration continued into the 1500s with the exploits of Cortes, Balboa, Pizarro, and Coronado.

Just as the Spanish sun had begun to set, other explorers and adventurers, notably English, Dutch, and French, opened up vast undiscovered areas of the New World. These explorations included the search for the Northwest Passage and led to the forerunner of the modern-day concept of adventure/exploration of the polar and subpolar regions.

One of the first of these journeys was led by the English explorer Henry Hudson, in search of the elusive shortcut to the Orient. Another exploration, led by Russian-born Vitus Bering, (1725–30, 1733–41) uncovered vast areas of Siberia and the northern seas. On January 17, 1773, the "Resolution" commanded by James Cook became the first ship in history to penetrate the Antarctic Circle.

BEGINNINGS OF MOUNTAINEERING

While the spirit of exploration for science and country was beginning to bloom, another era, "the Golden Age" of mountaineering, was also dawning. Early mountaineering efforts, as well as an increasing number of explorations at sea were done under scientific aegis. In 1760, the year "serious mountaineering" began (Scott, 1974, p. 3), Horace Benedict de Saussure, a wealthy scientist from Geneva, offered a handsome prize to the person who made the first ascent of Mt. Blanc. It was not, however, until 1786 that a local doctor, Michel-Gabriel Piccard, and his guide, Jacques Balmat, succeeded. As Scott (1974, p. 4) suggests, the flame had been kindled and it quickly spread as moun-

Lithograph from *Whymper's Scrambles Amongst the Alps* page 95.

taineering started in many alpine areas. It was a fervor pushed by a quest for knowledge, nation, and, ultimately—adventure. Starting with an early ascent of the Wetterhorn and culminating with Edward Whymper's first ascent of the Matterhorn in 1865 (Whymper, 1871), the next thirty years marked more climbs and successful summit attempts than any

Lithograph from *Whymper's Scrambles Amongst the Alps* page 54.

previous time. It was a time when mountaineering began to be pursued for its own sake rather than linking adventure with the search for scientific knowledge. As described by Nold in his monograph, "Profiles in Adventure" (1978), the scientific adventurer sought to bring back wealth in the form of accurate charts and maps instead of gold and spices. The adventure mountaineer, on the other hand, had brought back nothing but an experience and tales for the retelling.

By the 1850s it was common to see strings of "tourists" roped together on the glaciers of the more accessible peaks (Roberts, 1985). In 1857, the British Alpine Club was formed to help further the aims of mountaineering, with John Ball as its first president. It was the same John Ball who published one of the first guidebooks for climbing, *The Eastern Alps,* in 1868.

This emergence of adventure as a legitimate quest for its own sake coincided with a number of broader issues. One such issue was the growing dissatisfaction with the vision of the world as completely explainable by either religious dogma or social beliefs that were increasingly bombarded with assaults from empiricalism and reality. In addition, the image of the wilderness was changing from one of an unwholesome area to be conquered to one of a mystical, energizing place. Nash (1967, p. 44) believed that appreciation of the wilderness began in the cities. This appreciation was cultivated more by the writings and discussions of wilderness tourists and amateur naturalists than by the actual wilderness user. Indeed, the writings of Catlin (1841), Thoreau (1854), Isabella Bird (1879), and Muir (1894) served to spur interest in "the wilderness" and the inescapable adventure that goes with it, just as the more contemporary works of Carson (1962), Abbey (1968), and McPhee (1977) have sparked the interest of many since.

ADVENTURE AS AN END IN ITSELF

Slowly, as all the unexplored regions of the search were explored, the major summits all climbed, and the rivers run, the reason for adventuring shifted from a necessary by-product of searching for scientific knowledge to reasons related to an individual's own personal desires. The latter part of the 1800s and early 1900s brought about an increasing array of events which addressed this new awareness of the environment, the wilderness, and the emerging "need" for adventure. The formation of organizations such as the Appalachian Mountain Club (1876) and Sierra Club (1892) both represented and helped propel the movement toward conservation of the land and its resources. With the onset of agencies such as the Forest Service (1905) and United States Park Service (1916), the federal government became involved in land management and also, surreptitiously, the provision of adventure opportunities for an ever-growing portion of the public.

Just as Congress in 1894 funded a commission to inventory the state of outdoor recreation, the Congress of 1906 acted in a similar manner. By 1908, the report of this commission helped pave the way for the enactment of a substantial number of laws passed by both federal and state legislatures (Van Doren and Hodges, 1975). Many of the laws served to provide the settings and opportunities for future adventure

TABLE 2.1
Historical Events in the United States Supporting Outdoor Adventure Pursuits
(Robb and Ewert, 1987)

DATE	HISTORICAL DEVELOPMENTS
1821	Round Hill School
1832	Ouachita Mountainous Area in Arkansas set aside (Hot Springs)
1851	Young Mens Christian Association (YMCA)
1861	Gunnery School for Boys
1864	Yosemite Valley entrusted to State of California
1872	Yellowstone National Park
1876	Appalachian Mountain Club
1885	Adirondack State Park
1888	National Geographical Society
1892	Sierra Club
1899	Recreation is first recognized as legitimate leisure pursuit Mt. Rainier National Park
1905	Forest Service Recreation
1906	Devils Tower National Monument Yosemite ceded back to Federal Government
1907	Lassen Peak National Monument under U.S.D.A.
1910	Boy Scouts Camp Fire Girls
1911	Weeks Act purchased lands in headwaters of many eastern rivers
1912	Girl Scouts
1915	Agricultural Appropriations Act Recreation as legitimate use Trappers Lake Principle—no development in "Wilderness" areas
1916	National Park Service
1921	William Greeley/Major use of outdoor recreation in National Forests Quetico-Superior roadless area (boundary waters canoe area)
1924	First National Conference on outdoor recreation Gila Primitive area in New Mexico American Camping Association
1932	American Youth Hostels (AYH)
1933	Depression: CCC builds many trails, etc. presently used
1935	Wilderness Society
1936	First graduate/undergraduate course offered in recreation, New York University
1938	AAHPERD—American Alliance for Health, Physical Education, Recreation and Dance
1941	Outward Bound established at Aberdovy, Wales U.K.
1944	Flood Control Act—authorized outdoor recreation on federal water projects
1956/57	Operation Outdoors Mission 66 efforts to rehabilitate forests and parks
1958	Outdoor Recreation Resources Review Commission (ORRRC)
1960	Multiple Use Act
1962	Bureau of Outdoor Recreation
1964	Land Water Conservation Fund (LWCF) Wilderness Preservation Act
1965	National Outdoor Leadership School established (NOLS) National Recreation & Park Association (NRPA)
1968	Wild and Scenic Rivers Prescott College National Trails System Act Kelly & Baer Study
1970	Environmental Education Act
1974	First North American Conference on Outdoor Pursuits in Higher Education Association of Experiential Education
1978	Wilderness Education Association
1986	President's Commission on Americans Outdoors
1988	Oregon Wild Rivers Bill

North Carolina Outward Bound School is one of approximately thirty Outward Bound schools throughout the world.

recreationalists. These and other significant events are listed in Table 2.1. It was a time when various literature, organizations, and legislation combined in a synergistic fashion to spur the growth of adventure-based recreation. Narratives, mixed with how-to information, were the typical format of books describing some facet of adventure recreation, usually camping or mountaineering. Examples of these types of writings included: *Deep River Jim's Wilderness Trail Book* (Deep-River Jim, 1937), *Camping and Woodcraft* (Kephart, 1917), *Belaying the Leader* (Leonard et al., 1956), *Woodcraft* (Sears, 1920), *The Book of Woodcraft* (Seton, 1912), and *The Arctic Manual* (Stefansson, 1950).

FORMALIZED SCHOOLS OF OUTDOOR ADVENTURE

With the advent of World War II, the paths of three men crossed in Great Britain. This crossing led to one of the foremost organizations in the field of adventure-based education. It was a combination of the innovative vision of Kurt Hahn with the financial expertise of Lawrence Holt and the energy and ability to turn vision into reality of Jim Hogan that led to the formation of Outward Bound (Wilson, 1981). Since its inception as a training and educational system for strengthening an individual both physically and spiritually, Outward Bound has emerged as a leading organization in the field of adventure-based education.

It was not until twenty years later, however, that the concept of Outward Bound (by then an institution consisting of thirteen other schools throughout the world), finally reached the Western Hemisphere. Spearheaded by Charles Froelicher, the Colorado Outward Bound School emerged in 1962 with the purpose of:

> . . . developing apparent and latent capabilities through experience, both strenuous and testing, which demand an increase of initiative, self-confidence, understanding and respect for others. Using life in the mountains as the defying force, the students are taught the importance of cooperation and self-discipline in learning to cope with the hazards and emergencies of mountain living. They become acquainted with the great rewards of difficult and sustained efforts well done, the important spiritual value of service to others and self-respect for a well trained body. (James, 1980, pp. 8–9)

With a descriptive motto of "to serve, to strive, and not to yield" Outward Bound in the United States and Canada has grown to include eight individual schools.

Three years after the establishment of the Colorado Outward Bound School (1962), the chief instructor, Paul Petzoldt, stated he was:

> . . . shocked into the realization that nobody had really trained outdoorsmen in America. . . .we [Outward Bound] couldn't hire anyone that met my standards. We [Outward Bound] could hire people who knew how to do one thing well: climb mountains, fish, cross wild rivers, cook plain rations, recognize flora and fauna, read topographical maps, and teach and motivate. But we could not find a person who had been trained in all those things! They didn't exist. I thought the best thing I could do for American youth, if they were going to use the wild outdoors, was to prepare better leaders for such experiences. (Petzoldt, 1974)

From the desire emerged the concept of the National Outdoor Leadership School (N.O.L.S.), with the purpose of developing skilled outdoor leaders. Interestingly, Petzoldt and N.O.L.S. parted ways in the early 1980s, with Petzoldt forming another outdoor adventure organization, the Wilderness Education Association (W.E.A.). The purpose of the W.E.A. is to promote the safe and ecologically safe use of the wilderness through offering the certification of wilderness users and leaders. To date, the W.E.A. has failed to gain the same level of acceptance among outdoor enthusiasts as have Outward Bound and N.O.L.S.

What is apparent is that Outward Bound, N.O.L.S., and a substantial number of other neophyte outdoor adventure organizations such as the Dartmouth Outing Club, Brigham Young University's Outdoor Survival program, instructed by Larry Dean Olsen, and Prescott College emerged in the 1960s. This was the era of the "baby boomers" (large numbers of people under age 20), many of whom became affluent as adults and increasingly jaded by technology and urbanization (James, 1980, p. 5). The wilderness offered a setting that could provide the emotional catharsis and physical challenge which was increasingly lacking in contemporary, urbanized society. In a sense, adventure became likened to William James' "The Moral Equivalent of War" (Metcalfe, 1976, p. 5).

This desire for wild backcountry lands available for adventure-based activities coincided with the public's growing concern over the health of the environment and the protection of certain pristine areas. Together, these forces helped create the Wilderness Act of 1964. Land, untraveled by man, now became a legally protected resource.

Wallace Stegner, a wilderness advocate, wrote:

> . . . a headstrong drive into our technological termite life, the brave new world of a completely man-controlled environment. . . . Something will have gone out of us as a people if we ever let the remaining wilderness be destroyed; if we permit the last virgin forests to be turned into comic books and plastic cigarette cases; if we drive the few remaining members of that wild species into zoos or to extinction; if we pollute the last clear air and dirty the last clean streams and push paved roads through the last of the silence, so that never again will Americans be free in their own country from the noise, the exhausts, the stinks of human and automotive waste. (Stenger, 1961, p. 97)

By the very nature of wilderness, outdoor adventure activities such as backpacking and mountain climbing became accepted uses of these and other backcountry environments. This usage, combined with the phenomenal growth of organizations (e.g., Association of Experiential Education, 1974; First North American Conference on Outdoor Pursuits in Higher Education, 1974) and events (Earth Day, May 1, 1970) catering to the outdoor adventure resulted in the emergence of a new genre of recreationalists, a group which deliberately sought out the trials and dangers of outdoor adventuring.

More recent events which have impacted the outdoor adventure scene include: the First, Second and Third National Conferences on Outdoor Recreation (1984, 1986, 1988) and the emergence of adventure-based magazines such as *Outside, Backpacker, Outward Bound,* and *Outside Business.* Established in 1985, the President's Commission on Americans Outdoors (P.C.O.A.), like its earlier predecessor, the Outdoor Recreation Resources Review Commission (O.R.R.R.C.) of 1962, returned its report in 1987. This report spoke of overused outdoor recreation resources and burgeoning demands upon those finite resources. Many of these demands were in the area of outdoor adventure activities. How the government and country at large will deal with these findings and the subsequent recommendations of the P.C.O.A., including a $1 billion per year fund for the maintenance of facilities and land acquisition, remains to be seen.

Backpacking is an outdoor adventure pursuit that can be enjoyed regardless of one's age, background, or skill level.

OVERVIEW

In sum, we have traced the development of outdoor adventuring from the times of ancient Greece to contemporary civilization. It can be seen that, ostensibly, adventuring moved from a quest of one type of knowledge, namely that of new lands, spice routes, or wealth, to the search for a different type of information, that of one's own strength, abilities, and courage. Indeed, when reduced to the microcosm of the "individual," whether standing on the swaying deck of a small ship; peering up the white, windy expanse of a snow-covered slope; or nervously anticipating the next set of rapids in an unexplored river, what adventurer could escape these incredibly personal moments of adventure without the question: What awaits me? Thus, while mandating something else (i.e., science, wealth, colonization, or spreading the word of God) the individual explorer of the past is linked with the adventurer of the present and future by the nature of the quest itself: a bold undertaking in which the outcome, while uncertain, can often be influenced by the individual and/or circumstance. In a sense, the history of adventuring represents a thread of humanity linked today with generations long past. It provides a link every bit as important as the structures, philosophies, and knowledges forged by our ancestors. Through adventuring, an individual, while engaging in the activity, can *feel* the emotions, excitement, and concern that those who have gone before felt.

The ultimate measure of a man is not where he stands in moments of comfort and convenience, but where he stands at times of challenge and controversy. (Martin Luther King)

MAIN POINTS

1. The systematic search for new lands and wealth was an important impetus for early exploration and subsequent adventuring.
2. With the development of Greece and Rome, outdoor adventure activities assumed a new purpose, that of training youth for military service.
3. To aid in this exploration and conquest, training programs were established, such as one to train navigators. In a sense, these programs could be considered the forerunners of the Boy Scouts or the National Outdoor Leadership School.
4. Almost subtly, the search for adventure became more of a primary purpose of exploration with science the legitimizing reason but of secondary importance.
5. With the "Golden Age" of mountaineering, adventure gained an even greater prominence as a type of pursuit worthy by itself.
6. The "adventure for its own sake" phenomenon coincided with the growing interest in conservation in the United States during the 1800s.
7. With the inception of Outward Bound and the National Outdoor Leadership School, the training of leaders for adventure-based programming assumed greater importance in the recreational and educational systems of a large number of countries, including the United States, Canada, Great Britain, Australia and New Zealand.
8. In addition, with the advent of numerous other organizations, including adventure-tripping agencies (e.g., SOBEK), educational programs, and commercial operations, the opportunities for larger segments of the general public to experience an adventure activity has grown dramatically in the last twenty years.
9. This increased involvement by the public has resulted in broadened support for the outdoor environmental resources including wilderness areas, land acquisition for parks and forests, and the acceptance of adventure activities, such as rock climbing, as legitimate leisure pursuits.

REFERENCES

Burke, J. (1985). *The Day the Universe Changed.* Boston: Little, Brown and Company.

Deep-River Jim (1937). *Wilderness Trail Book.* Boston: Open Road Publishing Company.

Fitzgerald, R. (Trans.) (1963). *The Odyssey.* New York: Doubleday Anchor Books.

Hackensmith, C.W. (1966). *History of Physical Education.* New York: Harper and Row.

James, T. (1980). *Education At the Edge.* Denver, CO: Colorado Outward Bound.

Jones, G. (1964). *A History of the Vikings.* Cambridge: Oxford University Press.

Kephart, H. (1917). *Camping and Woodcraft.* New York: Macmillan.

Lacey, P. (Ed.) (1978). *Great Adventures that Changed the World.* Pleasantville, NY: Readers Digest Association, Inc.

Leonard, R., Wexler, A., Siri, W., and Bower, D. (1956). *Belaying the Leader.* San Francisco: Sierra Club.

Metcalfe, J. (1976). *Adventure Programming.* Austin, TX: National Educational Laboratory Publishing.

Murphy, J. F. (1975). *Recreation and Leisure Services: A Humanistic Perspective.* Dubuque, IA: William C. Brown.

——— (1981). *Concepts of Leisure,* 2d ed. Englewood Cliffs, NJ: Prentice-Hall.

Nash, R. (1967). *Wilderness and the American Mind.* New Haven, CT: Yale University Press.

Newton, A. P. (Ed.) (1968). *Travel and Travelers of the Middle Ages.* London: Barnes and Noble.

Nold, J. (1978). "Profiles in Adventure." Denver, CO: Colorado Outward Bound. Staff Development Paper, 21 pages.

Noyce, W. (1958). *The Springs of Adventure.* New York: The World Publishing Company.

Petzoldt, P. (1974). *The Wilderness Handbook.* New York: W. W. Norton and Company.

Robb, G. and Ewert, A. (1987). Risk Recreation and Persons with Disabilities. *Therapeutic Recreation, XXI,* First Quarter, pp. 58–69.

Roberts, D. (1985). The Growth of Adventure Travel. In *1000 Adventures: with Tales of Discovery.* New York: Harmony Books.

Scott, D. (1974). *Big Wall Climbing.* New York: Oxford University Press.

Sears, G. R. (1920). *Woodcraft.* New York: Forest and Stream Publishing.

Seton, E. T. (1912). *The Book of Woodcraft.* Garden City, NY: Garden City Publishing Co.

Severin, T. (1978). *The Brendan Voyage.* New York: McGraw-Hill.

Shorey, P. (Trans.) (1953). *Plato-The Republic.* Cambridge: Loeb Classical Library, Harvard University Press, 1930.

Stefansson, V. (1950). *Arctic Manual.* New York: Macmillan.

Stegner, W. (1961). The Wilderness Idea. In P. Brower (Ed.) *America's Living Heritage,* pp. 97–102. San Francisco: Sierra Club.

Stromberg, R. W. (1969). *A History of Western Civilization.* Homewood, IL: The Dorsey Press.

Whymper, E. (1871). *Scrambles Amongst the Alps: In the Years 1860–1869.* Reprinted by Ten Speed Press, Berkeley, CA, 1981.

Wilson, R. (1981). *Inside Outward Bound.* Charlotte, NC: The East Woods Press.

Van Doren, C. S. and Hodges, L. (1975). *America's Park and Recreation Heritage.* Washington, DC: U.S. Government Printing Office.

Zweig, P. (1974). *The Adventurer: The Fate of Adventure in the Western World.* New York: Basic Books.

OTHER RECOMMENDED READING

Darst, P. and Armstrong, G. (1980). *Outdoor Adventure Activities for School and Recreation Programs.* Minneapolis: Burgess Publishing.

Gibbons, M. (1974). Walkabout: Searching for the Right Passage from Childhood and School. *Phi Delta Kappan,* 55(9): pp. 596–602.

Meier, J., Morash, T., and Welton, G. (Eds.) (1987). *High Adventure Outdoor Pursuits,* 2d ed. Columbus, OH: Publishing Horizons, Inc.

Meldrum, K. I. (1971). Participation in Outdoor Activities in Selected Countries in Western Europe; Climbing, Canoeing, Caving and Skiing. *Comparative Education,* 7: pp. 137–142.

Miner, J. L. and Boldt, J. (1981). *Outward Bound U.S.A.: Learning Through Experience in Adventure-based Education.* New York: William Morrow and Company.

Mortlock, C. (1975). *Adventure Education and Outdoor Pursuits.* Colin Mortlock.

Parker, T. (1970). *An Approach to Outdoor Activities.* London: Parkam Books Ltd.

Scorsby, W. D. (1971). *A Survey of the National Outdoor Leadership School, Lander, Wyoming.* Master's Thesis. Montclair State College, Upper Montclair, NJ.

3

OUTDOOR ADVENTURE PURSUITS AND EDUCATION

A NEW DIMENSION[1]

Outdoor adventuring has been a recent entry in the health, physical education, recreation (HPER) field. Hendee and Roggenbuck (1984) report that out of 417 colleges and universities conducting wilderness-related courses, over 32 percent (n =77) were in the HPER field. Similarly, out of the 123 colleges and universities listed in the 1985-86 Society of Park and Recreation Educators Curriculum Catalog, 85 institutions (70 percent) had courses which were specifically related to outdoor adventure.

In considering activities such as canoeing, climbing, or backpacking, individuals are often in a unique natural environment, where they learn and use a variety of cognitive, motor, and social skills. Being part of a small group setting, receiving immediate feedback on the efficacy of their skills, and problem-solving tasks are also typical of outdoor adventure activities. Potential benefits that are related to the HPER objectives include skill development for life-long recreational activities and improved physical and emotional health components such as coordination, strength, cardiovascular response, and catharsis from the normal routine. Several psychological and sociological components that are often enhanced through outdoor adventure activities include self-concept, confidence, compassion for others, group cooperation, and respect for oneself and others. These benefits are discussed in detail in chapter 4.

These activities and their potential benefits are in tune with a growing

[1]This section is modified from an article that originally appeared in the *Journal of Physical Education, Recreation and Dance,* 57(5), May/June 1986.

Many HPER departments offer canoeing as part of the curriculum.

trend in our society to seek noncompetitive, personal growth activities in a small-group context. Consumers of HPER offerings will demand courses that are wellness-promoting, exciting, and different. In addition, these potential benefits correspond to the goals of most physical education and recreation programs, namely, the development of physical fitness, motor abilities, mental abilities, and social-emotional abilities (Darst and Armstrong, 1980).

INTERRELATIONSHIPS

Outdoor adventure activities can play a role in each of the sub-disciplines of HPER. These interrelationships go beyond having similar benefits and goals; they involve the process by which these goals and benefits can be achieved. Moreover, through outdoor adventure there can be an effective link between cognitive knowledge and actual application through behavior or attitude change. This is important in the HPER field as, increasingly, the goal is not just to improve an individual's physical performance but also to enhance the person's cognitive, attitudinal, and behavioral skills in order to achieve life-long physical and emotional well-being.

HEALTH

Outdoor adventure activities can provide opportunities to contribute to a health program in three ways: (1) providing specific health knowledge, (2) developing desirable attitudes toward good health, and (3) providing meaningful opportunities to use effective health procedures. Health information that can be specifically related to the health field includes such items as the recognition and treatment of hypothermia, nutritional practices, and emergency care. Because of the physical movement, outdoor natural setting, and generally socially supportive atmosphere, the participant usually feels a sense of accomplishment and well-being after an adventure experience. As Hamrick and Anspaugh (1983) suggest, these feelings of well-being and accomplishment can help develop attitudes that are often more important in the process of making health-related decisions than actual knowledge. People have to practice effective personal hygiene, keep themselves warm, if not dry, and be concerned with a multitude of factors that usually go unnoticed in their everyday life-styles. Failing to do so will often result in some immediate, personally relevant feedback, that is, they will be cold, wet, or hungry. Bucher and Koenig (1974) report that avoiding discomfort and disturbances to achieve optimal health can be powerful motivators for individuals.

PHYSICAL EDUCATION

Traditionally, outdoor adventure programs such as SCUBA and canoeing have been a part of physical education departments. Along with regular activity courses, outdoor adventure can be an area of study similar to exercise physiology or teacher education (Siedentop, 1980, p. 194). The demand for physical educators who have expertise in outdoor adventure activities has grown in response to both student and societal interest, providing a potential market for trained outdoor adventure educators. Outdoor adventure skill development through physical education can also be integrated into other disciplines such as geology or natural resource management. Outdoor adventure activities can be used to augment the traditional physical education program by providing human movement and performance activities in a noncompetitive atmosphere.

RECREATION

Increasingly, successful recreational experiences are being seen as complex phenomena with a variety of personal and external factors. Kelly (1982) suggests a new ecology of leisure in which recreational activities will become more diverse, time-intensive, and linked to geographical location. Outdoor adventure will play an important role in many recreational settings in terms of participation rates, user conflicts, economic impacts, and program design. As the recreation and leisure field tilts toward a private-sector orientation, providing outdoor adventure opportunities will account for a substantial portion of the recreation market. Supporting this claim is the 1985 National Outdoor Outfitters

Motor skill development is an important part of the outdoor adventure experience.

Market Report which describes a continuing increase in sales, profits, store expansions, and numbers of employees over previous seasons (Bishoff, 1985).

While it is clear that outdoor adventure has an important role to play in many of the recreational delivery systems in our society, the recognition of that importance afforded by the recreation profession is more obscure. In a recent issue of *Leisure Today* (Gray and Ibrahim, 1985), entitled the "Recreation Experience," twenty articles were included that described individual perceptions of recreation. Nine of those articles were clearly related to outdoor adventure activities.

It is paradoxical that, while much of the public defines its most significant recreational experiences as being related to activities or feelings commonly associated with outdoor adventure, many recreation and leisure textbooks have failed to adequately address the issue of risk taking in our leisure pursuits. One of the emerging mandates for the recreation profession will be to clearly identify the value and importance of outdoor adventure activities in leisure delivery systems.

There are a number of strong links between outdoor adventure and the field of HPER. These interrelationships include similar goals and methods, historical placements, available trained personnel, and appropriate facilities. Each section of the HPER curriculum can effectively use outdoor adventure programming as an additional method of achieving its goals. Programmers and instructors must recognize this changing market for HPER services in the 1990s.

OUTDOOR ADVENTURING AND THE SCHOOLS

Primary and secondary schools have always been a fertile but relatively untilled ground for the adventure programmer. Historically, the greatest penetration has been in the area of outdoor education. Recently, however, these types of programs have failed to attract much interest and may actually be in a phase-out situation.

Because of the inherent excitement and "attraction" that outdoor adventure activities have for youth, the adventure setting, such as day camps featuring ropes courses, has partially filled the void left by the outdoor education or conservation education curriculum. The following section presents several beliefs and concerns related to the role of outdoor adventure pursuits in the educational system from the perspective of a classroom teacher.

ADVENTURING AS AN EDUCATIONAL ANALOG[2]

For the eighteen years that I have been a classroom teacher I have spent part of each summer as a wilderness canoe guide in the Canadian northwoods, leading groups of high school-age students through the labyrinth of remote lakes and rivers that are to be found in Ontario's Quetico-Superior Area. In talking with friends and colleagues, I had often shared that I felt *I had done some of my best teaching* on those wilderness trips. I was convinced that there was something special about the teaching and learning environment that existed there.

However, because the wilderness was so very different from the classroom experience, I gave little thought to the possibility that the two experiences might be analogous in some important and interesting ways. In my classroom I was often responsible for thirty or more young people. In the wilderness, I had only eight charges on whom to focus my attention. At school, I saw my pupils for fifty-five minutes a day. On the trips we were often in each other's company for sixteen or more hours a day for ten consecutive days. In the classroom, our relationship was shaped by the written rules and cultural conventions of the school. On the lakes, rules were simple and few and the culture was of a different time and place. In the classroom, I was the final evaluator. *On the portage trails, there was no grade to be won or lost.* Because of these and many other major differences, it had never occurred to me to try and understand what the one experience might have to say about the other.

OUTDOOR ADVENTURE AND THE LEARNING PROCESS

What was it about the adventure experience that made learning seem so meaningful to young people? What was it about being a guide that made me feel like a good teacher? Once I decided to take the time to

---

[2]Portions of this section were written by Jim Rowley of Ohio State University, College of Education.

reflect on those specific questions I found that it was relatively easy to identify what I considered to be the fundamental forces that were at work.

In the final analysis, I was able to focus on five specific and interrelated characteristics of the wilderness adventure experience that I felt were collectively responsible for creating that positive teaching and learning environment in which both students and teacher were intellectually challenged, personally stimulated, and emotionally rewarded. Those same five conditions were also present in my classroom on those occasions when I felt that I had done my best teaching, and when my students seemed to be the most involved and satisfied with their learning experience. This was an important insight, because, by seeking to purposefully create those conditions in my classroom, I was able to construct an optimal teaching and learning environment on a more consistent basis. I began to think of *learning as adventure* and I began to consider the *role of the teacher as guide.*

As I discuss each condition I will not attempt an interpretation, for if the analogy is a useful one the possible applications to classroom teaching will be evident.

The Emergence of Shared Meaning

Young people decide to participate in an outdoor adventure experience for a variety of reasons. Some, for example, may well see the experience as a way of testing their physical endurance or their emotional resolve. Simply stated, they want to see if they can "do it." Can they meet the challenge? Others choose to participate because a best friend is going and they want to share the experience. These participants may believe that the adventure experience will be "fun" when shared with a friend. Still others are attracted by a vision of living in a world of pristine beauty. Or they sign up because they like to fish and want to try their luck in a remote lake or stream, or because they enjoy photography and want to capture some wilderness scenes, or because mom and dad believe that the experience will be a good one for their son or daughter.

Importantly, the different motivations that bring a group of young people together to share an adventure experience does not preclude the possibility that they may arrive at a common understanding of that experience. In fact, the nature of the adventure experience is such that it can, and often does, have a kind of bonding effect on the participants. By sharing the physical challenges, the humorous events, or common struggle to master new skills, a sense of camaraderie develops. By the end of the trip, the group has often developed a shared understanding of their experience. There is something special, and perhaps unforgettable, about that collective feeling that says "we did this together."

What is the process that allows such a shared *understanding* to emerge? First, it seems important to recognize the significance of the word emerge. To recognize that the phenomenon of shared *meaning* is

Mountaineering offers ideal opportunities for groups to develop "shared experiences".

one that must evolve over time and as a result of shared *experience* is a critical first step. The guide who begins the trip by attempting to impose his or her interpretation of what the experience will mean for the group fails to understand the important role that only time can play. In other words, the pretrip pep talk or statement of goals may have little to contribute except that it may be the first shared experience.

Where the guide can play an important role in the construction of shared meaning is by seizing the opportunities to promote discussion and interpretation of shared experience. Imagine that a group has just completed a difficult portage on a wilderness canoe trip. The map was in error and the trail was considerably longer than expected. In addition, half of the trail was through a mosquito-infested swamp. All group members eventually completed the portage, but not with the same grace or speed. Nonetheless it was a collective triumph. However, that shared accomplishment was made up of personal experiences. The guide who takes time to encourage the group to share those personal experiences does much to help build shared meaning.

A Spirit of Cooperation

As I thought about the idea of shared meaning I began to recognize the important role that cooperative behavior had to play in the construction of such meaning. When young people begin an outdoor adventure experience, they bring with them attitudes that define the way in which they expect to behave with other group members.

In the 1940s, Morton Deutsch, working from Lewin's theory of motivation, identified three possible behaviors: *competitive, individualist,* and *cooperative.* This framework seemed to accurately define the range of behaviors that could be expected in groups of young people given opportunities to demonstrate their superior strength, knowledge, or skill. To them, the trip will produce winners and losers. Maybe they fully expect to be winners. Or perhaps they hope to avoid being losers. As the canoes move down the lake they are uncomfortable if they are not in the lead. On the first few portage trails, those who stop to rest or accept help are labeled losers. Only one person can finish first and so the trip is viewed as a race.

The second type of participant operates from a predominantly individualistic frame of reference. These participants tend to see the experience as an opportunity to accomplish personal goals that are in no way related to other members of the group. The participant seeks outcomes that are personally beneficial and are not contingent upon whether other group members achieve their goals or not. The young man who wants to enjoy some wilderness fishing and perhaps learn some new techniques is rewarded by his own catch, not beaten by his tent mate who lands the bigger walleye. The individualistic participant often has no vision of needing to interact with other group members except in the most superficial way.

Experience has taught me that the majority of young people who participate in an outdoor adventure approach the expedition with a competitive or individualistic attitude. Such attitudes are not necessarily undesirable; to the contrary, they can be important and positive forces. However, participants are soon confronted with the reality that the adventure experience also demands that they consider the *value of cooperative efforts.*

When the value of cooperation is discovered, an important lesson is learned that can often have a positive carry-over effect on other trip activities. Helping someone build the campfire when it is not your "turn" means that everyone who is hungry, including you, eats sooner. Stopping to help someone who is struggling with a bad portage may mean that the whole group will get to camp earlier, or that you may be helped tomorrow if it turns out to be your day to fight an upset stomach or a temporary loss of confidence. It can actually feel good to know that you are a part of a group of people that care about each other, a group that celebrates its collective achievements while allowing room for individual successes and failures.

In straightforward terms, groups that developed strong cooperative spirits are groups that I associate with my best adventure experiences. These groups seemed to be hungrier for new knowledge and skills, and demonstrated an ability to master them more easily (Johnson, Johnson, and Tauer, 1979). The individual members of such groups tended to feel better about themselves and their experience (Johnson and Johnson, 1983).

High Levels of Engagement

The outdoor adventure experience almost always invites, and frequently demands, high levels of student engagement. Participants who choose to take part in an adventure outing may or may not anticipate the amount of physical and mental energy that they will be required to expend if they are to experience success. However, once they are in the wilderness they are soon confronted with new knowledge, skills, and attitudes which they must quickly process and practice if they are to avoid failure. In many cases, the newly acquired information must be applied immediately to real-life situations which may well involve some degree of real or perceived risk.

When traveling in bear country, for example, there is real risk to the group if one member fails to learn the lessons involved in the proper disposal of food waste. The guide who explains the proper techniques and the reasons why such techniques are employed may get better results than the guide who just explains the techniques themselves. However, the guide who explains the techniques, gives a reasoned explanation, and then discusses the potential problems of attracting a bear into camp will likely get the best performance from his group. The important point to be made is not that fear can be a powerful motivator, but that there is a definitive relationship between what is being taught and learned and the life of the student.

Confronted with the real possibility of success and failure, the learning experience often takes on an element of excitement or what has been referred to as optimal arousal (Fowler, 1966; Ellis, 1973). Students are engaged in the learning process because it is perceived to have real meaning. The participant who spends a cold, wet night because she failed to follow the guide's suggestions on how to properly pitch a tent is likely to be genuinely interested in discovering what went wrong and how the problem can be corrected.

The good guide recognizes and understands the importance of creating a teaching and learning environment where there is a balance between the newly acquired knowledge, skills, and attitudes and the real-like challenges against which they are tested. When there is a balance between boredom and anxiety, and the challenges confronted are real and appropriate to their skills, a kind of "flow" takes place (Czikszentmihalyi, 1975). Work, whether physical or mental, becomes more like play. Perhaps this is the phenomenon that young people try to describe by using the word fun. When work and play become one, it is a special experience that is not easily forgotten.

Dealing With Dissonance or Uncertainty

Learning new skills, or applying old skills to new situations, almost always involves some degree of dissonance. And it is normal for the level of dissonance to increase as the degree of risk increases. Risk, and the suspense that is associated with it, is central to the idea of the adventure experience. The participant who stands at the beginning of a mile-long portage trail may well wonder if she will be able to find the strength to carry her eighty-pound load to the next lake without accident, injury, or loss of self-confidence. What if she is the only one in the group who doesn't make it without help? These fears, and many others, real and imagined, are a part of the adventure experience. They are the source of dissonance, anxiety, and doubt. But, beaten, they hold the promise of pride, satisfaction, and a renewed or expanded sense of self-efficacy (Bandura, 1977). Importantly, the guide can actually help in the process of building that sense of self-efficacy by helping the participant attribute her success to her personal ability and efforts and not to some external forces (Heider, 1958).

Adventure pursuits can provide unique interactions between people and the natural environment.

Risk and fear, and the dissonance that accompany them, are a part of the human experience. Importantly, in the adventure experience their reality is acknowledged as an expected part of the process. They can be anticipated but not planned for, controlled but not eliminated (Ewert, 1986). If ignored and permitted to reach dangerous levels, they can have a kind of paralyzing effect that is counterproductive from a teaching and learning perspective. When anticipated and controlled by the leader, they can contribute to creating a productive learning environment where group members feel more excitement than fear, more anticipation than anxiety.

Leading from Behind

Leadership is an elusive and difficult concept to define and has been the subject of academic investigation, scholarly discussion, and workplace debate for many years. Despite the fact that journal articles and books on the subject abound, the search for a way to define the good leader continues.

Nonetheless, as a wilderness guide, I knew that I was in a position of leadership. Perhaps more importantly, I felt like a leader. I knew that I was responsible for taking a group of young people somewhere that they had never been before. In the simplest terms, that is why they needed me—*to take them someplace they had never been before.* I was someone who could, by the virtue of his greater experience, advise and direct them and, perhaps, serve as a model.

As I thought about the value of shared meaning, cooperation, constructive dissonance, and high levels of engagement, I began to appreciate the vitally important role a guide has to play in creating, controlling, and, in a sense, orchestrating those experiences. I gradually came to understand that my peak adventure experiences as a guide were those where I felt accepted as a part of the team and where I felt most comfortable *leading from behind.* More importantly, they were the experiences where the young people had developed a powerful sense of group and self-efficacy. In the final analysis, they were the experiences where the group came to an expanded understanding of the true meaning of adventure as an experience characterized by suspense, excitement, and risk.

MAIN POINTS

1. Outdoor adventure pursuits have become popular activities in a substantial number of educational institutions, including colleges, universities, and high schools.
2. In addition to this popularity, outdoor adventure pursuits can contribute to the health, physical education, and recreational endeavors of the student population.
3. One of the important benefits, from an educational perspective, is the shared experience and meanings that develop between the teacher and student through an outdoor adventure activity.
4. Outdoor adventure pursuits in an educational setting typically demand a high level of engagement and cooperation on the part of the participants.
5. Learning to cope and deal with feelings of uncertainty and dissonance are important virtues that can be experienced in an outdoor adventure setting.
6. Through outdoor adventuring, students can experience opportunities

to practice leadership and decision making within the context of a supportive group atmosphere.

REFERENCES

Bandura, A. (1977). Self-efficacy: Toward a Unifying Theory of Behavior Change. *Psychologist,* 37: pp. 122–147.

Bischoff, G. (ed.). (1985). National Outdoor Outfitters Market Report. *National Outdoor Outfitters News,* 10(8): pp. 10–13.

Bucher, C. and Koenig, C. (1974). *Secondary School Physical Education.* St. Louis: C. V. Mosby.

Csikszentmihalyi, M. (1975). *Beyond Boredom and Anxiety.* San Francisco: Jossey-Bass.

Darst, P. and Armstrong, G. (1980). *Outdoor Adventure Activities for School and Recreation Programs.* Minneapolis, MN: Burgess.

Ellis, M. (1973). *Why People Play.* Englewood Cliffs, NJ: Prentice-Hall.

Ewert, A. (1986). The Therapeutic Modification of Fear Through Outdoor Adventure Recreation Activities. *Bradford Papers Annual,* 1: pp. 1-10.

Fowler, H. (1966). *Curiousity and Behavior.* New York: MacMillan.

Gray, D. and Ibrahim, H. (eds.). (1985). Recreation Experience—the Human Dimension. *Journal of Physical Education and Recreation,* 56(8): pp. 28–58.

Hamrick, M. and Anspaugh, D. (1983). *Activities for Health Decisions.* Winston-Salem, NC: Hunter Textbooks.

Heider, F. (1958). *The Psychology of Interpersonal Relations.* New York: Wiley.

Hendee, J. and Roggenbuck, J. (1984). Wilderness-Related Education as a Factor Increasing Demand for Wilderness. Paper presented at the International Forest Congress Convention, Quebec City, Canada, August 5, 1984.

Johnson, R., Johnson, D., and Tauer, M. (1979). The Effects of Cooperative, Competitive, and Individualistic Goal Structures on Students' Attitudes and Achievement. *Journal of Psychology,* 102: pp. 191-198.

Johnson, D. and Johnson, R. (1983). The Socialization and Achievement Crises: Are Cooperative Learning Experiences the Solution? In L. Bickman (ed.). *Applied Social Psychology Annual,* 4. Beverly Hills, CA: Sage Publications.

Kelly, J. (1982). *Leisure.* Englewood Cliffs, NJ: Prentice-Hall.

Siedentop, D. (1980). *Physical Education: Introductory Analysis,* 3d ed.. Dubuque, IA: Wm. C. Brown.

4

THE BENEFITS OF OUTDOOR ADVENTURE PURSUITS

Many of the benefits, consequences, and expected outcomes from participation in outdoor adventure pursuits are similar to those realized through outdoor education, environmental education, or outdoor recreation. However, because of the element of risk, uncertainty of outcome, and personal influence on these outcomes, outdoor adventure programs have traditionally been associated with personal growth and development of the individual or group. Cullingford (1979) has called this exploration of one's self through physical and mental parameters "Innerlichkeit." He suggests that personal outdoor adventure becomes an exploration in self-discovery. In understanding this sociopsychological foundation, Meier (1977) and White (1978) maintain that there are constraints and requirements placed on individuals participating in outdoor adventure. These constraints consist of:

1. The need for an adequate fitness level and stamina of the individual.
2. A need to learn technical skills that become more complex and involved as the individual expands his or her adventure experiences.
3. The ability to deal with stress and uncertainty—the inherent aspects of outdoor adventure pursuits. Meier (1977) suggests that there is a definitive physical and/or mental barrier which must be crossed.
4. A willingness to invest a significant amount of time, commitment, money, and energy if an individual decides to move beyond the novice phase of an adventure activity. (See Figure 1.2, Chapter 1)
5. The ability to develop and maintain a strong communal bond that forms among participants within a given adventure experience

(White, 1978). Bonding is considered a benefit in itself and is translated into increased levels of trust, commitment to others, and compassion.

6. A willingness to use technical language and specialized equipment, and acknowledge professional instruction and leadership.

Rockclimbing involves seeking benefits through a challenging outdoor environment.

These and other requirements create an ambiance surrounding outdoor adventuring which is one of personal involvement and direct application of skills. For the participant to be successful, a combination of talents is required, including mental, physical, and emotional elements. Individuals must think through a solution to a given task, such as finding the way out of a cave; have the physical skills to accomplish the task;

and the emotional strength to persevere. It is this interaction between the physical, emotional, and mental requirements of an adventure experience that has led individuals to anticipate certain benefits and expectations concerning outdoor adventuring.

The benefits of participation in outdoor adventure can be divided into the categories of psychological, sociological, educational, and physical. These benefits are listed in Table 4.1. To date, most of the research has typically centered on such constructs as self-esteem and self-concept. This may be due to the fact that much of the research is affiliated with psychology.

TABLE 4.1
Potential Benefits of Outdoor Adventure Pursuits

Psychological	Sociological	Educational	Physical
Self-concept	Compassion	Outdoor education	Fitness
Confidence	Group cooperation	Nature awareness	Skills
Self-efficacy	Respect for others	Conservation education	Strength
Sensation seeking	Communication	Problem solving	Coordination
Actualization	Behavior feedback	Value clarification	Catharsis
Well-being	Friendship	Outdoor techniques	Exercise
Personal testing	Belonging	Improved academics	Balance

PSYCHOLOGICAL BENEFITS

The following psychological constructs involve those areas that may benefit the individual on a personal (as opposed to group) basis. These areas include self-concept, self-confidence and self-efficacy (perceived levels of abilities), self-actualization and well-being (Zuckerman, 1979).

SELF-CONCEPT

Of all the benefits ascribed to outdoor adventure activities, self-concept has received the most attention. It is defined as the way in which a person views or perceives himself, his attitudes, beliefs, feelings, and personal expectations (Patterson, 1972). Participation in outdoor adventure activities has usually been considered a method of enhancing or strengthening one's self-image. Survival courses were the first type of adventure medium through which the goal was to enhance a participant's self-concept positively (Clifford and Clifford, 1967; Ewert, 1983; Moses and Peterson, 1970; Howard, Heaps, and Thorstenson, 1972). With very few exceptions, these studies and later ones, such as Robbins (1976), George (1984), and Bacon (1988) suggested that after participation in an outdoor adventure program (e.g., a survival training school) a participant's self-concept did show significant improvement and strengthening.

Other types of programs from which self-concept studies have emerged include wilderness schools (Cave and Rapoport, 1977; Kaplan and Talbot, 1983; McDonald, 1983) and educational programs utilizing outdoor adventure activities (Fornader, 1973; Jones, 1978; Crume, 1983). The self-concept of participating individuals was positively enhanced in the vast majority of these studies.

SELF-EFFICACY/SELF-CONFIDENCE

Harmon and Templin (1987) reported that outdoor adventure can be an important methodology for improving one's feelings of confidence and self-efficacy. In addition, Darst and Armstrong (1980) suggest that one reason for the growth in popularity of outdoor adventure activities is in the feelings of success, even for those with limited physical abilities, that can arise with participation. Other authors and studies have supported the belief of a linkage between self-efficacy, self-confidence, and outdoor adventure (Katz and Kolb, 1968; Wetmore, 1972; Harmon, 1974; Ewert, 1986).

SELF-ACTUALIZATION/WELL-BEING

Based on Maslow's theory of self-actualization, several studies have indicated that outdoor adventure participation can play a role in feelings of personal well-being. Literary analyses of a number of great conservation and wilderness writers, such as John Muir, led Graber (1976) and Scott (1974) to propose that wilderness recreational encounters could create opportunities for self-expression and enhanced feelings of psychological health. These ideas were supported by other studies (Vanderwilt and Klocke, 1971; Young, 1983; Kaplan, 1974; Young and Crandall, 1984; Kaplan and Kaplan, 1983). It should be noted that, while these and other studies have suggested the potential for achieving a state of well-being, characterized as self-actualization, the findings are preliminary and subject to the contradictory findings of other works.

SOCIOLOGICAL BENEFITS

Benefits which have been categorized as sociological include compassion, group cooperation, respect for others, communication skills (particularly in a small-group setting), behavior while in the company of others, and developing friendships. To date, most of the research has focused on group cooperation.

Intrinsic in many outdoor adventure settings is the necessity of working within a small-group environment to accomplish required tasks and safely engage in the activity (Walsh and Golins, 1975). Given this

Successful engagement in outdoor adventure pursuits often results in feelings of well-being, self-confidence, and self-actualization.

fact, it is not surprising that a number of studies have demonstrated a positive effect on levels of cooperation from participants in small-group settings (Frant, Roland, and Schempp, 1982; Orlick, 1982; Roland and Hoyt, 1984). In addition, Harmon (1974) suggests that adventure programming can be effective in measuring group interaction by providing opportunities for listening to others' ideas, being offered and accepting leadership responsibilities, and becoming a member of a clearly identifiable team with clear-cut goals and tasks.

Individuals in trouble with the law have long been the subject of many research efforts in outdoor adventure programming. One of the first systematic efforts at determining the impact of adventure participation

Through outdoor adventure pursuits, an effective and well-functioning team can often result from an initial group of strangers.

upon the recidivism rate (returning to a juvenile institution after parole) of delinquents was made by Kelly and Baer (1971). Later research studies by Willman and Chun (1973), Kelly (1974), Cytrynbaum and Ken (1975), Bacon (1988), and Roberts (1988) also demonstrated a significant reduction in the rate of return to prison or a juvenile institution for those who participated in an outdoor adventure program. While there are a number of methodological problems, such as the lack of good baseline data or the weaknesses of the "self-report" questionnaire, the number of rehabilitative programs using outdoor adventure activities in their programs has grown rapidly (Wright, 1983; Hunter, 1984; Havens, 1985). This fact alone suggests that something of a positive nature is occurring in these programs that take place in an outdoor environment.

EDUCATIONAL BENEFITS

A substantial number of educational benefits can be accrued from outdoor adventure participation. A partial list of these positive consequences includes improved academic abilities, education about the environment, nature awareness, problem solving, outdoor skills, and value clarification. While many of these items can be taught in a traditional classroom, the outdoor environment may enhance an element of reality in the teaching situation.

A number of studies have indicated that participation in outdoor

Group decision-making and problem-solving become integral components of the outdoor adventure pursuits experience.

adventure programs may be helpful in motivating students to improve their future academic performances (Hammerman, 1978; Gass, 1987; Stogner, 1978). An earlier study by McNamara (1971) suggested that the outdoors may be particularly effective in helping a student learn to develop concepts rather than rote memory.

Other educational benefits include the development of problem-solving skills and value clarification. A study by Project Backstop in 1973 studied the relationship between participation in an outdoor adventure program and racial prejudices. The results, in part, seemed to indicate reduced prejudice and racial tension.

A number of other works have also suggested that outdoor adventure activities could be useful in enhancing problem-solving skills or values (Godfrey, 1972 and Knapp, 1986). For example, the components of problem solving—identifying the problem, identifying and reviewing solutions, picking and implementing a solution, and evaluating that solution—lend themselves particularly well in an outdoor adventure situation. In the outdoors there are concrete obstacles to overcome, such as crossing a river, navigating in the wilderness, planning or rationing food, or expedition and logistical planning. Not only are problems encountered that need to be resolved, but they are often time-critical. Communication and cooperation, enhanced by a small-group setting, are essential to solving a problem. In addition, problem solving in the outdoors is usually "rewarded" by seeing the immediate result of the group's decision—be it correct or incorrect.

More recently, Zook (1986) suggested that outdoor adventure programs may help provide opportunities to clarify the distinction between needs and wants. In the outdoors, amenities are often nonexistent. Individuals must prioritize what is actually *needed* and obtainable versus what they would like (i.e., a warm, soft bed; comfortable place to sit; watching T.V.; air conditioning, etc.).

PHYSICAL BENEFITS

By their very nature, many outdoor adventure activities demand a high degree of physical exertion and movement. One area of potential benefits that is often forgotten is the improvement of the physical fitness of the participant. Such benefits as improvement in skills, strength, coordination, exercise, and balance may result from outdoor participation.

Siedentop et al. (1984) write that one of the reasons for the popularity of outdoor adventure programs is that they allow the student a chance to participate, regardless of skill level and in a noncompetitive atmosphere. This active participation can often lead to improvements in a variety of fitness-related benefits. A recent study by Wright (1983) demonstrated significant improvement in cardiovascular values after participation in an outdoor adventure program. Moreover, Cordell (1985) suggests that recreation managers need to consider the growing influence of fitness activities involved in a natural outdoor setting.

Some writers have indicated that outdoor adventuring can provide a physical and emotional catharsis. Progen (1979) illustrates this point in the following statement:

> I see this trend toward natural sports not so much as an escape from daily life as an escape to nature: not so much to forget, but rather to remember. (p. 237)

Catharsis and physical exercise were also two important factors in describing the motivations for mountain climbing (Ewert, 1985) and other adventure recreation activities (Schreyer and White, 1979).

The benefits previously discussed do not, however, account for all the possible reasons for participation in outdoor adventure recreation. There are a number of contributions to society and the individual that are integral to outdoor adventure pursuits.

INHERENT CONTRIBUTIONS

One aspect of outdoor adventure pursuits that is related to benefits, but often overlooked, is the inherent contributions they offer to society, education, and the individual. Because of their unique interaction with the natural setting, the element of risk taking, their tangible objectives or tasks, and the social setting, outdoor adventure pursuits can provide a wide range of contributions. These contributions are listed in Table 4.2.

TABLE 4.2
Inherent Contributions of Outdoor Adventure Pursuits

- Opportunities for learning and experiencing with other students in a unique social and physical setting
- Developing skills for life-long participation in specific activities
- A unique opportunity to interlink attitude and value formation with behavioral change
- The provision of a personally and socially acceptable medium for personal testing
- Opportunities for reconstructing feelings, experiences, and problems faced by our ancestors
- Opportunities to gain a more intimate view of one's strengths, weaknesses, and character
- Multi-dimensional learning opportunities
- Opportunity to experience excitement in a controlled atmosphere

As can be seen, outdoor adventuring can provide a number of opportunities difficult to obtain in everyday life. In addition, outdoor adventure pursuits provide a noncompetitive atmosphere that is often very appealing, particularly to young people. Related to this sense of noncompetitiveness is the marked absence of spectators. The individual is faced with accomplishing only the assigned task and the regard of his or her group, rather than being exposed to the adulation or scorn of a large number of spectators. In outdoor adventure, most of the group members are faced with the same problems and challenges, with no one group being allowed to sit back and critique. Everyone will get a chance to perform according to his or her own ability. Some may fail and have to try again, while some may succeed well beyond their expectations. What seems to be essential to this success is often the support of the group. Progen (1979) elaborates on this sense of accomplishment within the group.

> Sometimes man finds a deep union with other men after sharing an [adventure] experience in nature, particularly because man is dependent upon his fellow man and is depended upon in a survival, life-death situation. Mountaineering provides a very vivid example. Together, two or three or four can do what is impossible for one to accomplish.

PERSONAL TESTING

Despite a supportive group atmosphere and lack of competitiveness with others, the individual still must perform the given task by himself.

Top-roped rockclimbing involves trust as well as physical and technical skills.

Outdoor adventure activities seem to demand a sense of self-centeredness within the individual. This may be due to the "aloneness" inherent in the activities. While the other members of the group can help and provide encouragement, individuals still have to perform the task by themselves. Rappelling down a 150-foot cliff is not like being on the football team, where individual performance can be enhanced or diluted by the actions of the team. In rappelling, the *individual* can be supported by the team (i.e., group) but has to perform alone. Furthermore, once that individual starts over the cliff, or down the rapids, or jumping out of the plane, what happens to him or her is usually directly attributable to his or her own actions. Slusher (1967) states that, in life, cooperation may provide quality but in survival a person just wants to exist. He goes on to suggest that mountain climbing may be one example of an activity that combines group altruism with individual selfishness.

CONCLUSIONS

In summary, participation in outdoor adventure pursuits has been linked with a number of potential benefits. These benefits have traditionally centered around psychological, sociological, educational, and physical dimensions. From a psychological perspective, benefits from participating in outdoor adventure pursuits include self-concept, esteem building, self-efficacy, and self-actualization.

Sociological benefits involve compassion for others, group cooperation, and respect for others. In addition, a number of educational benefits include enhanced GPAs and problem-solving skills, and heightened knowledge about the environment. Also of educational significance is the greater affinity of teachers and students after an outdoor adventure pursuit. Physical benefits include increased physical fitness, catharsis, and coordination/balance concerns.

Related to benefits are the inherent contributions associated with outdoor adventure pursuits. Among these contributions are opportunities for personal testing, multidimensional learning, and a chance to experience excitement in a somewhat controlled fashion. Other contributions include providing opportunities for learning and experiencing with other people in a unique social and physical setting.

MAIN POINTS

1. The benefits realized through outdoor adventure pursuits is one of the most widely researched and documented components of these types of activities.
2. In understanding participation and expected benefits through outdoor adventure pursuits, the constraints on the individual must also be understood, including:
   - The need for physical fitness.
   - The need to learn technical skills.
   - A willingness to invest significant amounts of time and financial resources.
   - The ability to deal with stress and uncertainty.
3. Despite these constraints, a number of benefits can be anticipated through outdoor adventure pursuits. These benefits can be categorized into psychological, sociological, educational, and physical benefits.
4. In addition, there are a number of inherent contributions associated with outdoor adventure pursuits. These contributions include:
   - Opportunities for learning and experiencing in a unique social and physical setting.

- The development of skills and attitudes for participation in life-long sports.
- A unique opportunity to interlink a person's attitude and value formation with behavioral change.
- The provision of multidimensional learning opportunities.

REFERENCES

Bacon, S. (1988). "Outward Bound and Troubled Youth." Greenwich, CT: Outward Bound.

Cave, S. and Rapoport, E. (1977). *The Wilderness Experience: A Conceptual and Theoretical Understanding.* Santa Fe, NM: New Mexico Department of Hospitals and Institutes.

Clifford, E. and Clifford, M. (1967). Self-Concepts Before and After Survival Training. *British Journal of Social and Clinical Psychology,* 6: pp. 241–248.

Cordell, B. (1985). Fitness as a Life-Style: The Trend Toward Commitment. *Proceedings: 1985 National Outdoor Recreation Trends Symposium II.* Atlanta, GA: National Park Service, pp. 171–181.

Crume, C. (1983). A Study of the Effect of Group Outdoor Activities on the Self-Concept of Physical Education and Recreation Majors. Ed. D. Dissertation. Lexington, KY: University of Kentucky.

Cullingford, C. (1979). The Philosophy of Adventure Education. *Outdoors,* 10: pp. 4–5.

Cytrynbaum, S. and Ken, K. (1975). The Connecticut Wilderness Program: A Preliminary Evaluation Report. Report submitted to the State of Connecticut Council on Human Services, Hartford, CT.

Darst, P. and Armstrong, G. (1980). *Outdoor Adventure Activities for School and Recreation Programs.* Minneapolis. MN: Burgess.

Ewert, A. (1983). *Outdoor Adventure and Self-Concept: A Research Analysis.* Center of Leisure Studies, University of Oregon, Eugene, OR.

Ewert, A. (1985). Why People Climb: The Relationship of Participant Motives and Experience Level to Mountaineering. *Journal of Leisure Research,* 17(3): pp. 241–250.

Ewert, A. (1986). The Therapeutic Modification of Fear Through Outdoor Adventure Recreation Activities. *Bradford Papers Annual,* 1: pp. 1–10.

Fornader, G. (1973). Report on Mitchell Senior Seminar. Master of Education Report. Boulder, CO: University of Colorado.

Frant, R.; Roland, C.; and Schempp, P. (1982). Learning Through Outdoor Adventure Education. *Teaching Exceptional Children,* 2: pp. 145–151.

Gass, M. (1987). The Effects of a Wilderness Orientation Program on College Students. *Journal of Experiential Education,* 10(2): pp. 30–33.

George, R. (1984). Learning Survival Skills, Solo Camping and Improvements in Self-Image: Is There a Relationship? *Psychological Reports,* 55: pp. 168–170.

Godfrey, R. (1972). Outward Bound: A Model for Educational Change and Development. Ph.D. Dissertation. Greeley, CO: University of Northern Colorado.

Graber, L. (1976). *Wilderness as Sacred Space.* Washington, DC: Association of American Georgraphers.

Hammerman, D. (1978). Outdoor Education. *Journal of Physical Education and Recreation,* 1: p. 28.

Harmon, P. (1974). *The Measurement of Affective Education: A Report of Recent Work by Outward Bound Prepared for the Conference on Outdoor Pursuits in Higher Education.* Denver: Colorado Outward Bound.

Harmon, P. and Templin, G. (1987). Conceptualizing Experiential Education. In J. Meier, T. Morash, and G. Welton (eds.). *High Adventure Outdoor Pursuits,* 2d ed., pp. 69-77. Columbus, OH: Publishing Horizons.

Havens, M. (1985). Ethical Challenges in the Outdoor Setting. *Therapeutic Recreation Journal,* 19(4): pp. 75–80.

Howard, G.; Heapes, R.; and Thorstenson, C. (1972). Self-Concept Changes Following Outdoor Survival Training. Provo, UT: Brigham Young Academic Standards Office (Mimeographed).

Hunter, R. (1984). The Impact of Voluntary Selection Procedures on the Reported Success of Outdoor Rehabilitation Programs. *Therapeutic Recreation Journal,* 3: pp. 38–44.

Jones, C. (1978). *An Evaluation of the Effects of an Outward Bound Type of Program Upon the Self-Concepts and Academic Achievement of High School Students.* Ph.D. Dissertation. Boston University School of Education.

Kaplan, J. (1974). Cognitive Learning in the Out-of-Doors. Master's Thesis. The Pennsylvania State University.

Kaplan, S. and Kaplan, J. (1983). Psychological Benefits of a Wilderness Experience. In I. Altman and J. Wohlwill (eds.). *Behavior and the Natural Environment,* pp. 163–204. New York: Plenum.

Kaplan, S. and Talbot, J. (1983). Psychological Benefits of a Wilderness Experience. In I. Altman and J. Wohlwill (eds.). *Behavior and the Natural Environment,* pp. 163–204. New York: Plenum.

Katz, R. and Kolb, D. (1968). Outward Bound and Education for Personal Growth. In F. Kelly and D. Baer (eds.). *Outward Bound Schools as an Alternative to Institutionalization for Adolescent Delinquent Boys.* Boston: Fandel Press.

Kelly, F. (1974). Outward Bound and Delinquency: A Ten Year Experience. In *Major Papers Presented at the Conference on Experiential Education.* Estes Park, CO, October 1974. Denver: Colorado Outward Bound.

Kelly, F. and Baer, D. (1971). Physical Challenge as a Treatment for Delinquency. *Crime and Delinquency,* 17: pp. 437–445.

Knapp, C. (1986). The Science and Art of Processing Outdoor Experiences. *The Outdoor Communicator,* 16(1): pp. 13–17.

McDonald, D. (1983). The Effect of Participation in an Outdoor Experiential Education Program on Self-Concepts. Ph.D. Dissertation. Oklahoma State University.

McNamara, E. (1971). A Comparison of the Learning Behaviors on Eighth and Ninth Grade ESCP Earth Science Students: One Half Experiencing Laboratory Investigations in the Indoor Environment, the Other Half Experiencing Laboratory Investigations in the Outdoor Environment. PH.D. Dissertation. The Pennsylvania State University.

Meier, J. (1977). Risk Recreation. Exploration and Implications. Paper delivered at the Congress for Recreation and Parks, Las Vegas, NV.

Moses, D. and Peterson, D. (1970). Academic Achievement Helps Program. Provo, UT: Brigham Young University. (Mimeographed).

Orlick, T. (1982). *The Second Cooperative Sports and Games Book.* New York: Pantheon Books.

Patterson, C. (1972). *Humanistic Education.* Englewood Cliffs, NJ: Prentice-Hall.

Progen, J. (1979). Man, Nature and Sport. In E. Gerber and M. Nillian (eds.). *Sports and the Body: A Philosophical Symposium,* pp. 237-242. Philadelphia: Lea and Febiger.

Robbins, S. (1976). Outdoor Wilderness Survival and its Psychological and Sociological Effects upon Students in Changing Human Behavior. Ph.D. Dissertation. Provo, UT: Brigham Young University.

Roberts, A. (1988). Wilderness Programs for Juvenile Offenders: A Challenging Alternative. *Juvenile and Family Journal,* 39(1): pp. 1-2.

Roland, C. and Hoyt, J. (1984). Family Adventure Programming. In G. Robb (ed.). *The Bradford Papers,* IV, pp. 19-28. Bloomington, IN: Indiana University Press.

Schreyer, R. and White, R. (1979). A Conceptual Model of High-Risk Recreation. *Proceedings: First Annual Conference on Recreation Planning and Development.* New York: American Society of Civil Engineers.

Scott, N. (1974). Toward a Psychology of Wilderness Experience. *Natural Resources Journal,* 14: pp. 231-237.

Siedentop, D.; Herkowitz, J.; and Rink, J. (1984). *Elementary Physical Education Methods.* Englewood Cliffs, NJ: Prentice-Hall.

Slusher, H. (1967). *Man, Sport and Existence: A Critical Analysis.* Philadelphia: Lea and Febiger.

Stogner, J. (1978). The Effects of a Wilderness Experience on Self-Concept and Academic Performance. Ph.D. Dissertation. Blacksburg, VA: Virginia Polytechnic Institute and State University.

Vanderwilt, R. and Klocke, R. (1971). Self-Actualization of Females in an Experimental Orientation Program (Experimental Studies Program at Mankato State College, in Conjunction with the Minnesota Outward Bound School). *National Association of Women Deans and Counselors Journal,* 34(3): pp. 52-58.

Walsh, V. and Golins, G. (1975). *The Exploration of the Outward Bound Process.* Denver: Colorado Outward Bound.

Wetmore, R. (1972). The Influence of Outward Bound School Experience on the Self-Concept of Adolescent Boys. Ph.D. Dissertation, Boston University.

White, B. (1978). Risk Recreation: Exploration and Implications. Paper delivered at the Congress for Recreation and Parks, Las Vegas, NV.

Willman, H. and Chun, R. (1973). Homeward Bound: An Alternative to the Institutionalization of Adjudicated Juvenile Offenders. *Federal Probation,* 37(3): pp. 52-58.

Wright, A. (1983). Therapeutic Potential of the Outward Bound Process: An Evaluation of a Treatment Program for Juvenile Delinquents. *Therapeutic Recreation Journal,* 17(2): pp. 33-42.

Young, R. (1983). Toward an Understanding of Wilderness Participation. *Leisure Sciences,* 4: pp. 339-357.

Young, R. and Crandall, R. (1984). Wilderness Use and Self-Actualization. *Journal of Leisure Research,* 16(2): pp. 149-160.

Zook, L. (1986). Outdoor Adventure Programs Build Character Five Ways. *Parks and Recreation,* 21(1): pp. 54-57.

Zuckerman, M. (1979). *Sensation-Seeking: Beyond the Optimal Level of Arousal.* Hillsdale, NJ: Lawrence Erlbaum Associates.

5

RISK SEEKING, MOTIVATIONS, AND FEAR IN OUTDOOR ADVENTURE PURSUITS

RISK/SENSATION SEEKING

Risk is an obvious component of many outdoor adventure activities. These risks can be real or apparent based on the perceptions of the participant. In addition to this taxonomic classification, there are a tremendous variety of risks that the individual feels or perceives. In the outdoor adventure pursuits setting, most are attributed to physical risks, such as falling, fast water, or cold temperatures. Carney (1971) suggests that the social risks should also be considered. In the outdoor setting, these types of risks include conflict within the group, appearing inept, or being perceived as a burden to the group.

Meier (1977) posits that risk in the recreation setting (a.k.a., outdoor adventure pursuits) contains the characteristics of:

- A large measure of interest, time and energy.
- A knowledge of equipment and locale.
- The elements of instruction and leadership.
- The relative need for physical strength and conditioning.

Meier goes on to state, "When we combine the terms risk and recreation we most likely visualize any number of leisure activities which provide exposure to physical danger" (p. 3). To this, one can add the concept of emotional danger. Taken together, the perceived level of physical and emotional danger or risk is partially dependent on the individual's appraisal of those dangers (Klausner, 1968; Huberman, 1968). In other words, how dangerous the activity may actually be may not be as important as how dangerous the participants "perceive" it to be.

In attempting to explain risk seeking, Allen (1980b) developed an interesting conceptual framework of risk recreation. Within this model the antecedents (predispositions), behavior, and consequences are interlinked to explain who the participants or risk seekers will be, for what purposes they seek out risk, and what the possible outcomes of those actions are. This model is illustrated in Figure 5.1.

FIGURE 5.1
Allen's (1980) Model of Risk-Taking Outdoor Recreation

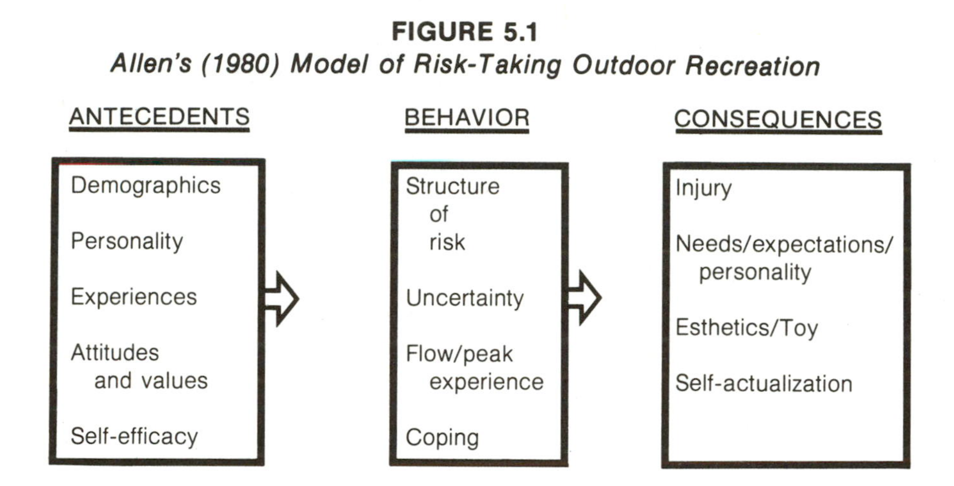

The antecedents section of the model is of particular interest in the description of who the risk seekers are. Within these antecedents are the components of demographics, personality, activities, experience, and attitudes. Research findings suggest that the outdoor risk taker is usually relatively young, middle class, and male (Klausner, 1968). With respect to personality, Allen (1980a) reports that the research findings are relatively consistent with risk seekers scoring consistently higher than nonrisk seekers in the areas of confidence (Cober, 1972), need for achievement (Huberman, 1968; O'Connor, 1971), sensation seeking (Zuckerman, 1979), and risk-taking propensity (Allen, 1980b).

While the benefits of enhanced self-confidence and need for achievement are self-evident, sensation seeking and risk taking are of particular import to researchers in outdoor adventure pursuits. Sensation seeking, as described by Zuckerman (1971, 1979, 1985), refers to a need for varied, novel, and complex sensations, and the willingness to take physical and social risks for the sake of the experience. Closely linked to optimal arousal, the concept of sensation seeking is of obvious relevance in outdoor adventure pursuits. Past research suggests that

Risk-taking is an integral part of the mountaineering experience.

the high sensation seeker may be less fearful than the low sensation seeker (Zuckerman, 1979). An interesting recent characterization of sensation seeking is that proffered by Farley (1986) entitled the Big T, Little T theory of thrill seeking. Farley suggests that personality can be categorized along a continuum anchored by Big T and Little T types of people. Individuals with a Big T personality deliberately seek out thrill and novel sensations. On the other hand, Little T personalities seek to avoid risks and overt stimulation. Farley suggests that the Big or Little T personality is partly determined by genetic makeup and early experiences. Farley goes on to explain that Big T personalities can make either a constructive or destructive contribution to society. While both seek out sensation and thrill, constructive Big T personalities usually seek their stimulation through outdoor adventuring or physical risk taking, and may often become scientists, entertainers, or artists. Destructive Big T personalities seek out sensation through antisocial activities such as delinquency and criminal acts and may often become criminals, schemers, and con artists.

While Type T personality research is in its infancy, the concept is not new in outdoor adventure pursuits. Indeed, most outdoor adventure educators have long recognized that youth will seek adventure one way or another. The long-time motto of the National Outdoor Leadership School is an example of this intuitive understanding:

> We believe that youth demand adventure, and if adventure is not provided, then youth will seek it out, often in illegal and unsocial ways.

Risk and sensation seeking are but two of a wide variety of motives in the quest for outdoor adventuring. The following section discusses the concept of motivation in relation to outdoor recreation and outdoor adventure pursuits.

MOTIVATIONS IN OUTDOOR RECREATION

A number of approaches have been used to investigate why people engage in both outdoor recreation and, more recently, outdoor adventure pursuits. As might be expected, the preponderance of studies and literature has focused on the issue of motivations for participation in outdoor recreation. Within this context, the earliest research efforts concentrated on the types of outdoor recreation activities in which people engaged. It was found that people engaged in outdoor recreation because they liked to fish or hike or camp (Driver and Toucher, 1970). While useful from a descriptive standpoint, it did little to further the understanding as to *why* people engaged in these activities.

A more recent approach has addressed the concept of need satisfaction. Manning (1986) suggests that the most widely recognized expression of the concept of need satisfaction is that of Maslow's (1943) hierarchy of needs. Participation (behavior) is a result of a desire to obtain a psychological or sociological outcome. Thus, as Manning (1986) suggests, people select and participate in particular types of recreation to meet certain goals or to satisfy certain needs. These goals and needs can be considered satisfactions or desired outcomes.

Haas et al. (1980) expanded on this idea by developing four levels of hierarchies of demand for outdoor recreation: activities, settings, experiences, and benefits. These levels are hierarchial in the sense that each level becomes more pervasive and abstract than the previous one. Thus, level 1—*activities*—implies that participants engage in outdoor recreation for the sake of doing or learning the activity. *Settings* implies a social, environmental, or managerial context that includes difficult terrain, isolation, or a lack of rules and regulations. Level 3—*experiences*—suggests a combination of the setting, the individual, and the activity. These "experiences" lead to the realization of benefits or outcomes. These *benefits* can be for the individual (e.g., self-concept), group (e.g., improved communication and trust), or society (e.g., reduced recidivism or increased work production).

Manning (1986) suggests that, in most cases, more than one type of experience is sought and more than one benefit realized. Iso-Ahola (1980) supports this contention with a belief that the reasons for which people seek outdoor recreation are based on two dimensions: attempts to achieve something and attempts to avoid something. A number of studies on outdoor recreation have supported that view (Rossman and Ulehla, 1977; Fridgen and Hinkelman, 1977; Kaplan and Talbot, 1983). Indeed, one of the earliest studies in outdoor recreation (Wildland Research Center, 1962) suggested that two of the strongest motives for seeking outdoor recreation are a wish to escape from the routines and crowds of daily life and a desire to be close to nature. Intuitively, this fact may be related to the previously described concepts of optimal arousal or sensation seeking. Petrie et al. (1958) labeled this concept *reduction* or *argumentation* and considered it a component of individual personality.

Beyond the generalized concept of reducing or increasing stimulation, a number of other categories (or clusters) have emerged as motivations for participation in outdoor recreation (Crandall, 1980; Tinsley and Kass, 1979). These categories include a variety of concepts and are listed in Figure 5.2.

FIGURE 5.2
Motivational Clusters in Leisure Pursuits

Tinsley and Johnson (1984)	Ewert (1985)	PCOA (1986)
LEISURE ACTIVITIES	MOUNTAIN CLIMBING	OUTDOOR RECREATION
• Intellectual stimulation	• Challenge/risk	• Excitement seeking
• Catharsis	• Catharsis	
• Expressive compensation	• Physical setting	• Escapism
• Hedonistic companionship	• Recognition	• Fitness
• Supportive companionship		• Sociability
• Secure solitude	• Locus of control	
• Routine, temporary indulgence		
• Moderate security		
• Expressive aestheticism	• Creativity	

Clearly, the possible motivations for engaging in outdoor recreation are diverse. A typical methodology for generating these types of factors includes the questioning of users regarding the importance they place on various motivations and then the combination of these factors into underlying "dimensions" through factor and cluster analysis techniques. Of additional importance to the generation of various underlying dimensions, or clusters, is the linking of these clusters with user groups and specific activities. This type of research suggests that motives for participation, the setting for the participation, and the specific activity may be linked (Driver and Rosenthal, 1982). At this point, it appears that there is some commonality among the reasons why people seek out outdoor recreation activities. Chief among these reasons are the factors of viewing the scenery, for peace and calm, to escape crowds, to learn new skills, and for exercise (Knopf and Lime, 1984).

MOTIVATIONS IN OUTDOOR ADVENTURE PURSUITS

While a substantial amount of research has now been directed toward the motivations for outdoor recreation, the same cannot be said for participating in outdoor adventure pursuits. One could legitimately ask if the motivations for engaging in outdoor adventure differ significantly from those of the more traditional outdoor recreation activities. While a lack of research data precludes any firm conclusions, the literature does suggest that there are both similarities and some differences in the motivations of outdoor adventure seekers and outdoor recreationalists (Ewert, 1985b; Kaplan, 1974; Hammitt, 1982). These commonalities are expressed in Figure 5.2.

As can also be seen in Figure 5.2, there are some potential differences in these motivations. The primary differences between these two constructs lie in the areas of challenge and risk and the specific setting. People seeking outdoor adventures through recreation are *specifically* interested in participating in activities that feature risk and potential danger. This danger, as mentioned earlier, can be translated into actual or perceived threats of physical or emotional harm. While the outdoor recreationalist may occasionally experience similar circumstances, these types of occurrences are usually not deliberately sought out. In addition, the settings of the outdoor adventurer and outdoor recreationalist often differ, with the former seeking out settings such as white water and steep cliffs which are not usually the habitat of the typical outdoor recreationalist.

Just as the activities and settings provide the backdrop for the outdoor recreator to obtain specific benefits or outcomes, so do the specific outdoor adventure settings and activities produce desired benefits for the outdoor adventurer. While the insensitivity of instruments for measuring motivations often produces similar motivations for the two types of user groups, a closer scrutiny often reveals subtle but important differences. For example, the desire to escape from crowds, everyday routine, and be alone, is often expressed by both groups (Ewert, 1985b; Knopf and Lime, 1984). The adventure seeker, however, is usually less interested in simply seeking solitude and more concerned with being alone or in a self-autonomous, small group while being engaged in an activity that contains an element of risk. The lack of people provides the outdoor recreationalist with a chance to escape from something, while solitude for the outdoor adventurer represents a potential increase in the risk associated with an activity. Thus, the solitary fisherman and rock-climber may both be alone but not necessarily for the same reasons.

Rafting down a white-water river provides an exhilarating experience for many outdoor participants.

Another example of these often overlooked differences is the achievement factor. Achievement in outdoor recreation often means catching a fish, bagging a deer, or spotting a bald eagle. For the person engaged in outdoor adventure pursuits, achievement is more often associated with the accomplishment of less tangible, more abstract goals, such as climbing a mountain or rafting down a class IV river. Thus, while both groups will usually report achievement as a motivating factor, achievement for the outdoor adventurer is associated more with the completion of a self-imposed, personal goal than with a tangible outcome. It is the seeking of the less tangible and more implicit goals of outdoor adventure pursuits that often creates confusion and misunderstanding, especially when compared to more traditional and/or consumptive forms of outdoor recreation. Of course, the same could be said of the less consumptive forms of outdoor recreation which are also intrinsically motivated but with less tangible goals such as birding, enjoying the serenity of a setting sun over a lake, or collecting. The difference, once again, becomes one of deliberately seeking out risk and challenge through an outdoor setting. This fact brings us to the concept of risk-taking propensity.

PROPENSITY FOR RISK TAKING

Risk-taking propensity, or the willingness to take risks, is an inherent phenomenon of outdoor adventure pursuits. Allen (1980a) suggests that risk-taking propensity is strongly related to a preference for uncertainty. This search for uncertainty may be a result of an innate drive to acquire knowledge about interactions with the environment. While it would seem reasonable to assume that adventure risk takers would also be risk takers in everyday life, Slovic (1972), and more recently, Zuckerman (1979) have suggested that this may not always be the case. Carney (1971) offers a similar view with his belief that risk taking for people is relative to the individual and the activity. In other words, while an outdoor adventure pursuit such as mountain climbing may seem risky, even foolhardy, to some, the mountaineer will often view it as a controllable and even non risky situation. Carney goes on to describe propensity of risk taking as "risk hunger" and distinguishes between Level I and Level II risk taking. This classification is based on the level of fear. Level I risks are described as highly stimulating, often physically dangerous, exciting, and usually very intense but of short duration. On the other hand, Level II risks are longer lasting, of less intensity, and involving risk to the ego rather than the body. While outdoor adventure pursuits has traditionally been associated with Carney's Level I risk taking, as we shall see in the following section, fear in the risk recreation setting can involve both emotional as well as physical risks.

FEAR IN AND THROUGH OUTDOOR PROGRAMS

Several years ago this writer heard an outdoor instructor mention that she taught a successful course because there was enough fear in it. Although the instructor probably meant that the participants had a challenging and exciting course, her statement suggested that fear-provoking activities were good for people. Using fear in an educational setting poses questions of both function and form, not to mention ethics. More specifically, what is gained by using activities that may be somewhat frightening to the participant and, if these activities produce desirable outcomes, how can they be structured to be effective and ethical? The next section addresses these questions of fear by utilizing a recent research study based on the fear of outdoor adventure participants.

The "edge" in rapelling is often the place where people learn to deal with their fear of heights.

A CONCEPTUAL REFERENCE

Fear has always been a companion of the human race, regardless of the society or cultural epoch. Historically, fear often served as a survival mechanism, by warning animals and people of dangerous situations. In contemporary terms, transitory and intense fears such as fear of starvation and fear of disease have been replaced by a more subtle but constant level of unfocused fear, more properly referred to as *anxiety*.

Many of us have varying levels of anxiety, ranging from nuclear holocaust to financial disaster. We experience fear over these issues but they seem more or less distant and uncontrollable rather than immediate and resolvable. Levitt (1980) reports that this "anxiety is the most pervasive psychological phenomenon of our time." Nevertheless, fear has not totally lost its survival-enhancing capability, for it can impel one toward self-improvement and achievement. A closely related term often mistakenly interchanged for fear is stress. *Stress* can be defined as a condition which arouses anxiety or fear. This stress can elicit different affective stages in people, including precognition, warning, impact, and recoil.

One measure of progress in any civilization has been the ability to insulate itself from both environmental (e.g., cold, dark, hunger) and societal/psychological (e.g., confrontation, alien cultures) fears. When the sources of these fears cannot be reduced or eliminated, societies and individuals learned to adapt to a fearful situation. This adaptation has been considered a hallmark of successful life (Seyle, 1950). Periods of fear and anxiety often proved to be great catalysts for successful change. World Wars I and II and the Great Depression are but a few examples of this influence.

Paradoxically, as our societal institutions have sought to counteract fear, many of our educational and recreational systems have sought to provide opportunities for people to experience fear, or at least the illusion of fear. The fact that many people deliberately seek out these types of activities will surprise no one who has recently taken a look at many college and recreational offerings. Several of these organizations have incorporated ropes courses, rock-climbing, wilderness camping, or white-water activities as methods to help their participants develop skills, experience personal development, improve interaction among each other, and achieve personal testing.

Golins suggests that using fear and stress in an outdoor program will enhance decision making, discipline, and personal awareness (Emerson and Golins, n.d.). Underlying these outcomes is the assumption that, by dealing with fear or stress in an educational or recreational sense, some transfer mechanism will develop which will enable the individual to better handle future fearful experiences. Historically, this transference has been described in a variety of terms: freeze-thaw-refreeze (Rhoades, 1972), adaptive dissonance (Walsh and Golins, 1975), attractive enemies (Kleinman, 1984), or transderivational searches (Bacon, 1983). In understanding this transference, one must first understand the construct of fear.

THE CONSTRUCT OF FEAR

We have all had firsthand experience in learning what fear is, for we have all been afraid. However, experiencing fear and being able to operationally define it have proved to be two different things. Compounding the situation even further are the terms anxiety and stress. These constructs are grounded in both physiological and sociological concerns. We know fear through biophysical responses such as sweating palms, dry throat, and "butterflies" in the stomach. We also know fear through the anticipation of certain experiences or social situations. Fear and the surrounding constructs of anxiety and stress are bound up with emotions, perceptions, and feelings. This "affectiveness" tends to blunt the sharp measuring instruments of science. Rachman (1974) reports that subjective reports of fear are often quite different from the observed physiologic responses. Previous studies using written instruments or interviews suggest that people will usually underestimate their courage. Conversely, their behaviors will generally underestimate the fear they have for a particular activity. In other words, participants will be more likely to say they are more fearful than they actually are and engage in activities in which they are more afraid than they appear.

According to Rachman (1978), fear is made up of four components: the subjective experience of fear, associated physiological changes, outward expressions of fear, and attempts to eliminate the source of the fear. Stated differently, an individual enters a situation in which he feels afraid, his body reacts toward that fear, there are often expressions of fear, and finally the individual will usually make some attempt to rectify the situation.

Elaborating on this idea of rectification, Ratner (1975) proposes four responses to the fear situation: freeze, fight, flee, and feigning death. In the outdoor setting, feigning death can be replaced by the often-fallacious belief in equipment failure. We have all heard the cliche, "frozen with fear" and in outdoor adventure it sometimes happens. However, many other responses usually take place. If the outdoors is to effectively use activities which may be fear-provoking, these other responses must also be recognized. Panic is not a typical group response in most adventure or disaster settings, despite media reports (Resnik and Ruben, 1975; Abraham, 1970), nor is being paralyzed with fear the norm. More likely, behaviors which the instructor may interpret as expressions of fear include talkativeness or extreme introversion, irritability or increasing hostility, inability to concentrate (flighty behavior), forgetfulness, and detachment. These components and others are listed in Table 5.1. Behaviors are considered even more suspect if they represent something which is not a usual response for that individual.

RECENT FINDINGS IN FEAR RESEARCH

Obviously, fear is one of the most powerful emotions known to both animals and humans. While animals are primarily faced with environmental dangers, people face both environmental and social perils. Epstein (1976) suggests that fears in animals are related to life and limb,

TABLE 5.1
Behavior Components of Fear in Outdoor Adventure Activities

Physiological Changes	Expressions of Fear	Resolutions
Perspiration	Talkativeness	Participation
Heart rate	Irritability	Freeze
Muscle tension	Lack of focus	Flight
Elevated respiration	Hostility	Nonparticipation
Elevated blood pressure	Overly precise	Alternatives
Glycemia	Forgetfulness	Inhibitions
Pupil dilation	Unusual behavior	
Increased temperature	Pointless activity	
Gastromotility	Seeking reassurance	
	Rationalization for inaction	
	Diminished performance	

but fears in people are primarily linked to threats to one's ego. In turn, these threats are associated with an inability to cope and with self-esteem. Hauck (1975) suggests that the most common types of fear are related to rejection and failure. When placed in an outdoor setting, there are several other considerations. Ewert (1985a) reports a factor analytic study of outdoor participants which isolated six underlying factors or dimensions surrounding the construct of fear. These dimensions included lack of control, personal inadequacies, personal skills, homeostasis (state of physiological equilibrium), level of comfort, and program inadequacies. The results of this analysis are listed in Table 5.2.

Upon examining the individual dimensions, items which were deemed to be particularly important in terms of causing concern were not getting enough to eat, keeping others from reaching their objectives, not fitting in with the group, and not getting their money's worth from the course. The mean scores for each item are listed in Table 5.3. Mean scores suggest that many of the fears expressed by the participants were centered around social and programmatic concerns.

Further observation of the data suggests that social fears are of great concern for most individuals in an outdoor adventure setting, where as a natural assumption would be that situational fears would be of greatest concern. This finding lends support to Hauck's (1975) original contention that social fears are of paramount importance to individuals in our contemporary society.

ABUSES IN USING FEAR

Having gained an understanding of fear and its relationship to the outdoor adventure setting, the abuses of fear that sometimes occur

TABLE 5.2
Factor Analysis of Fears in Outdoor Environment

	Rotated factor loadings						
Items	Lack of Control (I)	Personal Inadequacies (II)	Homeo-stasis (III)	Personal Skills (IV)	Level of Comfort (V)	Program Inadequacies (VI)	Commu-nality (H^2)
Unable to control environment	0.69						0.78
Surprise	0.67						0.71
Venomous animals	0.61						0.72
Physically entrapped	0.60						0.88
Unexpected emergencies	0.59						0.56
Imposed personal beliefs	0.41						0.67
Making wrong decisions		0.83					0.86
Letting myself down		0.67					0.67
Not accepted by group		0.67					0.74
Going unrecognized		0.55					0.76
Confrontation with others			0.80				0.72
Tasks too demanding			0.58				0.51
Extremes in temperature			0.57				0.68
Boredom			0.49				0.79
Poisonous plants			0.49				0.60
Being injured			0.45				0.69
Not enough strength				0.88			0.89
Insufficient experience				0.63			0.86
Becoming lost				0.55			0.69
Not trained enough				0.40			0.81
Fast-moving water				0.40			0.80
Lack of sleep					0.83		0.80
Bothered by insects					0.53		0.51
Inadequate clothing					0.46		0.71
Being uncomfortable					0.46		0.62
Instructor impatience						0.79	0.80
Not enough information						0.53	0.71
Not getting money's worth						0.51	0.49
Insufficient food						0.42	0.71
Eigenvalues	11.55	2.79	2.44	2.01	1.71	1.26	
Percentage variance	40.60	9.80	8.60	7.10	6.00	5.30	
Cummulative variance	40.60	50.40	59.00	66.00	77.10	77.40	

NOTE: Overall reliability (Cronbach's Alpha) = 0.94

need to be discussed. Because fear can be such a powerful emotion, the potential for abuse is immense. Imagine, if you will, a first-time rock climber. What might at first appear to be a relatively straightforward situation can be immensely complex if one considers that a variety of fears may be involved. These fears may include obvious ones such as falling, being struck by rockfall, or being injured. The individual may also experience more covert fears, including lack of ability, appearing foolish, or being afraid. The emotion of fear can also be abused by the instruc-

TABLE 5.3
Means of Fear Items

Item	Mean (0–5)
Not getting enough to eat	3.53
Keeping others from reaching objectives	3.31
Not fitting in with group	3.06
Bothered by insects	3.04
Not getting money's worth	3.00
Falling	2.92
Being isolated	2.88
Not being recognized by the group	2.86
Not given enough information	2.76
Making wrong decisions	2.75
Lack of sleep	2.74
Instructor being impatient	2.73
Inadequate clothes	2.73
Inadequately trained	2.67
Not being accepted by peers	2.66
Letting myself down	2.63
Becoming lost	2.53
Becoming unkempt and dirty	2.49
Confrontation with others	2.41
Becoming bored	2.41
Being uncomfortable	2.37
Imposed beliefs	2.29
Emergencies	2.28
Becoming physically entrapped	2.26
Venomous animals	2.06
Lack of privacy	2.04
Forced to interact with group	2.04
Tasks too demanding	2.04
Not enough strength	1.98
Insufficient experience	1.98
Sexually harassed	1.86
Being injured in violent act	1.86
Poisonous plants	1.67
Constant surprise	1.66
Temperature extremes	1.62
Sharp edges	1.57
Unable to control environment	1.45
Darkness	1.24
Deep water	1.22
Fast water	0.92

tor, who simply does not pay any attention to it, or more likely, discounts the fear as something easily overcome. The cliche "no problem, you can do it," spoken to an individual who has a problem and doesn't think he or she can do it, is, to say the least, somewhat limited in its effectiveness.

Injecting fear or stress unnecessarily is another abuse situation. A thorough understanding on the instructor's part as to why fear is useful in the *particular* situation is imperative. The level of fear must be congruent with the stated objectives of the program. To have incongruency is tantamount to indefensible teaching methods, and could even be considered as outright harrassment. Templin (n.d.) suggests that a lack of connectedness between the using of fear or stress and the hoped-for results is detrimental to student trust toward the instructor.

As previously stated, the social aspect of fear is made up primarily of rejection and failing. To avoid abusing the concept of fear, it becomes vitally important to separate success and failure within the activity with personal self-worth. While this is an often-stated protocol within an outdoor adventure program, problems arise when instructors fail to see the hidden self-efficacy mechanisms in their students. Failing at an activity can be devastating for an individual, particularly if he or she is already prone to fear of failure. Merely telling the individual that it is all right does not necessarily alleviate those feelings of failure nor does it rectify the fear of *future* failures. According to the Bandura (1977) model of self-efficacy, verbal persuasion is the least effective pathway through which people gain information about their ability levels. Rather, the instructor should rely on actual performance-based activities to inhibit the failure cycle, that is, one failure creating an attitude which creates more failure. Abuse can occur when the instructor allows a lack of success in some activity to grow into a fear and expectation for future failure. Fear abuse can also develop if the group is allowed to use activity failure as a basis for rejecting an individual. Younger students are particularly prone to this fear syndrome and will go to great and often dangerous lengths to avoid this situation.

What about the physical, situational fears that can develop with any program? There are certainly obvious physical dangers in many outdoor adventure activities and to discount them would not only be foolish but counterproductive. We want our participants to foster a healthy respect for both the environment and the activities in which they may be engaged. Where abuse can come into play is in the degree to which we exacerbate those fears. Healthy fear is displayed when the individual recognizes the danger but also feels a sense of personal control and ability. This perception of control is of great importance to the individual in an outdoor adventure setting, since it is the controlling of danger which often attracts the risk recreator (Allen, 1980a). Totally removing a sense of effectiveness from the individual will expose him to the whim of nature or fate. The instructor, who when questioned whether the group can make it through a particular activity, answers by saying something like, "Some of you will and some of you won't," might be creating an exciting setting but could also be creating unnecessary and unhealthy fears.

Fear can be manipulated through the withholding of information, operationalized by the equation $F = Pr(Ir - Is)$, where

F = fear
Pr = the perceived risk
Ir = the information required
Is = the information supplied

It can be seen that the greater the perceived risk the greater the felt need for information. In practice, this means that the instructor can create feelings of anxiety and fear merely by failing to supply enough information. While students can play a question-and-answer game with the instructor by creating a constant barrage of questions, usually with the hidden purpose of seeking reassurance, instructors need to be cognizant about the tremendous power the *information giver* has over the *information needer.* An often-used technique by the instructor is the question reversal, in which the question is turned back to the student for an answer. If used tactfully, students become more aware of their own problem-solving abilities. When used indiscriminately, instructors can create an aura of unconcern, or worse, discourage students from coming to them if they are having problems.

USING FEAR IN THE OUTDOOR ADVENTURE SETTING

While fear is a powerful emotion, subject to abuse, it also has tremendous value in the adventure setting. The key to its successful usage is in remembering that function follows form. There are two main purposes in using fear: teaching people about themselves, and learning to overcome fear. Any use of the fear paradigm must relate back to one or both of these concepts or the activity may be ethically unsound and programmatically indefensible. Issues which are amenable to using fear-provoking activities include personal testing, self-imagery, stress coping, optimal arousal, sensation seeking, and learning. With respect to any of these items, several considerations must be taken into account. First, most of the above items, such as learning and stress coping, are subject to the Yerkes-Dodson law (Levitt, 1980) which suggests a curvilinear relationship between fear and the item in question. More simply stated, some fear may be useful in facilitating learning or self-concept, but too much fear can actually inhibit both learning and performance. Hackman (1970) reports that this inhibition may be affected by three factors: the amount of time available, the complexity of the task, and the consequences of failing to perform the activity successfully. The Yerkes-Dodson (1908) relationship is shown in Figure 5.3.

As can be seen, fear may be both a motivating and a debilitating influence. The determining factor is the level of intensity.

If the activity is designed to be generative, in that it will promote transferable behaviors or attitudes useful in some future situation, the instructor needs to understand the probable mechanism by which fear is actually overcome or coped with by the individual. *Fear stimuli* can be generalized into *four categories:* intensity, novelty, specific situational factors (e.g., darkness, cold, etc.). and social interaction (Gray, 1974). The individual's perception of fear is acquired through direct experience, instinct, or vicarious methods, such as being told not to do something because something frightening might happen. This state of mind manifests itself into a series of physical reactions such as increased heartbeat and respiration. This physical state creates a desire in the individual to act in some way to alleviate the fear. This fear creates behavior change or adaptation if its source cannot be removed. For the instructor to provide opportunities for his or her students to overcome fear, the construct must be approached from all four of these states.

Rachman (1974) suggests three techniques for modifying fear: systematic desensitization, flooding, and modeling. Within the outdoor adventure setting, a fourth technique can also be applied—rehearsal. Systematic *desensitization* involves a gradual exposure to the fearful situation, in which the individual attempts to modify not only his cognitive and emotional reactions but also physical responses. The outdoor instructor often unknowingly utilizes this technique by suggesting that a fearful student relax, slow down, or take it easy. Results are not always

FIGURE 5.3
Item Change as a Function of Level of Fearfulness

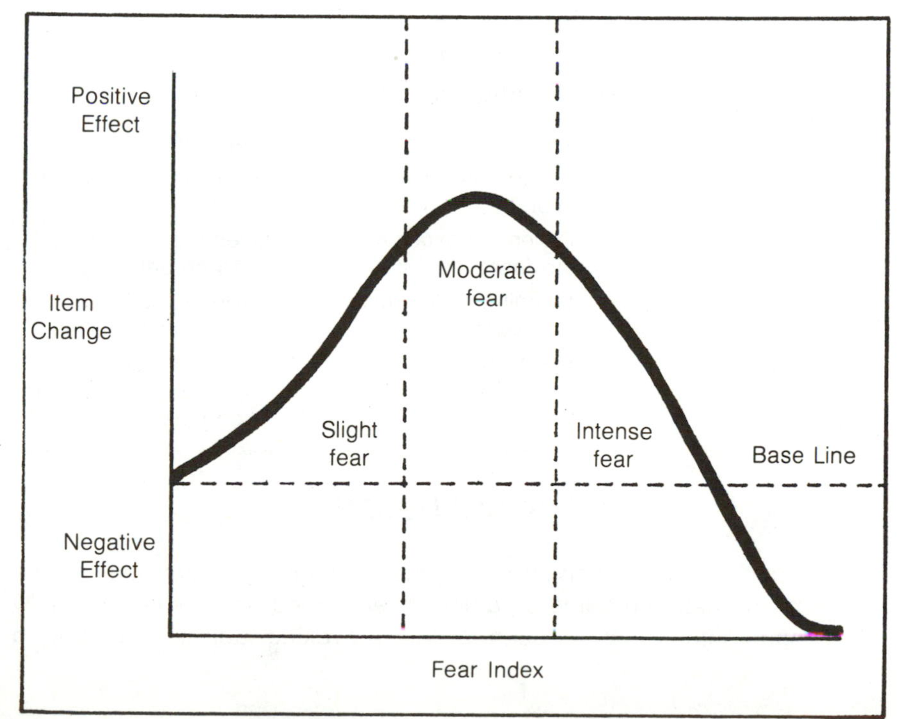

what they could be because the approach is often used too abruptly. To be effective, the student must be allowed to approach the situation gradually, forming positive coping mechanisms as he or she proceeds.

Flooding involves a prolonged exposure to a fearful situation, usually used in connection with combat or disaster settings. The instructor may occasionally use flooding in a programmatic situation where students are constantly exposed to fear. It is in this setting that great care must be used in providing coping mechanisms. Without these mechanisms, students' performances and attention to safety can drop radically. Several studies have indicated that prolonged stress and fear can have debilitating effects on individual performance (Powell and Verner, 1982; Hammerton and Tickner, 1968).

Related to the previous two methods is *modeling.* This fear-modification technique involves the transmitting of new coping behaviors which lead to the development of new adaptive behaviors. While modeling presents the individual with a new cognitive perception, the fourth fear-modification technique, *rehearsal,* provides the student with the direct experience necessary for effective learning. The instructor must show the students useful procedures to cope with fear and provide opportunities to practice these techniques. As can be seen, the most effective method of dealing with fear is not to dichotomize the various modification techniques but to combine them into logical formats geared to the specific outdoor setting. Table 5.4 illustrates these techniques.

TABLE 5.4
Fear Modification Techniques

Technique	Definition	Comments
Systematic desensitization	Gradual exposure to source	Useful, time-consuming
Flooding	Prolonged exposure to fear	Often inappropriate, can be debilitating
Modeling	Learning new coping methods	Powerful, can use instructor behavior
Rehearsal	Practicing different adaptive behaviors	Very useful but requires preplanning and time

CONCLUSION

Fear can play an important role in the outdoor adventure setting. The student who has overcome a particular fear or learned some personally meaningful information through a fear-provoking activity has had a valuable educational experience. The instructor has the responsibility of providing opportunities for this type of personal growth and of monitoring the student/activity mix to prevent a fearful situation that can inhibit learning. While intuition can play an important role in this process, the efficacy of the program can be enhanced if fear theories and protocol are understood. Fear has been with mankind since our beginning and our physical and sociopsychological makeup are, in part, geared around coping with fear. Only recently has civilization replaced short-term, intermittent fears with a more omnipresent anxiety. Paradoxically, this has not always been a healthy development. Through the use of outdoor adventure activities, the individual can be provided with a personal testing and learning arena, which is difficult to ethically obtain anywhere else in contemporary society.

MAIN POINTS

1. Risk and sensation seeking are other components in the adventure experience. Both concepts are, in part, affected by the demographics of the individual adventure. Relatively young males still comprise the largest user group.
2. While adventure recreationalists have reasons for participation which are similar to those of other users in outdoor recreation, the person seeking adventure also engages in these activities for the risk-taking and challenging aspects of the activities.
3. Studies in fear and anxiety in the outdoor adventure setting have become some of the more recent types of research. Findings from this type of research suggest that situational and trait fears can be reduced through participation in adventure activities.
4. Why people choose adventure pursuits has been a widely discussed issue. Research indicates that there are a multitude of reasons, including personal testing, catharsis, skill development, and to escape normal routine.

REFERENCES

Abraham, H. (1970). *Psychological Aspects of Stress.* Springfield, IL: Charles C. Thomas.

Allen, S. (1980a). *Risk Recreation: Some Psychological Bases of Attraction.* Ph.D. Dissertation. University of Montana.

Allen, S. (1980b). Risk Recreation: A Literature Review and Conceptual Model. In J. Meier, T. Morash, and G. Welton (eds.). *High Adventure Outdoor Pursuits,* pp. 52–81. Salt Lake City, UT: Brighton Publishing Company.

Bacon, S. (1983). *The Conscious Use of Metaphor in Outward Bound.* Denver: Colorado Outward Bound.

Bandura, A. (1977). Self-Efficacy: Toward a Unifying Theory of Behavioral

Change. *Psychological Review,* 84: pp. 191-215.

Carney, R. (1971). *Risk-Taking Behavior.* Springfield, IL: Charles C. Thomas.

Cober, L. J. (1972). A Personality Factor Study of Participants in High Risk Sports. Master's Thesis. The Pennsylvania State University.

Crandall, R. (1980). Motivations for Leisure. *Journal of Leisure Research,* 12(1): pp. 45-54.

Driver, B. and Rosenthal, D. (1982). *Measuring and Improving Effectiveness of Public Outdoor Recreation Programs.* USDA Forest Service, USDI Bureau of Land Management, and George Washington University.

Driver, B. and Tocher, R. (1970). Toward a Behavioral Interpretation of Recreational Engagements, with Implications for Planning. In B. Driver, (ed.). *Elements of Outdoor Recreation, pp.* 9-31. Ann Arbor, MI: University Microfilms.

Emerson, L. and Golins, G. (eds.). (n.d.). *Workbook on Adventure Based Education.* Denver: Colorado Outward Bound.

Epstein, S. (1976). Anxiety, Arousal, and the Self-Concept. In I. Sarason and C. Spielberger (eds.). *Stress and Anxiety,* Vol. 3. Washington, DC: Hemisphere Publishing Corporation.

Ewert, A. (1985a). Identifying Fears in the Outdoor Environment. In *Proceedings: Southeastern Recreation Research.* Athens, GA: Institute for Behavioral Research, University of Georgia.

Ewert, A. (1985b). Why People Climb: The Relationship of Participant Motives and Experience Level to Mountaineering. *Journal of Leisure Research,* 17(3): pp. 241--250.

Farley, F. (1986). The Big T in Personality. *Psychology Today,* pp. 44-52.

Frigden, J. and Hinkelman, B. (1977). Recreation Behavior and Environment Congruence. Paper presented at the NRPA Research Symposium, National Recreation and Park Association. Las Vegas, NV.

Gray, J. (1974). *The Psychology of Fear and Stress.* New York: McGraw-Hill.

Haas, G.; Driver, B.; and Brown, P. (1980). Measuring Wilderness Recreation Experiences. *Proceedings of the Wilderness Psychology Group Annual Conference.* Durham, NH: University of New Hampshire. pp. 20-40.

Hackman, J.R. (1970). Tasks and Task Performance in Research on Stress. In Joseph McGraph (ed.). *Social and Psychological Factors in Stress,* pp. 202-237. New York: Holt, Rinehart and Winston.

Hammerton, M. and Tickner, A. (1968). An Investigation into the Effects of Stress upon Skilled Performance. *Ergonomics,* 12: pp. 851-855.

Hammitt, W. (1982). Psychological Dimensions and Functions of Wilderness Solitude. In F. Boteler (ed.). *Wilderness Psychology Group,* pp. 50-60. Morgantown, WV: West Virginia University.

Hauck, P. (1975). *Ovecoming Worry and Fear.* Philadelphia: Westminster Press.

Huberman, J. (1968). *A Psychological Study of Participants in High Risk Sports.* Ph.D. Dissertation. University of British Columbia.

Iso-Ahola, S. (1980). *The Social Psychology of Leisure and Recreation.* Dubuque, IA: Wm. C. Brown.

Kaplan, R. (1974). Wilderness Perception and Psychological Benefits: An Analysis of a Continuing Program. *Leisure Sciences,* 6(3): pp. 271-290.

Kaplan, S. and Talbot, J. (1983). Psychological Benefits of a Wilderness Experience. In J. Altman and J. Wohlwill (eds.). *Behavior and the Natural Environment, pp. 163*-204. New York: Plenum.

Klausner, S. (ed.). (1968). *Why Man Takes Chances.* New York: Anchor Books.
Kleinman, G. (1984). The Attractive Enemy. Paper presented at Chautauqua Lecture Series. Chautauqua, NY.
Knopf, R. and Lime, D. (1984). *A Recreation Manager's Guide to Understanding River Use and Users.* USDA Forest Service General Technical Report WO-38.
Levitt, E. (1980). *The Psychology of Anxiety.* Hillsdale, NJ: Lawrence Erlbaum Associates.
Manning, R. (1986). *Studies in Outdoor Recreation.* Corvallis, OR: The Oregon State University.
Maslow, A. H. (1943). A Theory of Human Motivation. *Psychological Review,* 50: pp. 370-396.
Meier, J. (1977). Risk Recreation: Explorations and Implications. Paper at the Congress for Recreation and Parks, Las Vegas, NV.
O'Connor, C. (1971). *Study of Personality Needs Involved in Selection of Specific Leisure Interest Groups.* Dissertation Abstracts International, 31 (11-A), p. 5865.
Petrie, A.; Collins, W.; and Solomon, P. (1958). Pain Sensitivity, Sensory Deprivation and Susceptibility to Satiation. *Science,* 12(1): pp. 45-54.
Powell, F. and Verner, J. (1982). Anxiety and Performance Relationships in First Time Parachutists. *Journal of Sport Psychology,* 4: pp. 184-188.
President's Commission on American's Outdoors [P.C.A.O.]. (1986). *Americans Outdoors, The Legacy, The Challenge.* Washington, DC: Island Press.
Rachman, S. (1974). *The Meanings of Fear.* Baltimore, MD: Penguin Books.
Rachman, S. (1978). *Fear and Courage.* San Francisco, CA: W. H. Freeman and Company.
Ratner, S. C. (1975). Animal's Defenses: Fighting in Predator-Prey Relations. In P. Pliner, L. Krames, and J. Alloway (eds.). *Advances in the Study of Communication and Affect,* Vol. 2; *Non-Verbal Communication of Aggression.*
Resnik, H. and Reuben, H. (1975). *Emergency Psychiatric Care.* Bowie, MA: Charles Press Publishers.
Rhoades, J. (1972). The Problem of Individual Change in Outward Bound: An Applicaton of Change and Transfer Theory. Ph.D. Dissertation. University of Massachusetts.
Rossman, B. and Ulehla, J. (1977). Psychological Reward Values Associated with Wilderness Use: A Functional Reinforcement Approach. *Environment and Behavior,* 9: pp. 41-66.
Seyle, H.(1950). *The Psychology and Pathology of Exposure to Stress.* Montreal, Canada: ACTA Publishers.
Slovic, P. (1972). Information Processing, Situation Specificity, and the Generality of Risk-Taking Behavior. *Journal of Personality and Social Psychology,* 22: pp. 128-134.
Templin, G. (n.d.). The Element of Stress. In *Workbook on Adventure Based Education.* L. Emerson and G. Golins (eds.). Denver; Colorado Outward Bound.
Tinsley, H. and Johnson, T. (1984). A Preliminary Taxonomy of Leisure Activities. *Journal of Leisure Research,* 10(3): pp. 234-244.
Tinsley, H. and Kass, R. (1979). The Latent Structure of the Need Satisfying Properties of Leisure Activities. *Journal of Leisure Research,* 11(4): pp. 278-291.

Walsh, V. and Golins, G. (1975). *The Exploration of the Outward Bound Process.* Denver: Colorado Outward Bound.

Wildland Research Center, University of California. (1962). *Wilderness and Recreation—A Report on Resources, Values, and Problems.* ORRRC Report No. 3. Washington, DC: U.S. Government Printing Office.

Yerkes, R. and Dodson, J. (1908). The Relation of Strength of Stimulus to Rapidity of Habit-Formation. *Journal of Comparative and Neurological Psychology,* 18: pp. 459–482.

Zuckerman, M. (1971). Dimensions of Sensation-Seeking. *Journal of Consulting and Clinical Psychology,* 36: pp. 45–52.

Zuckerman, M. (1979). *Sensation Seeking: Beyond the Optimal Level of Arousal.* Hillsdale, NJ: Lawrence Erlbaum.

Zuckerman, M. (1985). Biological Foundations of the Sensation-Seeking Temperment. In J. Strelau, F. Farley, and A. Gale (eds.), *The Biological Bases of Personality and Behavior,* pp. 97–113. Washington, DC: Hemisphere.

6

MODELS AND THEORIES IN OUTDOOR ADVENTURE PURSUITS

Throughout history, civilizations have sought to guard themselves against a host of environmental and psychological threats. Migration, wars, intricate politics, and so on have typically evolved as an answer toward alleviating a real or perceived threat.

Ironically, as our society has sought to protect itself from risk, increasing numbers of individuals have sought the personal testing ground of outdoor adventure pursuits. Participating in outdoor adventure activities such as rock climbing, white-water rafting, sailboarding, and ropes courses has moved from the domain of daredevils to one in which a wide variety of people are interested. Society has responded to this growing trend through the development of schools, organizations, and businesses that cater to the outdoor adventurer. As early as 1975, over 200 outdoor adventure-based programs were operating within the United States (Hale, 1978). Hendee and Roggenbuck (1984) have estimated that there were 542 wilderness-related courses offered by American universities during the 1983–84 academic year. In a previously discussed study of outdoor adventure leaders (Ewert, 1987), a moderately strong increase in the number of colleges and universities offering outdoor adventure programs is anticipated by the year 2000. Given this increase of interest and institutional attention to outdoor adventure pursuits, this chapter addresses the theories and models that underlie the outdoor adventure pursuits experience. This chapter is divided into the following categories: (1) the importance of theory and model building, (2) optimal arousal, (3) competence-effectance, (4) self-efficacy, (5) attribution theory, (6) expectancy theory, (7) attitude and behavior mix, and (8) a causal model of behavior in outdoor adventure pursuits.

THE IMPORTANCE OF THEORY AND MODEL BUILDING

How do we "know" the world? How do we get a sense of cause and effect and what is real versus what is illusion? As the general public, we have the luxury of using hearsay and intuition to provide knowledge. On the other hand, program planners often employ the added techniques of reading and observation to understand their portions of the world. As researchers and evaluators, the questions are approached through systematic inquiry and testing. Foregoing systematic and scientific inquiry and relying merely on common sense and intuition limit the observer to the obvious. The development of theories and models can aid both the scholar and the practitioner in the quest to understand, predict, and control their specific areas of concern. While *theories* can be considered a collection of explanatory statements about observed and inferred relationships among variables (Kerlinger, 1973), *models* can be considered descriptions or analogies that provide descriptive patterns.[1] In addition, it should be recognized that the purpose of science is to develop these explanatory theories and models. In turn, these theories and models rely on the use of research questions and attendent hypotheses to investigate relationships between various factors and variables. Upon testing these hypotheses, the findings are used to support, refute, or redesign the original theories and models. DiRenzo (1967) suggests that the maturity of a science is reflected in the accumulation of its theory. This accumulative role of research is illustrated in Figure 6.1.

With respect to outdoor adventure pursuits, the systematic development and inquiry into applicable models and theories has had a relatively short history. Nevertheless, there are a variety of theories and models which can be used to better describe the outdoor adventure pursuits phenomenon. Examples of these theories are discussed in the following sections. It should be noted, however, that the theories and models presented do not exhaust the list but merely serve to illuminate several of the more important issues in outdoor adventure pursuits.

---

[1] For a more elaborate discussion of theories and models see Slawski (1981).

FIGURE 6.1
The Accumulative Role of Research

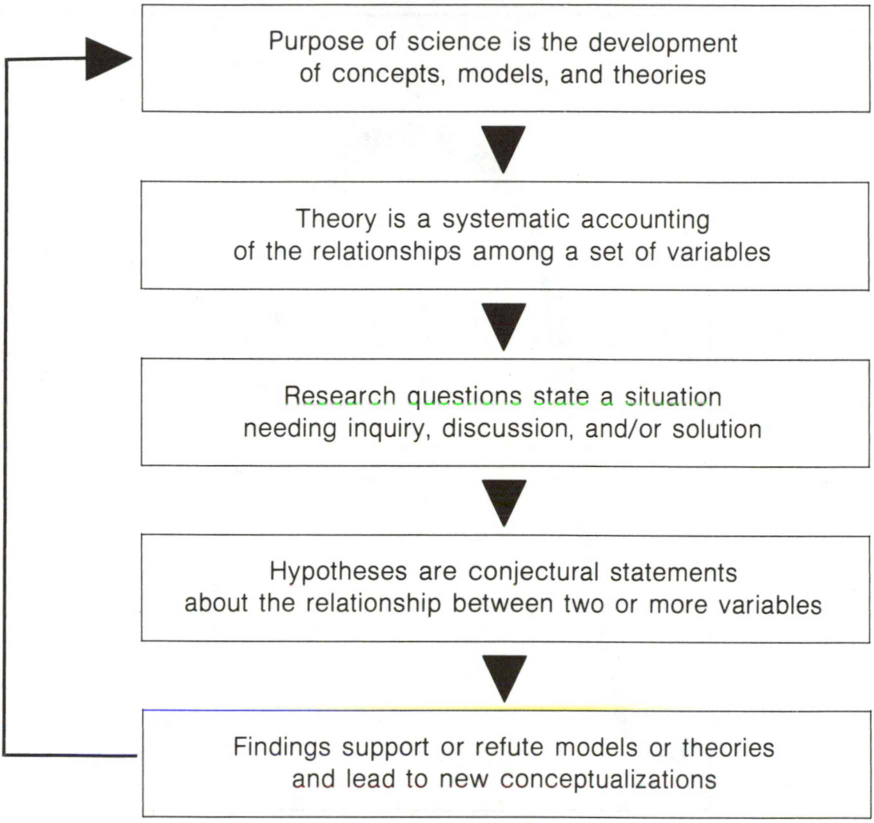

Purpose of science is the development of concepts, models, and theories

Theory is a systematic accounting of the relationships among a set of variables

Research questions state a situation needing inquiry, discussion, and/or solution

Hypotheses are conjectural statements about the relationship between two or more variables

Findings support or refute models or theories and lead to new conceptualizations

OPTIMAL AROUSAL

One of the most pervasive theories associated with outdoor adventure pursuits is that of optimal arousal. Originally conceived by Duffy (1957), optimal arousal refers to a level of arousal or sensation that is sought by the organism (person). It is dependent on both the organism-environment interaction and individual experience. In other words, individuals will seek levels of arousal that are congruent with their past experience, skill level, and situation. This relationship is quadratic in that it can best be represented by an inverted "U" shape, as illustrated in Figure 6.2.

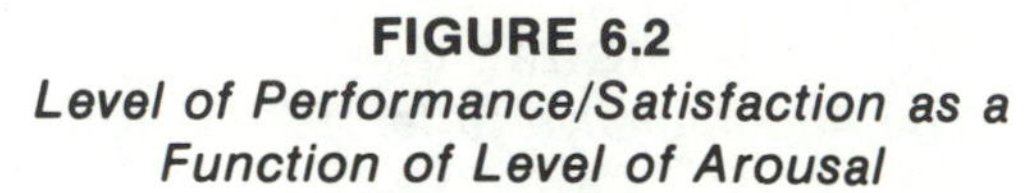

FIGURE 6.2
Level of Performance/Satisfaction as a Function of Level of Arousal

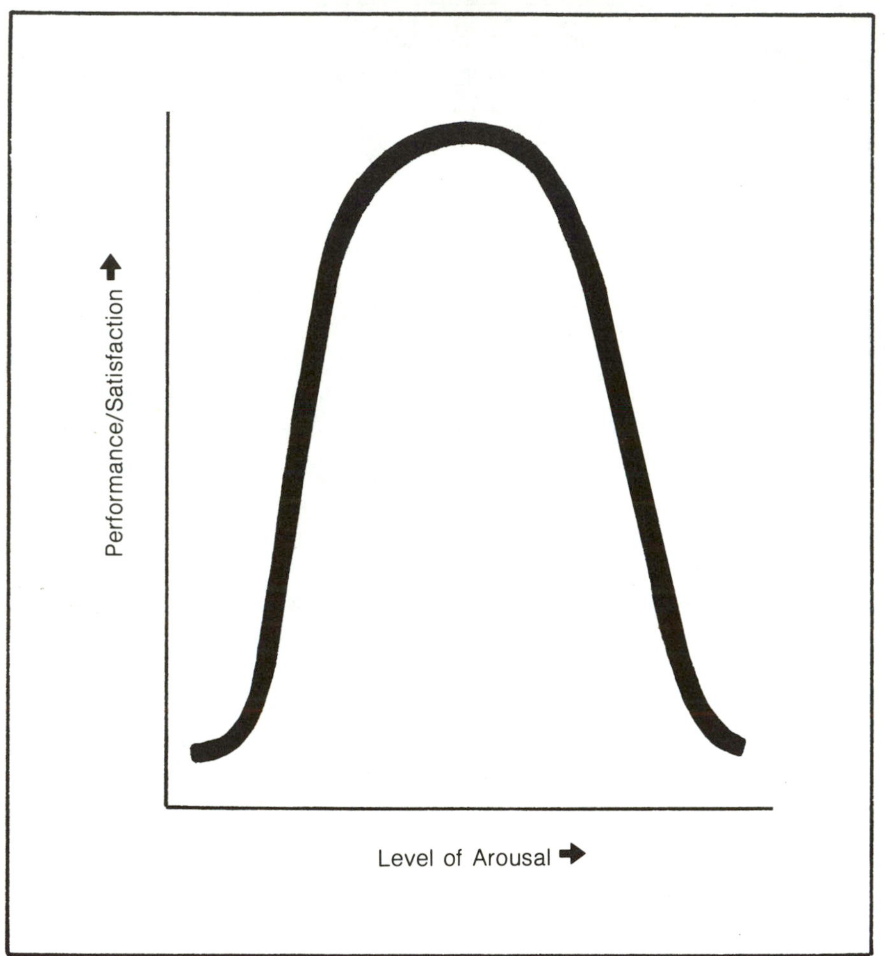

As depicted in Figure 6.2, levels of arousal for each individual can move from being too little through too intense. Along with this concept of differing levels of arousal, Berlyne (1960) has suggested that arousal contains the attributes of novelty, uncertainty (dissonance), and complexity. In other words, for an environment or situation to be optimally arousing it must contain the proper mix of new activities or old activities done in a new way (novelty). In addition, there must be an uncertainty of outcome (dissonance) and to a certain degree the individual must have a sense that he or she has enough ability to succeed at the task (complexity). Ellis (1973) suggests that the complexity of an event or situation can be modified by increasing the number of behavioral options, increasing the dissimilarity of the options, and intensifying the possible outcomes. As most outdoor leaders can attest, decisions are often difficult because there are a number of different possible actions and these actions can lead to a variety of different but critical outcomes. A good example of an individual seeking optimal arousal in outdoor adventure pursuits might be a mountain climber taking a "new" route or making a "first" ascent (see *Games Climbers Play* by Lito Tejada-Flores, 1973). A first ascent or new route implies that no one else has completed that particular climb and hence there are no guidebooks or past knowledge to completely aid the climber.

Fowler (1966) reports that arousal seeking may be linked to a survival instinct to gain information and mastery over an individual's environment

Ice-climbing is one way the outdoor pursuit specialist seeks optimal arousal.

through exploration. Specifically, exposure to something new creates uncertainty within the individual. This uncertainty necessitates a change in behavior which generates knowledge about the success of the new behavior. To be successful in meeting the demands of a new situation, a new behavior must often be learned; in essence something new must be tried. Thus the individual is "pushed" along to learn new, more successful and innovative behaviors that can be remembered and utilized in some future situation. Many outdoor pursuits programs utilize optimal arousal by casting students into new environments and creating situations that necessitate the learning of new personal and social skills. The keys to successful arousal are information load and intensity of motivation, with uncertainty and dissonance being increased in three ways:

1. Increasing the number of acceptable choices.
2. Increasing the complexity of the situation.
3. Creating an information overload.

Individuals respond in a variety of ways to these techniques. Some of the more common responses often seen by outdoor instructors include omission (ignoring the information), queuing (storing the information but not acting upon it), and selective discrimination (not dealing with information accurately enough). For example, a student may come to a fork in the trail and instead of "seeing" two trails, he or she will think, "I'm lost" even though there may be a trail sign at eye level.

While optimal arousal can provide an explanation for many situations in outdoor adventure pursuits, it does not address all the possibilities. For example, consider the recreationalist who continues to practice his or her activity even after the novelty or other aspects of optimal arousal have worn off. This type of behavior involves continued learning and interaction with the environment and can be related to the theory of competence and personal ability.

COMPETENCE-EFFECTANCE

Initially discussed by White (1959), competence-effectance involves a need to demonstrate an ability to affect or control the environment. A similar theory, later developed by Deci (1975), stated that there is a human need for feeling capable and self-determining. Consequently, individuals seek out optimally arousing situations and strive to successfully respond to those challenges. Iso-Ahola (1980) suggests that this need to seek out and successfully complete these challenges is an ongoing process with the end-product being feelings of satisfaction arising from a sense of competence and effect. Csikszentmihalyi (1975), however, suggests that this is a cyclic process, in which the individual will seek out greater challenges as his or her skill and competence level grows. He suggests that when challenges and levels of competence are congruent a feeling of "flow" develops. This concept of "flow" is illustrated in Figure 6.3.

FIGURE 6.3
Csikszentmihalyi's (1975) "Flow" Model of Play

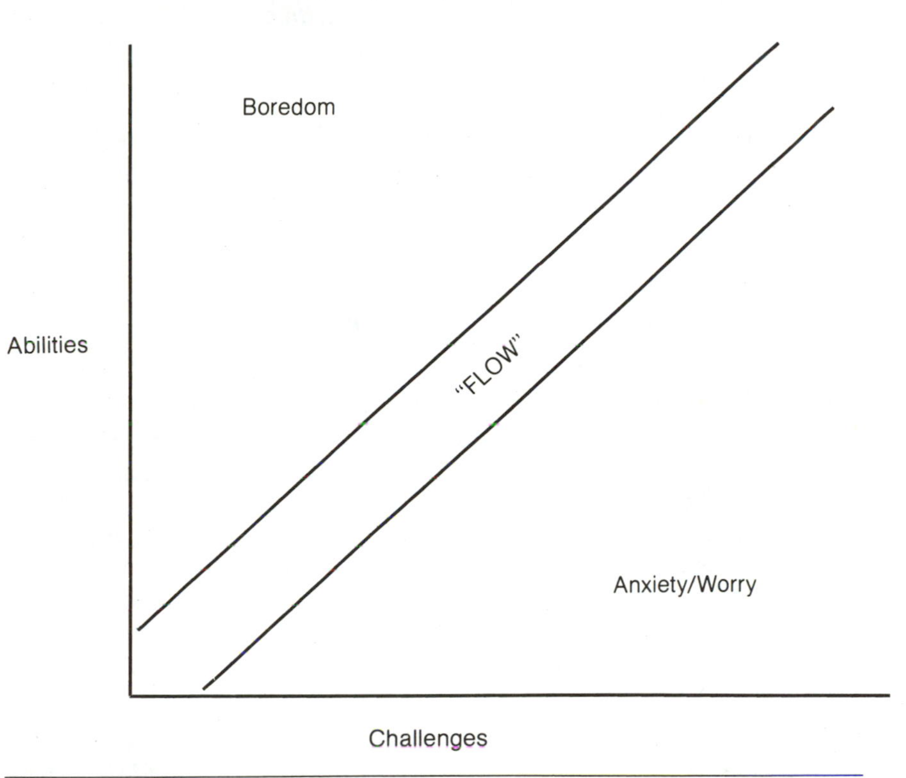

Indeed, it should surprise no one involved in outdoor pursuits that as individuals gain in experience they often change the types of activities they pursue.

Related to competence-effectance and "flow" is the concept of specialization advocated by Bryan (1979). Formally stating an intuitively logical idea, Bryan suggested that a mega-activity, such as watersports, involves a variety of subactivities, including canoeing, powerboating, and white-water kayaking. These subactivities fall on a continuum based on the required specialization of the activity. For example, powerboating generally requires less skill and specialization than activities such as white-water canoeing or kayaking. The illustration in Figure 6.4 depicts this relationship.

Concomittant to this change in specialization is a change in the motivations of the recreationalists. What this implies is that what motivates the powerboater is often different from what motivates the wilderness canoeist or kayaker. For example, the powerboat enthusiast may be more interested in the socialization and waterskiing aspects of the activ-

FIGURE 6.4
Bryan's Model of Specialization (1979)
Recreational Water Activities

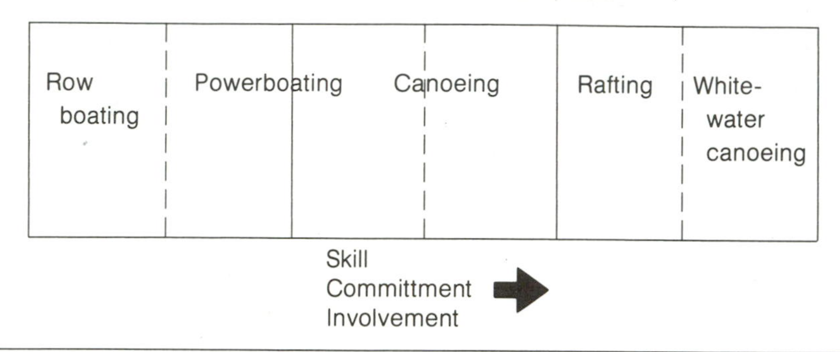

ity. In contrast, the canoeist may more often seek the solitude and challenge of the wilderness environment (Rossman and Ulehla, 1977; Ewert, 1985. Fridgen and Hinkelman (1977) supported this concept by suggesting that the search for challenge and solitude through recreational activities was increasingly correlated with the natural environment. These findings have implications for outdoor adventure pursuits as, with any outdoor activity, there may be a variety of skill and experience levels, motivations, and subactivities (e.g., rock climbing can involve bouldering, aid climbing, lead climbing, top-roping, and soloing).

Climbing Mt. Robson in the Canadian Rockies involves a high degree of specialization in mountaineering.

In sum, competence-effectance implies the dual concepts of ability and influence. In part, outdoor adventure pursuits is an increasingly popular form of recreation because these activities provide opportunities for people to seek out avenues to acquire and demonstrate competence and ability. DeCharms (1968) supports this idea by stating that

> Man's primary motivational propensity is to be effective in producing changes in his environment. Man strives to be a causal agent, to be the primary focus of causation for, or the origin of, his behavior; he strives for personal causation.

In a sense this process is related to problem solving (Ellis, 1973) and involves an awareness of one's abilities in or through the outdoor environment and a testing of those abilities. Through this testing and appraisal, individuals gain a sense of their personal ability to control their immediate environment. This sense of control, the perception that one can exercise control over his or her environment and affect personal choice, has been a cornerstone in Western man's thought process. In turn, critical components of competence-effectance are self-efficacy and attribution theory.

SELF-EFFICACY THEORY

One of the most heavily subscribed-to theories of human behavior in outdoor adventure pursuits is that of self-efficacy. Originally conceptualized by Bandura (1977), self-efficacy refers to personal judgments of how well one can perform actions in specific situations that may contain ambiguous, unpredictable, and stressful features (McGowan, 1986).

Whether an individual will choose to participate in an outdoor adventure activity is often determined by his or her perceived level of ability. This perception is based on a cognitive appraisal of one's level of competence in dealing with anticipated demands. Outdoor leaders will often work with students who opt not to participate under the premise that "it doesn't look like fun," when the real reason lies in his or her personal appraisal of not having the skills or abilities to complete the activity successfully.

Self-efficacy implies a personal appraisal and weighing of both ability and nonability factors such as:

- Perceived ability for the activity.
- Amount of effort to be expended.
- Perceived difficulty of the task.
- Amount of expected assistance to be received.
- Type of situational circumstances.
- Previous patterns of success or nonsuccess.

It should be expected that the participant in an outdoor adventure pursuit will make an appraisal of the potential for success involving some or all of these components. An efficacy expectation, then, refers to the belief that one can successfully execute the behavior required to produce the desired and expected changes. These efficacy expectations vary with respect to the magnitude of the task, the degree to which they are generalized or tranferred to new tasks, and their persistence in the face of disconfirming or unsuccessful experiences.

In addition, individual efficacy statements can be made and altered by four processes: (1) performance accomplishment, (2) verbal persuasion, (3) vicarious experience, and (4) emotional arousal. These techniques are illustrated in Figure 6.5.

FIGURE 6.5
Bandura's Theory of Self-Efficacy (1972)

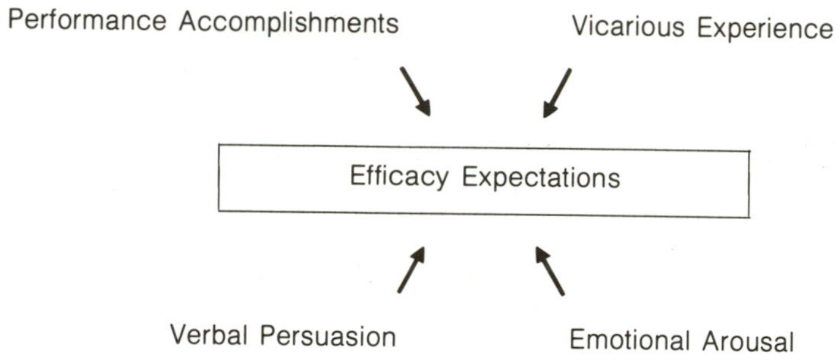

Performance Accomplishments → Efficacy Expectations ← Vicarious Experience

Verbal Persuasion → Efficacy Expectations ← Emotional Arousal

Self-efficacy—an individual's perception of his/her ability to perform anticipated demands

Weightings

1. Perceived level of ability
2. Effort needed to perform
3. Task difficulty perceived
4. Aid expected
5. Situational circumstances
6. Patterns of success

Efficacy statements are influenced by:

1. Magnitude (degree of difficulty expected)
2. Generality (degree to which these abilities are transferrable)
3. Strength (persistence)

Of these four, performance accomplishment is the most powerful technique. Performance accomplishment reinforces the usefulness of experiential learning as an educational technique for developing learning situations in which the learner can generalize from one experience to another. Bandura (1977) reports that, while verbal persuasion is the most often used technique for developing efficacy statements, it is weaker than performance accomplishment because it does not provide a genuine experiential base. A typical example of verbal persuasion involves an instructor *telling* beginning rock-climbing students that they can do the climb rather than creating successful situations where the more powerful efficacy source, performance accomplishment, can come into play.

Harmon and Templin (1980) elaborated on the efficacy of performance accomplishments, indicating that they are especially powerful influences because they are based on personal mastery and individual perceived competence. In turn, when these personal accomplishments are perceived to be significant to the individual, they tend to be generalizable to a variety of situations. That is, if a person does something she feels is very noteworthy, and she accomplished the task through her own effort and skill (such as completing an adventurous expedition or finishing an arduous course), the feelings of competence and ability that may arise can often be carried over to other situations and circumstances. Indeed, this ability to carry over feelings of competence to different situations is one of most important outcomes of many outdoor programs.

The assumption in self-efficacy is that successful performance in one group of activities is one of the best predictors of future performances. This assumption relates to another important theory (discussed in more detail later in the chapter), namely attribution theory. Attribution and self-efficacy theories provide congruence because, as individuals gain in ability and self-efficacy beliefs, they move toward internal, stable attributions. These, in turn, can create situations in which individuals participate in a given activity because they feel they are competent and capable.

Within an outdoor educational setting, self-efficacy theory is often applied through the use of rewards and goals. Rewarding experiences inform and motivate while goal setting establishes standards by which one's actions can be focused. In both cases, rewards seem to promote motivation when compared with offering no rewards. In a similar fashion, goals that incorporate specific performance-based standards lead to higher performance than no goals or goals that are too general. If the outdoor educator wishes to develop the self-efficacy feelings of a client through the use of rewards and goal setting, the following guidelines are suggested:

In sum, self-efficacy is a cornerstone of many outdoor pursuits programs. Most practitioners would agree that participants who emerge from a program with feelings of competence and higher perceived levels of skill are more likely to continue in some form of outdoor recreation and, hopefully, be willing to trade some of their mechanical leisure items, such as snowmobiles, for less mechanized and less consumptive forms of recreation.

Ultimately, the success of many outdoor adventure pursuits programs will rest not only on the skills and knowledge imparted to the students, but, just as importantly, the individual learner will need to feel competent and at ease with the skills just acquired.

However, self-efficacy does not fully explain participation in outdoor adventure activities. An individual may feel that he or she has the abilities to engage in the activity but still chooses not to participate. When considering participation, other factors or attributions must be considered.

	More Effective Than	Comments
Rewards	No rewards	Should be tied to actual accomplishments
Goal setting	No goals or very general goals such as "You can do it"!	Use specific performance standards
Proximal goals	Distant goals or no goals	Goals that are close and attainable

ATTRIBUTION THEORY

Iso-Ahola (1976) refers to attribution as the process by which an individual makes assumptions about the cause of certain events. Not getting to the top of a peak can be attributed to bad weather (external-situational), poor leadership (external-personnel), or lack of climbing skill (internal-ability). More importantly, these attributions are composed of two dimensions: *internality* and *stability*. Internality refers to intrinsic motivation or how compelled an individual feels toward doing an activity. Is she doing it because she wants to or somebody else wants her to? Stability refers to how likely it is that an individual will continue the activity. Using canoeing as an outdoor adventure example, consider Figure 6.6.

Clearly, in terms of keeping an individual engaged in the activity, the stable-intrinsic situation is preferred. The least desirable situation is someone participating for incidental reasons (unstable-extrinsic) such as being asked by friends to come along when he or she doesn't really want to. While this circumstance may lead to a life-long enthusiasm, it often does not because there is little psychological meaning placed on the event *after* the activity. In other words, the individual may end a white-water canoeing episode feeling excited and energized but without thinking that he or she could be a good white-water paddler. Making the link to internal-stable attributions, that is, "I can be good at this activity," is critically important in outdoor adventure programming—especially when learning new outdoor skills, as there are often moments of incompetence which necessitate the support and guidance of an outdoor staff member. Attribution theory suggests that, within a supportive environment, attributions can be altered to stable-intrinsic patterns. While learning outdoor adventure skills is a salient component of participation, making internal-stable attributions during and after the activity is necessary in encouraging a new learner to stay with the activity. Letting the experience "speak for itself" can often do an injustice to the participant.

FIGURE 6.6

Dimensions of Participating in Canoeing Using Attribution Theory

Adapted from Weiner et al. (1971)

Stability Dimension	Internality Dimension: Intrinsic	Internality Dimension: Extrinsic
Stable	I canoe because I am good at this activity	I canoe because it is a good way to get the family together
Unstable	I canoe because I like water activities and canoeing is relatively inexpensive	I canoe when my friends happen to invite me along

EXPECTANCY THEORY

It should surprise no one offering outdoor adventure activities that most participants come with a variety of expectations. These expectations can be divided into psychological (self-concept enhancement, confidence, sensation seeking, fun), sociological (compassion, socializing, respect for others, trust), and physical (fitness, outdoor skills, health, catharsis).

In addition to the expectations previously mentioned, a number of others can be associated with outdoor adventure pursuits. McAvoy (1978) and Progen (1979) suggest that excitement and challenge are two expectations of the adventure experience. Other expectations include individual and group challenges, opportunities for decision making, and participation in a small-group setting. Moreover, these expectations can be categorized into three general classifications of expectancy: avoidances, antecedents, and actual benefits.

Within the rubric of expectancy, what else can a participant expect from a formalized outdoor adventure experience? First, he or she should expect a high degree of safety with a minimum degree of exposure to *unnecessary* risks. Second, he or she should expect an appropriate meshing of activity with program objectives. If an individual is going on a

Participants in outdoor pursuits come with a variety of expectations, skills, and backgrounds.

TABLE 6.1
Potential Expectancy Components in Outdoor Adventure Programming

Avoidances	Antecedents	Benefits
1. Getting hurt	1. Money's worth	1. Enjoyment
2. Demeaning treatment	2. Safety	2. Self-concept
3. Unnecessary risks	3. Appropriate activities	3. Physical fitness
4. Rigorous work	4. Learning opportunities	4. Socialization
5. Failure	5. Souvenirs	5. Self-actualizing
6. Confrontation	6. Reasonable costs	6. Achievement
7. Illness	7. Quality equipment	7. Personal reflection

white-water trip for novices, being required to paddle through Lava Falls on the Colorado River (a technically difficult river) may very well be an inappropriate merging of stated objectives with performed activities.

The term *avoidances* implies items that individuals do not expect or want to have happen. Understandably, they do *not* expect to be injured or killed. Neither do they expect to feel foolish, incompetent, or unworthy.

They probably do not expect to be treated as one of many clients. *Antecedents* refer to positive or appropriate expectations when participating in an outdoor adventure experience. In other words, the necessary components to achieve a non-negative experience and feelings that one has gotten his "money's worth" must be present or anticipated to be present. For this to occur, certain perceived *"benefits"* must be realized. Examples of these benefits might include excitement, personal challenge, learning new skills, and meeting friends. Table 6.1 illustrates these expectancy components within outdoor adventure programming. Obviously, for a program to be successful, staff must stay cognizant of all three expectancy components.

ATTITUDE AND BEHAVIOR MIX

As stated previously, outdoor adventure has moved from the realm of a few daredevils to a much wider acceptance by society at large. This societal trend is manifested in the attitudes or learned predispositions to respond in a favorable or unfavorable manner toward outdoor adventure activities. In general, attitude is a product of past experience and can predispose future action or behavior (Iso-Ahola, 1980). Understanding an individual's attitudes can help explain his or her participation patterns in outdoor adventure activities. To more fully understand the effect of attitude, consider the following "Attitude-Behavior" model adapted from Fishbein and Ajzen (1975).

Attitude-Behavior Model

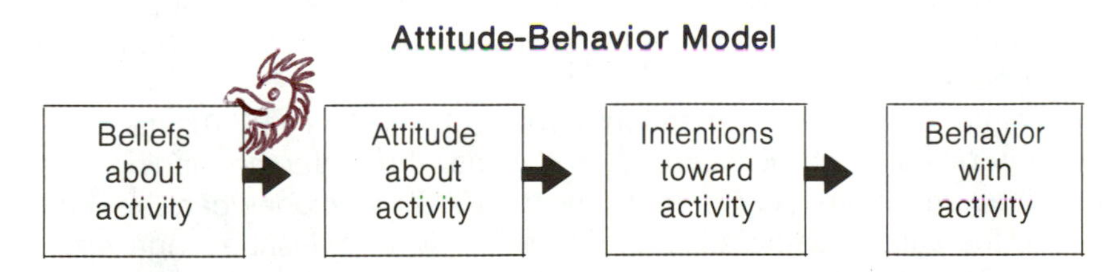

Clearly, the beliefs about the activity and the intentions toward it play important roles in the ultimate behavior displayed. Beliefs about outdoor adventure activities are formulated in two ways: (1) past experience and (2) situational/social influences. Fishbein and Ajzen (1975) suggested that an individual will generally hold from five to nine salient beliefs about a given object or activity at any one time. Outdoor adventure programmers would do well to consider identifying a potential client's specific beliefs about an activity since these beliefs, unless changed, will have a powerful influence on the person's behavior toward and during that activity. Both beliefs and their consequential attitudes can be changed through two primary mechanisms: *active participation* and *persuasive communication.* While active participation is the most powerful method and the raison d'etre for most programs, participants still have to be convinced to come to the program, thus often necessitating persuasive communication. This communication is empowered by the perceived trust in the message as well as its strength.

To summarize attitude theory and outdoor adventure—if the purpose is to *predict* an adventure behavior, such as participation, one should focus on the stated *intentions* of the participants, with regard to participation. However, if *understanding* the behavior is the goal, the factors which affect those intentions should be studied. While there are other theories that impact the outdoor adventure situation (such as intrinsic motivation and cognitive dissonance), the previously discussed theories lay a strong foundation for the development of a causal model for outdoor adventure.

A CAUSAL MODEL

A causal model attempts to resolve questions about causes and effects. To date, there are a plethora of studies suggesting that participation in outdoor adventure activities *can* enhance self-concept, stimulate personal growth, and create opportunities for self-actualization (Ewert, 1983). What is needed now is a better understanding of what factors influence these outcomes and to what degree. The ultimate goal is to produce a model of causes and effects (causal) that is consistent with both field observations and collected data. This is critical, as any concept or model without empirical meaning cannot serve any theoretically useful function (DiRenzo, 1967). Without this development of substantiated theories applicable to the field, outdoor adventure will continue to remain a concept analogous to electricity; we know that it works but we do not know how.

Building on the risk recreation paradigm of Allen (1980), the self-efficacy research of Bandura (1977), and the outcome findings as described in Shore (1977) and Ewert (1983), a model can be built around the substantiated attitudinal/behavior work of Fishbein and Ajzen (1975). This model attempts to explain the relationship between (a) the dimensions of predisposing conditions (antecedents), (b) beliefs about an outdoor adventure activity, (c) the individual's attitude about the activity, (d) his intention to elicit a particular behavior such as participating in the activity, and (e) the ultimate behavior exhibited by the individual. The framework of these dimensions is depicted in Figure 6.7.

As can be seen, each dimension is made up of a number of variables. When combined, these variables can collectively comprise an overall dimension such as predisposing factors (antecedents) or beliefs. In defining a possible pattern of these relationships, a path diagram is depicted in Figure 6.8, using participation as the outcome behavior.

As can be seen in Figure 6.8, predisposing factors and beliefs influence one another. Both dimensions influence an individual's attitude

FIGURE 6.7
Framework Relating Beliefs, Attitudes, Intentions, and Behaviors in Outdoor Adventure Recreation

Predisposing Factor[1]	Beliefs about Actvity	Attitude toward Activity	Intentions to Perform Desired Behavior	Behaviors with Respect to Outdoor Adventure Activities
Personality factors Demographics Preexisting activities Attributions Social/ psychological environment Sex role orientation Propensity for risk seeking Opportunity spectrum	Intrinsic feelings Information Expectations Perception of risk/danger • Frequency and magnitude • Risky shift • Protective measures • Hazard folklore[2]	Amount of affect • Positive • Negative • Neutral Belief strength Expectation values Image building	Participate Nonparticipation Extent of participation Time/location Willingness to assume costs • Financial • Time • Opportunities	Engage Nonengagement Disengagement Modification of engagement

[1] See Allen, 1980.
[2] See Helms, 1984.

FIGURE 6.8
Conceptual Model of Participation in an Outdoor Adventure Activity

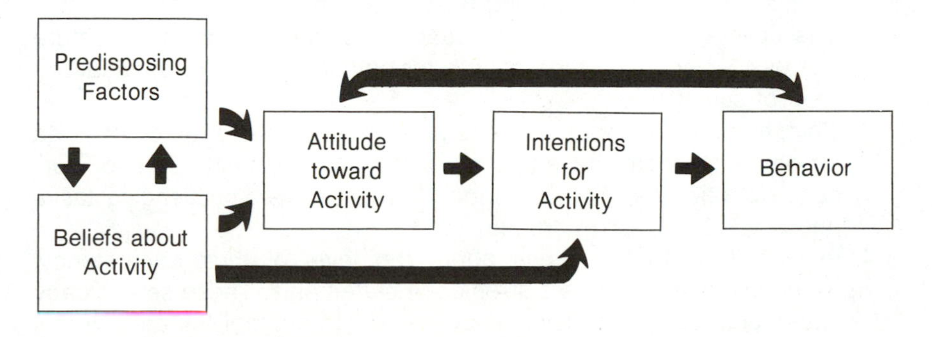

about an activity. Attitude affects the intentions for an activity or can bypass intentions and directly influence behavior. Intentions can also directly influence behavior. For example, an individual may believe that a particular activity is extremely dangerous and formulate the intention of never participating in that activity. In a similar fashion, a person may have developed some very positive attitudes about rock-climbing, through past experiences or collected information. In turn, these attitudes can influence a person to join a rock-climbing class or create intentions to do so. Behavior can also influence attitude, as suggested earlier in the optimal-arousal and attribution theories, by creating the opportunities for active participation, thereby constituting a potential attitude change.

The importance of this paradigm lies in its ability to predict and explain adventure behavior. However, describing a potential model and testing its validity are different things. While model testing can only disconfirm rather than prove (Pedhazur, 1982), the next step is to conduct some empirically based research on the validity of the proposed model.

CONCLUSIONS

Outdoor adventure activities have played an important recreational and educational role for many millions of individuals. The time has come for the field to take a more critical and astute view of what it does. The question needs to be extended beyond the point of "whether" something happens to one of "how" it happens. By exploring the theories that can glue our observations together, the field will be able to better explain how outdoor adventure activities impact an individual. In devising substantiated causal models, the field will move closer to realizing its ultimate goal: a healthier, more vibrant individual and society.

MAIN POINTS

1. Model and theory building are accumulative in the sense that they add to the body of knowledge in outdoor adventure pursuits by constantly verifying or refuting past ideas and beliefs.
2. It is believed that one of the reasons people engage in adventure pursuits is because of the search for optimal arousal or an idealized level of stimulation.
3. Competence-effectance refers to an individual's need to demonstrate an ability to control or effect his or her environment. Outdoor pursuits activities can provide opportunities to meet challenging tasks and a personal testing ground.
4. Individuals formulate ideas about the level of their competency, which are referred to as self-efficacy statements. These self-efficacy statements can be developed by personal accomplishments, verbal persuasion, arousal levels, and modeling.

5. Related to the theory of self-efficacy is the theory of attribution. Attribution theory refers to the process by which an individual makes assumptions about the cause of certain outcomes.
6. Using the attitude-behavioral model of Fishbein and Ajzen (1975), a model was developed to help explain and predict the behavior of people engaging in outdoor adventure pursuits.

REFERENCES

Allen, S. (1980). *Risk Recreation: Some Psychological Bases of Attraction.* Ph.D. Dissertation. University of Montana.

Bandura, A. (1977). Self-Efficacy: Toward a Unifying Theory of Behavioral Change. *Psychological Review,* 84: pp. 191–215.

Berlyne, D. (1960). *Conflict, Arousal and Curiosity.* New York: McGraw-Hill.

Bryan, H. (1979). *Conflict in the Great Outdoors.* Bureau of Public Administration, Sociological Studies No. 4., University, AL: University of Alabama.

Csikszentmihalyi, M. (1975). *Beyond Boredom and Anxiety.* San Francisco: Jossey-Bass.

DeCharms, R. (1968). *Personal Causation: The Internal Affective Determinants of Behavior.* New York: Academic Press.

Deci, E. (1975). *Intrinsic Motivation.* New York: Plenum.

DiRenzo, G. (ed.). (1967a). *Concepts, Theory and Explanation in the Behavioral Sciences.* New York: Random House.

DiRenzo, G. (1967b). "Conceptual Definition in the Behavioral Sciences." *Concepts, Theory, and Explanation in the Behavioral Sciences.* New York: Random House.

Duffy, E. (1957). The Psychological Significance of the Concept of Arousal or Activation. *Psychological Review,* 64: pp. 265–275.

Ellis, M. (1973). *Why People Play.* Englewood Cliffs, NJ: Prentice-Hall.

Ewert, A. (1983). *Outdoor Adventure and Self-Concept: A Research Analysis.* Eugene, OR: Center for Leisure Studies.

Ewert, A. (1985). Why People Climb: The Relationship of Participant Motives and Experience Level to Mountaineering. *Journal of Leisure Research,* 17(3): pp. 241–250.

Ewert, A. (1987a). Outdoor Adventure Recreation: A Trend Analysis. *Journal of Park and Recreation Administration* (in press).

Ewert, A. (1987b). Models and Theories in Outdoor Adventure Recreation. *Journal of Outdoor Recreation Research* (in press).

Fishbein, M. and Ajzen, J. (1975). *Belief, Attitude, Intention and Behavior: An Introduction to Theory and Recreation.* Reading, MA: Addison-Wesley.

Fowler, H. (1966). *Curiosity and Behavior.* New York: Macmillan.

Fridgen, J. and Hinkelman, B. (1977). Recreation Behavior and Environment Congruence. Paper presented at the NRPA Research Symposium, National Recreation and Park Association. Las Vegas, NV.

Hale, A. (1978). *Directory-Programs in Outdoor Adventure Activities.* Mankato, MN: Outdoor Recreation.

Harmon, P. and Templin, G. (1980). "Conceptualizing Experiential Education." *High Adventure Outdoor Pursuits,* pp. 42–49. J. Meier, T. Morash, and G.

Welton (eds.). Salt Lake City, UT: Brighton Publishing Company.

Hendee, J. and Roggenbuck, J. (1984). "Wilderness-Related Education as a Factor Increasing Demand for Wilderness." Paper presented at the International Forest Congress Convention, Quebec City, Canada.

Iso-Ahola, S. (1976). "On the Theoretical Link Between Personality and Leisure." *Psychological Reports,* 39: pp. 3–10.

Iso-Ahola, S. (1980). *The Social Psychology of Leisure and Recreation.* Dubuque, IA: Wm. C. Brown.

Kerlinger, F. (1973). *Foundations of Behavior Research.* New York: Holt, Rinehart and Winston.

McAvoy, L. (1978). Outdoor Leadership Training. *Journal of Physical Education and Recreation,* 4: pp. 18–19.

McGowan, M. (1986). Self-Efficacy: Operationalizing Challenge Education. *The Bradford Papers Annual,* 1: pp. 65–69.

Pedhazur, E. (1982). *Multiple Regression in Behavioral Research.* New York: Holt, Rinehart and Winston.

Progen, J. (1979). Man, Nature and Sport. In E. Gerber and M. Nillian (eds.). *Sports and the Body: A Philosophical Symposium,* pp. 237–242. Philadelphia: Lea and Febiger.

Rossman, B. and Ulehla, J. (1977). Psychological Reward Values Associated with Wilderness Use. A Functional Reinforcement Approach. *Environment and Behavior,* 9: pp. 41–66.

Shore, A. (1977). *Outward Bound: A Reference Volume.* New York: Topp Litho.

Slawski, C. (1981). *Social Psychological Theories: A Comparative Handbook for Students.* Glenview, IL: Scott, Foresman and Company.

Tejada-Flores, L. (1973). *Games Climbers Play.* Englewood Cliffs, NJ: Prentice-Hall.

White, R. (1959). Motivation Reconsidered: The Concept of Competence. *Psychological Review,* 66: pp. 297–333.

7

RESEARCH AND EVALUATION IN OUTDOOR ADVENTURE PURSUITS

It has been said that you can prove anything with statistics and certainly there is an element of truth in this statement. The opposite point of view is also true. T. H. Huxely most elegantly stated this position:

> The tragedy of science is the slaying of beautiful hypotheses with ugly facts.

Despite the misuse of research and statistics there is great value in the use of these tools. Without them, practitioners and scholars are left with intuition and conjecture as their only tools. Valuable as these tools may be, they have some obvious limitations.

As a natural outgrowth of outdoor recreation and outdoor education, research in outdoor adventure pursuits has been able to draw on a substantial amount of prior research studies and writings. Based on this foundation, there has emerged a growing body of research specifically concerned with outdoor adventure pursuits. This research has encompassed a wide range of topics and methodology.

Chapter 7 provides a discussion of the history of research in outdoor adventure pursuits. Following this is an overview and assessment of the completed research in the field. Finally, recommendations are provided to aid researchers in their future endeavors.

RESEARCH BEGINNINGS

Systematic inquiry and research into these outdoor adventure pursuit programs originated in the 1950s. It was during this time that efforts were first made to identify the extent and impact of adventure-based activities upon the individual. Schraer (1954) attempted to identify the number of public schools using survival training programs in their curricula. Three years later, Morse (1957) wrote one of the first "scientific" articles on the therapeutic values of outdoor camping. His points concerning the advantages of outdoor programs include control without institutionalization, real living situations, motor outlets for catharsis, creative learning, and adventures without antisocial behavior. These early findings serve to remind future researchers not to reinvent the wheel but rather to move on to more current areas of concern.

The 1960s marked the beginning of the *social benefits* phase of outdoor adventure recreation. The works by Kelly and Baer (1968, 1969, 1971), considered a foundational work in the field, provided some initial and relatively conclusive evidence that adventure-based activities can produce socially desirable benefits such as reduced recidivism rates. In addition, the work by Moses (1968) and Moses and Peterson (1970) provided additional support for the positive effects of participation in adventure-based survival courses with demonstrated improvements in G.P.A. and eligibility for academic readmission.

It was also during this time that the first of a long line of research efforts on *benefits to the individual* was seen. Beginning with Clifford and Clifford (1967), this research included many noteworthy studies such as those by Adams, 1970; Wetmore, 1972; Heaps and Thorstenson, 1974; Nye, 1976; Robbins, 1976; George, 1979; Stogner, 1978; and Black, 1983. The most prolific effort has been in the area of improved self-concept, followed by self-actualization (Vander Wilt and Klocke, 1971; Young and Crandall, 1984), modification of levels of fear (Ewert, 1986), and self-efficacy (McGowan, 1986).

A third area of research could be termed the wilderness experience. Efforts in this area have involved investigating topics such as motivations (Young, 1983; Mitchell, 1983; Kaplan, 1984; Ewert, 1985b), expected benefits (Lambert, 1978; Schreyer and White, 1979; Driver and Brown, 1987; Ewert, 1987), and levels of satisfaction (Manning, 1986; LaPage, 1983). Inherent in many of these studies is the underlying dimension of participation in some form of outdoor adventure recreation (e.g., backpacking, rock climbing, or white-water canoeing).

Subsumed within all three research areas (social benefits, benefits to the individual, and wilderness experience) is the theme that outdoor adventure may serve as a type of therapeutic intervention. A substantial research effort has been made linking outdoor adventure as a form of therapy with goals such as enhanced self-concept, improved social attitudes and behavior, improved physical health, and reduced emotional problems (Barcus and Bergeson, 1972; Wright, 1982; Smith, 1982, 1985a; Robb and Ewert, 1987).

There is a substantial amount of research literature currently available concerning outdoor adventure pursuits. In terms of numbers alone,

People in adventurous settings often provide excellent situations for psychological and sociological studies.

Thomas (1985) reported over 700 articles written on adventure education, many of which are research studies. There are also an additional number of concerns that have consistently appeared. The following section discusses these concerns and provides an assessment of the current state of research in outdoor adventure pursuits.

A RESEARCH ASSESSMENT

One of the earliest and most comprehensive attempts at assessing the quality of the research work done in outdoor adventure pursuits was conducted by Shore (1977). While focused primarily on Outward Bound, this work covered a variety of different types of programs and methods. Of greater use may be Shore's establishment of a comprehensive bibliography, which included a wide mix of bibliographic topics such as education, psychology, corrections, and other literature available at the time.

As a framework for discussion, Shore developed two categories of study. The two categories consisted of studies "included" for their quality and research methodology and those studies "not included." It should be noted, however, that one criticism of Shore's work has been the lack of explicitly stated criteria for categorizing the various research (Kraft, 1985). Studies which comprised the "not included" category were seen as too flawed or conceptually unsound to warrant an elaborate assessment. Shore's conclusions concerning the quality of the research completed up to that time were guarded and reserved. He states that:

> One must conclude, overall, that the research literature of Outward Bound [and the research literature up to that time in adventure education] is weak. It has focused on disciplinary issues (self-concept, self-esteem) to the virtual exclusion of their relationship to programmatic issues (length of course, mix of activities, and nature of instruction). There have been few attempts to link outcome measures with program components and very little statistical analysis in this sense as opposed to statistical reporting. (Shore, 1977)

Shore's work, while the most comprehensive, was only one of several studies occurring during the 1970s, a not-so-surprising fact when one considers that, after the change and experimentation in both education and recreation of the 1960s, there was much more to research and write about in the 1970s. One particularly popular form of reporting was the annotated bibliography. Within this form, a substantial number of studies were reported by Mattews (1976), Pollack (1976), Thomas (1985), and Colan (1986). Other useful bibliographies and listing of abstracts included the American Alliance of Health, Physical Education, Recreation and Dance series entitled, "Research in Outdoor Education: Summaries of Doctoral Studies," and the Educational Resources Information Center (ERIC) and Clearinghouse on Rural Education and Small Schools (CRESS) supplements entitled, "Selected Bibliographies in Outdoor Education."

While useful from a documentary perspective, the annotated bibliographies provide little guidance to the researcher concerning an evaluation of the conceptual basis of the studies, their methodologies, and the credibility of the findings. From a research perspective, greater use can be made of the works by Vogl and Vogl (1974), Iida (1975), Lowenstein, (1975), Shore (1977), Staley (1979), Burton (1981), and Ewert (1983). Critiques of the selected studies and suggestions for the

TABLE 7.1
Types of Current Research Methods in Outdoor Adventure Pursuits

• Historical	• Correlational
• Descriptive	• Experimental
• Case study	• Quasi-experimental
• Observational	• Critical-incident
• Causal	• Single-subject
• Behavioral analysis	• Time sampling
• Ethnographic	• Mechanized Collection

direction of future research efforts are provided within each of these works. Table 7.1 summarizes the observations of several of the aforementioned authors.

The general view of the research conducted in the field of outdoor pursuits has been reserved, due primarily to the overreliance on self-selected samples and measures using a self-report format. Despite these reservations, there have been literally hundreds of studies which have reported positive benefits from participation in outdoor pursuits. These studies, as listed in Table 7.2, have employed a number of methodologies, and have generated findings in a variety of areas. These areas have included therapeutic dimensions, individual and group benefits, behavior modification, and motivations for participation. The generalized findings of a selected group of studies in each of the above mentioned areas are presented in Tables 7.3, 7.4, and 7.5.

TABLE 7.2
Summary of Selected Research Analyses in Outdoor Pursuits

	Overall Impression of Completed Research	Specific Problems	Recommendations
Vogl and Vogl (1974)	Insufficient and limited Usually done by graduate students Few national reporting on findings	Few historical, philosophical, or course content studies Insufficient training in graduate programs	Larger samples More evaluation studies of program Distinguish between cognitive and affective
Iida (1975)	Generally positive benefits Wide range of paper and pencil instruments Self-theory framework	Overuse of standarized instruments Unsophisticated research designs "Ceiling effect" of participants Small sample size	More measurement of behavioral modifications Reasons for nonparticipation Presence of longterm effects
Shore (1977)	Focus on outcomes Lack of emphasis on program components Substantial supportive literature	Little statistical analysis Overemphasis on descriptive reporting	Identify effects of various program components More sophisticated statistical analysis
Ewert (1983)	Mixed but generally supportive Substantial convergent validity	Few causal comparative designs Overreliance on convenience sampling Overprojected expectations	Development of causal models Studies using more "main stress" populations Construction and testing of explanatory theories

TABLE 7.3
Therapeutic Dimensions

• The therapeutic outdoor camp	Morse (1957)
• Self-acceptance	Vander Wilt and Klocks (1971)
• Coping rather than defensive strategies	Bechtel (1972)
• Reentry problems	Robbins (1976)
• People with disabilities	Roland and Havens (1981) Smith (1982; 1985)
• Self-actualization	Young and Crandall (1984)
• Wilderness group therapy	Nurenberg (1985)
• Risk recreation and persons with disabilities	Robb and Ewert (1987)

TABLE 7.4
Individual/Group Behavior

• Reduced recidivism	Kelly and Baer (1969; 1971)
• Reduced drop-out rates	Moses (1968)
• Increases in G.P.A.	Moses and Peterson (1970)
• More realistic perceptions of self	Yenser (1972)
• Reduced racial conflict	Potts (1974) Nelson and Martin (1976)
• Reduced deviant behavior	Gaston, et al., (1978)
• Long-term environmental attitudes	Crompton and Sellor (1981)
• Effectiveness in substance abuse	Stich (1983)

TABLE 7.5
Self-Concept/Self-Esteem/Locus of Control

• Improved self-concept with lower initial levels	Clifford and Clifford (1967)
• Enhanced internal locus of control	Borstelman (1970)
• Higher levels of self-concept after one-year follow-up	Heaps and Thorstenson (1974)
• Significant improvement in self-concept when compared to control	Nye (1976)
• Equalizing on pretest (covariate) significant improvement	George (1978)
• Increases in self-esteem	Bertolami (1981)
• Positive relationship between program length and self-concept	Ewert (1982)
• Situational specific self-concept	Wright (1982)
• Increases in multidimensional self-concept	Marsh (1986)

While the studies listed in the tables were selected because of their "representativeness," there are many other studies which were not listed. As Iida (1975) correctly notes, however, most of the studies done in the area of outdoor adventure pursuits revolve around a self-theory framework. This theory suggests that individuals behave in a manner congruent with how they perceive themselves. Where outdoor adventure pursuits come into play is in the ancillary corollary of this theory, which states that an individual's response to a situation both reflects and determines his or her current state of self-concept. In outdoor adventure pursuits, an underresearched postulate of this theory suggests that an unsuccessful or debilitating adaptation to this outdoor situation may cumulatively affect the self-concept in a negative way. Little is known, for example, as to what happens to an individual if he or she fails to complete a course component such as rock-climbing.

As previously stated, the primary thrust of most research efforts, to date, in outdoor adventure pursuits has been with some permutation of the self-theory concept. There are, however, a variety of additional areas and issues in need of investigation. These areas are listed in Tables 7.6 and 7.7.

TABLE 7.6
Current Research Topics in Outdoor Adventure Education

Participation rates
Demographics
Program availability
Cost/benefit analyses
Physical fitness
Social integration
Level/types of fears
Self-efficacy
Motivations/benefits
Price elasticity
Staff selection and development
Program components:
- Length
- Order of activities
- Type of activities
- Location and topography
- Participant characteristics
- Season

Model testing and verification
Historical events and emerging trends
Transfer/generalization
Staff burn-out and turn-over
Certification
Marketing

TABLE 7.7
Research and Evaluation Issues in Outdoor Pursuits

Latent vs. measuring variables
Model testing
Single-subject designs
Naturalistic inquiries
Behavioral/archival analysis
Documentary evidence
Validity concerns: Triangulation techniques
Computer applications
Mutivariate statistics
Experimental/quasi-experimental designs
Matching/blocking procedures
Multivariate analysis
Goal evaluation
Sample size and type
Implementation/measurement problems in programs
Attrition/nonrespondents
Multiple indicators
Scale/Instrument development

It should be noted that, while it may appear redundant to list self-concept as a topic in need of further research, it is suggested that greater sophistication be taken in the type of analysis. While studies in self-concept have historically used a self-report psychological measure, little has been found concerning the nature or reasons for any observed change. Future studies of self-concept changes through outdoor adventure pursuits can contribute to a greater overall understanding by focusing on how, why, and when any change occurs.

The lesson generated by this historical perspective on the research done in outdoor adventure is that the future of meaningful and "acceptable" research lies in the arena of methodological pluralism or using a variety of approaches and techniques. In addition, there is a need for more sophisticated analytic procedures and methods. What we know about the effects of participation in outdoor adventure pursuits upon individuals has generally been derived from (1) their everyday conduct (naturalistic-ethnographic studies and direct involvement of the researcher as a participant), (2) the impressions made on other (observation techniques), (3) self-characterizations and reports (personality inventories and surveys), (4) what others have written (documentary and literature inquires), and (5) their observed behaviors (behavioral analyses and mechanized data collection). Given the complexity of the human organism, including the affective, behavioral, and cognitive components of the human experience, the inherently diverse agenda for research in outdoor adventure pursuits must encompass as many different sources of information as possible.[1]

Unfortunately, this need for methodological pluralism has been transformed in reality to an overreliance on paper and pencil measurement of attitudes, most notably self-concept, using a self-report format. Webb et al. (1966) have elegantly summed this overreliance in the statement:

> Almost everything we know about attitudes [in the social sciences] is also suspect because the findings are saturated with the inherent risks of self-report information. One swallow does not make a summer; nor do two "strongly agrees," one "disagree," and "I don't know" make an attitude. (p. 172)

These statements imply that present and future researchers need not automatically cast aside the techniques of self-report or questionnaires, but rather use these methods in conjunction with others. What will continue to impede these efforts will be the problem of integration of the findings of a cross-method study. Cattell (1968) and Glancy (1986) offer interesting procedures to account for these difficulties. In other words, the findings of behavioral, anecdotal, and self-report research generally produce different measurement units and will need to be integrated into generalized findings.

If research in outdoor adventure pursuits is to move beyond the earlier criticism of Shore (1977), that is, too few analytical studies, the development, testing, and modification of theories and concepts must play a more pivotal role. To date, there is an overemphasis on measurement and a corresponding deficiency in conceptualization. Given the substantial amount of research already done in outdoor adventure pursuits, there can be little doubt that participation in these types of programs and activities may provide a variety of benefits for the individual and group. These benefits, however, are outcomes and the raison d'etre of outdoor adventure programming. Documenting these outcomes often does little in explaining how and why they have occurred.

Moving beyond description into explanation will prove to be as difficult as it is necessary. This involves a more in-depth understanding of the related fields of psychology, sociology, and education. In addition, this movement will entail the excruciating task of formulating and testing theories. According to Slawski (1981), to be effective a theory must be relatively easy to apply, provide valuable information, enhance predictability of a phenomenon, and have explanatory power.

In outdoor adventure pursuits, what is needed is the development of a body of knowledge on which future research can be grounded. This entails moving away from the compilation of independent, unrelated studies and toward an integration of and building upon past research work. Theory-based research can contribute to this continuity within the body of knowledge surrounding outdoor adventure pursuits.

---

[1] For a similar analysis in the area of personality research see Craik (1986).

Furthermore, there are four distinct but complementary perspectives in outdoor adventure pursuits research. First, there is the *psychological perspective.* While the most widely used viewpoint, this perspective subsumes the behavior of the individual as well as his or her attitudes, feelings, and so on (Tinsley and Johnson, 1984). Studies on leadership training and development also fall into this category of research.

The second framework from which to conduct outdoor adventure pursuits research is the *sociological perspective.* From this perspective, the researcher is concerned with what happens in a group context. Of particular interest may be the hedonistic tone of the group and the communication patterns or the support structures that develop. Similar to the psychological, this perspective has obvious implications for research in outdoor adventure pursuits.

The *economic perspective* is the third framework on which researchers can base their inquiries. This perspective includes the allocation of resources such as land areas, in addition to the most commonly thought of cost-benefit and income-generating studies. For example, recent articles by Schreyer and Knopf (1984) and Dustin and McAvoy (1982) have examined the concepts of succession and displacement (i.e., how outdoor adventure recreationalists are moved out or leave a particular area) and their implications for participation in outdoor adventure pursuits.

The fourth perspective, *interaction with the natural environment,* implies the generation of information which is focused on how outdoor

Understanding and mediating the impact adventure-seekers have on the environment is an important area of study for future research efforts.

adventure pursuits activities use, impact, and interact with the environment. One topic of current interest is the impact outdoor programs have on a natural area over a period of time.

While there may be other perspectives of outdoor adventure research which could be added, present and future researchers need to ensure that their particular work provides for continuity and contributes to the knowledge base. There must be a greater relatedness between the

TABLE 7.8
Recommendations for Future Research Directions in Outdoor Adventure Pursuits*

- Comprehensive studies done on the penetration of adventure programming within recreational and educational systems
- The development of more scholarly investigations into the phenomenon of outdoor adventure recreation
- Greater attention and recognition from the academic recreation community concerning the uniqueness and contributions of adventure programming
- A heightened awareness by both the federal and state governments about the purposes, requirements, and importance of outdoor adventuring within the total recreation picture
- A detailed study of the major delivery systems for outdoor adventure programs (Vogl and Vogl, 1974)
- Investigate the descriptive aspects of outdoor adventure recreation, including the attitudes of the participant, perceptions of risk and danger, resource management options, environmental impacts, and motivations for participation
- Collect information on the sociological effects of crowding, carrying capacity for a successful experience, and developing a satisfaction model for adventure participation
- Develop explanatory models for engagement in the activity, expected benefits, and future rates of participation
- Increase the research efforts in other potential benefits besides the global self-concept and simple return rates to prison or incarceration
- Analysis of the need for and demand of outdoor pursuits in contemporary society
- Studies of the various systems for the delivery of outdoor pursuit programs and activities
- Identification of the trends and emerging patterns in outdoor pursuits
- The development of explanatory and predictive models of outdoor pursuits participation and behavior
- The application of more studies using an interdisciplinary approach

* For a similar discussion on recommendations for leisure research see Smith and Ng (1982).

various past and present studies. This current state of research affairs is symptomatic of research done primarily by graduate students rather than professional researchers. Other recommendations for enhancing the research effort in the field are listed in Table 7.8.

PROGRAM EVALUATION

Evaluating outdoor adventure programs is becoming increasingly important in this era of cost/benefit analyses and "accountability." Evaluation in outdoor adventure pursuits programs can be considered a two-purpose methodology: determining the worth or effectiveness of a program and getting information to make decisions (Theobald, 1979). There have evolved a number of different approaches to program evaluation involving the use of expert judges, need indexes, discrepancy evaluation, goal attainment evaluation, and systems models.

Using expert judges involves having other professionals observe a program. These observations are often based on making comparisions between similar programs. The need index approach usually attempts to place a monetary value on some facet or benefit believed to accrue to the participant(s) of the program (Wilder, 1977). Discrepancy evaluation measures the intended goals of the program with the goals actually realized. Goal attainment usually focuses on a thorough understanding of the benefits and goals of the program and how to measure whether they are accomplished. Evaluation using a systems model focuses on the optimum distribution of resources. In addition, this method attempts to understand how the program actually works.

Whatever the specific method used, evaluation can be summative or formative. *Summative evaluation* involves using evaluation to investigate the final outcomes or overall effectiveness of the program. *Formative evaluation* seeks to collect information as a continuous process, with the information being used to make decisions concerning how the program is conducted.

As mentioned previously, evaluation can be used to aid decision making or help determine the worth of a program. However, the specific purposes of program evaluation are much more complex for they involve both overt and sometimes covert reasons. The specific reasons might be concerns about the organization, administration, funding agency, consumer, and evaluator. A sampling of the covert and overt reasons for program evaluation are included in Table 7.9.

This table suggests that evaluation is to be used but not abused. Findings from evaluation can be effective tools in designing programs that are more responsive to the needs of the participants. Moreover, with the specter of limited resources, evaluation of programs can be useful in determining what things a specific program can do and what should be attempted elsewhere. Using evaluation to increase one's status, because it is an in-vogue procedure, or to satisfy the require-

TABLE 7.9
Reasons for Evaluation

Organization
- Demonstrate program effectiveness
- Justify expenditures
- Determine costs
- Gain support
- Satisfy funding agencies
- Determine future course of action

Program Administrators
- Being favorable or unfavorable attention to a program
- Increase one's status
- Promotion
- In-vogue procedure
- Greater program control
- Supporting evidence

Funding Agency
- Efficiency of program
- Impact of effectiveness

Consumer
- Tax-dollar expenditure
- Specific benefits provided
- Value of planned change
- Increased community participation

Evaluator
- Desire to contribute to knowledge
- Professional or financial advancement
- Belief in importance of evaluation

ments of a college course or degree are not justifiable reasons for going through the effort.

In sum, the purpose of this section has been to suggest ways to enhance the effectiveness of research in outdoor adventure pursuits. This is desirable because ultimately the participant and the natural environment will benefit. Systematic and rigorous investigation can be used to help sharpen the focus of outdoor-based programs and strengthen the intuition of the program staff. This is an important consideration when one considers that this intuition, coupled with observation and personal involvement, ultimately provides the motivation to continue these types of activities and research. People and organizations offer outdoor adventure programs because they feel that there is something intrinsically beneficial and productive that happens when humans and adventure meet. Better utilization of the available research tools can help support that process and avoid the dilemma poised by Reinharz (1979) where research generates data instead of meaningful findings.

MAIN POINTS

1. Systematic inquiry and research into outdoor adventure pursuits began in the 1950s with some early works on Outward Bound in England and on survival training.
2. By the 1960s, outdoor adventure pursuits were considered useful in rehabilitating troubled youth and providing other social benefits.
3. During the 1970s, research efforts began to look at the effects of outdoor adventure pursuits upon the individual. Heavily researched topics included self-concept and self-esteem.
4. A substantial amount of research literature has been dedicated to improving the quality of research in outdoor adventure pursuits.
5. To date, concerns about the quality of research in outdoor adventure pursuits have focused primarily on issues of validity. More specifically, questions concerning how generalizable the findings are to other populations and whether the treatments (i.e., participation in outdoor adventure pursuit activities) created the change, are often directed at research in this area.
6. A number of techniques are currently available to the outdoor adventure pursuits researcher, including surveys and questionnaires, historical research, case studies, and naturalistic inquiry.
7. In addition, there are a number of issues that are important for research at this time. These issues involve the effect of ordering of course components, the effects of stress, and course length upon the outcomes of the course.
8. Given the relative undeveloped state of research in outdoor adventure pursuits, there are tremendous possibilities for systematic investigation. It is hoped that a number of research tracts will develop that can be systematically added to by different researchers. For example, the concept of stress and its effect upon the individual currently needs more long-term investigation.

REFERENCES

Adams, W. (1970). Survival Training: Its Effects on the Self-Concept and Selected Personality Factors of Emotionally Disturbed Adolescents. *Dissertation Abstracts International, 1970–71,* 31: p. 388B.

Barcus, C. and Bergeson, R. (1972). Survival Training and Mental Health: A Review. *Therapeutic Recreation Journal,* 6(1): pp. 3–8.

Bechtel, A. (1972). A Behavioral Comparison of Urban and Small Town Environments. In A. Berstein, Wilderness as a Therapeutic Behavior Setting, *Therapeutic Recreation Journal,* 4: p. 160.

Bertolami, C. (1981). *Effects of a Wilderness Program on Self-Esteem and Locus of Control Orientations of Young Adults,* ERIC Report No. 266 928.

Black, B. (1983). The Effect of an Outdoor Experiential Adventure Program on the Development of Dynamic Balance and Spatial Veering for the Visually Impaired Adolescent. *Therapeutic Recreation Journal,* 17(3): pp. 39–49.

Borstelman, L. (1970). Psychological Readiness for and Change Associated with the Outward Bound Program. Morganton, NC: North Carolina Outward Bound School. Mimeographed, 9 pgs.

Burton, L. (1981). A Critical Analysis and Review of the Research on Outward Bound and Related Programs. *Dissertation Abstracts International,* 42: p. 1581B.

Cattell, R. (1968). Trait-View Theory of Perturbations in Ratings and Self-Ratings (L(BR)- and Q-data): Its Application to Obtaining Pure Trait Score Estimates in Questionnaires. *Psychological Review,* 75: pp. 95–113.

Clifford, E. and Clifford, M. (1967). Self-Concepts Before and After Survival Training. *British Journal of Social and Clinical Psychology,* 6: pp. 241–248.

Colan, N. (1986). *Outward Bound: An Annotated Bibliography, 1976–1985.* Denver: Colorado Outward Bound.

Craik, K. (1986). Personality Research Methods: An Historical Perspective. *Journal of Personality,* 54(1): 18–51.

Crompton, J. and Sellar, C. (1981). A Review of the Literature: Do Outdoor Education Experiences Contribute to Positive Development in the Affective Domain? *Journal of Environmental Education,* 12(4): pp. 21–29.

Driver, B. and Brown, P. (1987). Probable Personal Benefits of Outdoor Recreation. In *Proceedings: President's Commission on Americans Outdoors,* 1987, U.S. Government Printing Office, pp. values 63–20.

Dustin, D and McAvoy, L. (1982). The Decline and Fall of Quality Recreation Opportunities and Environments? *Environmental Ethics,* 4: pp. 49–57.

Ewert, A. (1983). *Outdoor Adventure and Self-Concept: A Research Analysis.* Eugene, OR: Center for Leisure Studies, University of Oregon.

Ewert, A. (1985a). Risk Recreation: Trends and Issues. *Trends,* 22(3): pp. 4–9.

Ewert, A. (1985b). Why People Climb: The Relationship of Participant Motives and Experience Level to Mountainerring. *Journal of Leisure Research,* 17(3): pp. 241–250.

Ewert, A. (1986). The Therapeutic Modification of Fear Through Outdoor Recreation Activities. *Bradford Papers Annual,* 1: pp. 1–10.

Ewert, A. (1987a). Values, Benefits and Consequences in Outdoor Adventure Recreation. In *Proceedings: President's Commission on Americans Outdoors,* 1987, U.S. Government Printing Office, pp. values 63–20.

Ewert, A. (1987b). Research in Outdoor Adventure Recreation: Analysis and Overview. *The Bradford Papers,* 2: pp. 15–28.

Gaston, D.; Plouffe, M.; and Chinsky, J. (1978). An Empirical Investigation of a Wilderness Adventure Program for Teenagers: the Connecticut Wilderness School. ERIC Report No. ED 178 250.

George, R. (1979). Learning Survival Self-Sufficiency Skills and Particpating in a Solo Camping Experience Related to Self-Concept. *Dissertation Abstracts International,* 40: p. 106A.

Glancy, M. (1986). Participant Observation in the Recreation Setting. *Journal of Leisure Research,* 18(2): pp. 59–80.

Hamilton, L. (1981). The Changing Face of American Mountaineering. *Review of Sport and Leisure,* 6(1): pp. 15–36.

Heaps, R. and Thorstenson, C. (1974). Self-Concept Changes Immediately and

One Year after Survival Training. *Therapeutic Recreation Journal,* 8(2): pp. 60–63.

Iida, M. (1975). Adventure Orientated Programs: A Review of Research. In *Research in Camping and Environmental Education.* Proceedings from the National Research Workshop, Pennsylvania State University.

Kaplan, R. (1984). Wilderness Perception and Psychological Benefits: An Analysis of a Continuing Program. *Leisure Sciences,* 6(3): pp. 271–290.

Kelly, F. and Baer, D. (1968). *Outward Bound: An Alternative to Institutionalization for Adolescent Delinquent Boys.* Boston, MA: Fandel Press.

Kelly, F. and Baer, D. (1969). Jesness Inventory and Self-Concept Measures for Delinquents Before and After Participation in Outward Bound. *Psychological Reports,* 25: pp. 719–724.

Kelly, F. and Baer, D. (1971). Physical Challenges as a Treatment for Delinquency. *Crime and Delinquency,* 17: pp. 437–445.

Kraft, R. (1985). Towards a Theory of Experiential Learning. In R. Kraft (ed.). *The Theory of Experiential Education,* pp. 4–85. Boulder, CO: Association for Experiential Education.

Lambert, M. (1978). Reported Self-Concept and Self-Actualizing Value Changes as a Function of Academic Classes with Wilderness Experience. *Perceptual and Motor Skills,* 46: pp. 1035–1040.

LaPage, W. (1983). Recreation Resource Management for Visitor Satisfaction. In S. Lieber and D. Fesenmaier (eds.). *Recreation Planning and Management.* State College, PA: Venture Publishing Company.

Lowenstein, D. (1975). *Wilderness Adventure Programs: An Activity Profile.* ERIC Report No. ED 127 102.

Manning, R. (1986). *Studies in Outdoor Recreation.* Corvallis, OR: Oregon State University.

Market Opinion Research, 1986. *Participation in Outdoor Recreation Among American Adults and the Motivations Which Drive Participation.* New York: National Geographical Society.

Marsh, H.; Richards, G.; and Barnes, J. (1986). Multidimensional Self-Concepts: The Effect of Participation in an Outward Bound Program. *Journal of Personality and Social Psychology,* 50(1): pp. 195–204.

Mattews, B. (1976). Adventure Education and Self-Concept—an Annotated Bibliography with Appendix. ERIC Report ED 160 287.

McGowan, M. (1986). Self-Efficacy: Operationalizing Challenge Education. *Bradford Papers Annual,* 1: pp. 65–69.

Mitchell, R. (1983). *Mountain Experience: The Psychology and Sociology of Adventure.* Chicago: The University of Chicago Press.

Morse, W. (1951). An Interdisciplinary Therapeutic Camp. *Journal of Social Issues,* 13(1): pp. 3–14.

Moses, D. (1968). *Improving Academic Performance.* Provo, UT: Brigham Young University.

Moses, D. and Peterson, D. (1970). *Academic Achievement Helps Programs.* Provo, UT: Brigham Young University, Academic Office.

Nelson, N. and Martin, W. (1976). *Project BACSTOP Evaluation Report. 1974–1975.* ERIC Report No. ED 198 992.

Nurenberg, S. (1985). Psychological Development of Borderline Adolescents in Wilderness Therapy. *Dissertation Abstracts International,* 46(11): p. 3488A.

Nye, R. (1976). The Influence of an Outward Bound Program on the Self-Concept of the Participants. *Dissertation Abstracts International,* 37: p. 142A.

Pollack, R. (1976). *An Annotated Bibliography of the Literature and Research on Outward Bound and Related Programs.* ERIC Report No. 171 476.

Potts, V. (1974). *Project BACSTOP Evaluation Report, 1973-1974.* Battle Creek, MI: Michigan Department of Education, Battle Creek Public Schools.

Reinharz, S. (1979). *Social Science.* San Francisco, CA: Jossey-Bass.

Robb, G. and Ewert, A. (1987). Risk Recreation and Persons with Disabilities. *Therapeutic Recreation Journal*, Vol. XXI, No. 1, pp. 58-69.

Robbins, S. (1976). Outdoor Wilderness Survival and its Psychological and Sociological Effects Upon Students in Changing Human Behavior. *Dissertation Abstracts International,* 37: p. 1473A.

Roland, C. and Havens, M. (1981). *An Introduction to Adventure: A Sequential Approach to Challenging Activities with Persons Who Are Disabled.* Loretto, MN: The Vinland National Center.

Schraer, H. (1954). Survival Education: A Survey of Trends in Survival Education in Certain Public Schools and Teacher Training Institutions and a Detailed Study of the Elements of Survival Education Found in the Programs of the Boy Scouts and Girl Scouts of America. *Dissertation Abstracts International,* 14: p.1966A.

Schreyer, R. and White, R. (1979). A Conceptual Model of High-Risk Recreation. In *Proceedings, First Annual Conference on Recreation Planning and Development.* New York, NY: American Society of Civil Engineers.

Schreyer, R. and Knopf, R. (1984). The Dynamics of Change in Outdoor Recreation Environments—Some Equity Issues. *Journal of Park and Recreation Administration,* 2(1): pp. 9-19.

Shore, A. (Comp.). (1977). *Outward Bound: A Reference Volume.* New York: Topp Litho.

Slawski, C. (1981). *Social Psychological Theories: A Comparative Handbook for Students.* Glenview, IL: Scott, Foresman and Company.

Smith, T. (1982). Self-Concept, Special Populations and Outdoor Therapy. In G. Robb (ed.). *The Bradford Papers,* Vol. 2, pp. 1-15.

Smith, T. (1985a). Outdoor Therapy: Dangling Ropes and Solid Foundations. In G. Robb and P. Hamilton (eds.). *The Bradford Papers,* Vol. 5, pp. 63-68.

Smith, T. (1985b). Issues in Challenge Education. In G. Robb and E. Hamilton (eds.). *Issues in Challenge Education and Adventure Programming.* Martinsville, IN: Bradford Woods, Indiana University Press.

Smith, S. and Ng, D. (1982). *Perspectives on the Nature of Leisure Research.* Waterloo, Canada: University of Waterloo Press.

Staley, F. (1979). The Research, Evaluation and Measurement Dragons in Outdoor Education. Paper presented at the National Outdoor Education Association Meeting, Lake Placid, NY.

Stich, T. (1983). Experiential Therapy for Psychiatric Patients *Journal of Experiential Education,* 5(3): pp. 23-30.

Stogner, J. (1978). The Effects of a Wilderness Experience on Self-Concept and Academic Performance. *Dissertation Abstracts International,* 39: p. 4704A.

Theobald, W. (1979). *Evaluation of Recreation and Park Programs.* New York: John Wiley and Sons.

Thomas, S. (Comp.) (1985). *Adventure Education: A Bibliography.* Amherst, NY: Institute on Classroom Management and School Discipline at State University of New York at Buffalo.

Tinsley, H. and Johnson, T. (1984). A Preliminary Taxonomy of Leisure Activities. *Journal of Leisure Research,* 16(3): pp. 234-244.

Vander Wilt, R. and Klocke, R. (1971). Self-Actualization of Females in an Experimental Orientation Program. *National Association of Women's Deans and Counselors Journal,* 34(3): pp. 125–129.

Vogl, R. and Vogl, S. (1974). *Outdoor Education and Its Contributions to Environmental Quality: A Research Analysis.* Austin, TX: National Educational Laboratory Publishers, Inc.

Webb, E.; Campbell, D.; Schwartz, R.; and Sechrest, L (1966). *Unobtrusive Measures: Nonreactive Research in the Social Sciences.* Chicago, IL: Rand McNally and Company.

Wetmore, R. (1972). The Influence of Outward Bound School Experience on the Self-Concept of Adolescent Boys. *Dissertation Abstracts International,* 33: p. 1498A.

Wilder, R. (1977). EEI: A Survival Tool. *Parks and Recreation,* 12(8): pp. 22–24, 50–51.

Wright, A. (1982). *Therapeutic Potential of the Outward Bound Process: An Evaluation of a Treatment Program for Juvenile Delinquents.* Unpublished Doctoral Dissertation. Pennsylvania State University.

Yenser, S. (1972). *Personal and Interpersonal Effects of Outdoor Survival.* Unpublished Master's Thesis. Brigham Young University.

Young, R. (1983). Toward an Understanding of Wilderness Participation. *Leisure Sciences,* 4: pp. 339–357.

Young, R. and Crandall, R. (1984). Wilderness Use and Self-Actualization. *Journal of Leisure Research,* 16(2): pp. 149–160.

8

TRENDS IN OUTDOOR ADVENTURE PURSUITS[1]

> The important thing to predict is not the automobile but the parking problem. (Isaac Adimov)

Having presented an overview of the historical events surrounding outdoor adventure pursuits, it is now appropriate to discuss the current and emerging trends in the field. While predicting trends in any profession can be a hazardous undertaking, correctly anticipating the "right" trends and developments can be of distinct benefit in the planning process.

To accomplish this task, this chapter is divided into four sections. These sections are composed of an analysis of the socioeconomic factors that can affect outdoor adventure pursuits, trends as perceived by the instructors and administrators in the field, business-related trends, and a summary of the findings of the first three sections.

MAJOR INFLUENCING FACTORS

That some people deliberately choose to engage in life-threatening recreational activities should surprise no one involved in the delivery of outdoor recreation services (Wilson, 1977). What may be surprising is that the popularity of these types of activities has dramatically increased in the last twenty years (Darst and Armstrong, 1980). McLellan (1986) reports that activities such as white-water sports, rock-climbing, and adventure-oriented exploration are some examples of the outdoor recreational endeavors expected to increase in popularity. She bases this prediction on the belief that governmental, social, and economic factors will combine to create more opportunities for outdoor adventure pursuits.

Clawson (1985) describes four "fueling factors" that can increase the demand for outdoor recreation. These factors include:

---

[1] Portions of this chapter were taken from a paper delivered at the Outdoor Recreation Trends Symposium II (Ewert, 1985a).

- A growing population that will ultimately increase demand levels.
- A persistent trend in per capita income that makes outdoor recreation affordable to more people.
- The development of blocks of leisure time (e.g. holidays, weekends, etc.) for large segments of society.
- The availability, relative comfort, and affordable cost of transportation that increases the ability for many people to reach outdoor recreation sites.

Clawson (1985) suggests that the effect of these factors, combined with an underlying interest in the outdoors, has led to a steady increase in outdoor recreation participation rates. Indeed, the recent findings of the President's Commission on Americans Outdoors (1986) indicated that over 75 percent of the American public considered itself "outdoors" people.

Hornback (1985) tempers this estimation with an analysis of several mega-socioeconomic trends, which he believes may lessen the demand for outdoor recreation in the near future. For example, while the "baby boomers" or the people currently in the 35 to 44-year-old range are entering their peak earning years, the aspects of delayed childbirth and time constraints of the dual-income household will diminish the opportunities to participate in outdoor recreational activities. Income patterns will be further complicated by the shift from an industrial to a service-centered economic base. This shift will create the kinds of jobs that often require little training or apprenticeship, are usually poorly paid, have a high turnover rate, and frequently do not include fringe benefits such as paid vacations. In addition, Hornback (1985) argues that many outdoor recreation facilities, such as the national parks, are not equipped either administratively or philosophically to effectively compete for the consumer's dollar when faced with promotional approaches to the travel-tourism industry.

Current and projected use information seems to support a general flattening in the growth rate. However, it is at this point that caution is needed. A closer analysis of these growth-rate projections reveals some interesting insights. Van Doren (1984) reports that, while overnight stays in the national park system have shown an erratic but slight increase since 1961, the use of recreational vehicles to facilitate those stays has exceeded that of tent camping. When one considers the typical park service campground with accommodations that are specifically designed for the travel trailer, there can be little wonder that the tent camper has sought a more private, less structurally developed atmosphere.

In addition, between 1950 and 1980 total attendance at state parks had increased steadily (Coffin, 1985; Van Doren, 1984). Other indices pointing to the popularity and impact of outdoor adventure pursuits are also present. In a recent issue of *Trends,* Petty and Norton (1987) reported that mountaineering and hiking accounted for 6 percent of the total number of visitor days in the national forest system in 1986. This 6 percent amounted to over 13,000,000 visitor days.

Elsner (1985) reports that there has been a significant change in the mix of recreation activities in the national forest system. This mix has been in the proportion of total use that occurred in dispersed recreation areas, with use in these areas (e.g., wilderness and primitive areas) amounting to a tenfold increase (4.5 percent of the total).

GROWING POPULARITY OF OUTDOOR ADVENTURE PURSUITS

Society has responded to the increased interest in adventure by developing and organizing agencies and institutions that cater to the individual in search of outdoor adventures. As early as 1975, over 200 colleges and universities offered courses or degrees in outdoor adventure pursuits (Hale, 1978). This is but one example of the many indicators that suggest the increased popularity of outdoor adventure activities. Other indicators of the extent and pervasiveness of outdoor adventure are listed in Table 8.1.

TABLE 8.1
Indicators of Popularity of Outdoor Adventure Activities
(Ewert, 1985b)

Indicator	Implications
Increase in:	
Regulations	Greater use of resources with subsequent damage
Organizations/camps	Heightened use of facilities and programs
Sales/expenditures for equipment, travel, etc.	More participants and/or participants using more equipment and clothing
Universities/colleges offering courses/programs in outdoor adventure pursuits	Greater interest in outdoor adventure education
Advertising/commercials featuring outdoor adventure activities	Increasing public awareness and acceptance as desirable activities or traits
Literature/media	Same
Ropes courses/localized adventure activities	Supplying a need to experience "adventure" despite geographical or financial limitations
Workshops/courses/programs	Demonstrates a public desire to seek greater knowledge and skills
Legislation	Increased attention being paid by government agencies

These indicators are part of a larger picture that suggests that North Americans are becoming more self-conscious in their leisure time. What this implies is that individuals are turning away from a quantity orientation (i.e., material goods) and moving toward greater emphasis on concerns such as self-improvement, increased physical fitness, or family/community activities (Kelly, 1982, p. 12). This movement away from material-based leisure pursuits is reflected in outdoor recreation statistics, with categories such as camping, hiking, mountain climbing, and SCUBA diving all showing markedly increased participation rates (Clawson and Van Doren, 1984).

Cordell and Hartmann (1983), upon reviewing the A.C. Nielson national surveys, reported that the ten most popular sports and outdoor recreation activities are, in order: swimming (45 percent of U.S. population), bicycling (32 percent), fishing (28 percent), camping (27 percent), boating (19 percent), bowling (18 percent), physical conditioning with equipment (15 percent), jogging/running (15 percent), roller-skating (13 percent), and pool/billiards (13 percent). Among these and other sports surveyed, ice-skating, swimming, and pool/billiards decreased while bicycling, boating, skiing, and sailing increased strongly.

Along similar lines, Brady and Skjemstad (1974) reported that the number of cross-country skiers rose from 2,000 to 500,000 between

Cross-country skiing is rapidly growing in popularity.

1964 and 1974. Similarly, between 1971 and 1973 the Southern California Hang Glider Association increased from 25 to 4,000 members (Dunn and Gulbis, 1976). Other participation indices for outdoor adventure pursuits are presented in Tables 8.2 and 8.3.

TABLE 8.2
Indices of Future Participation Rates for Selected Outdoor Adventure Activities 1977-2030 (base year = 1977 = 100 percent)

Activity	Projection Level[1]	Projections By Year					
		1977	1990	2000	2010	2020	2030
Population Index[2]	Medium	100	112	120	127	134	139
Camping–undeveloped sites	High	100	130	161	207	254	311
	Medium	100	116	133	157	182	205
	Low	100	111	121	132	145	155
Hiking	High	100	124	149	187	225	270
	Medium	100	109	117	132	146	159
	Low	100	101	102	103	107	109
Horseback riding	High	100	125	151	194	233	284
	Medium	100	109	118	137	155	173
	Low	100	102	102	105	113	119
Canoeing and white-water boating	High	100	140	182	243	305	384
	Medium	100	121	140	170	200	233
	Low	100	109	117	128	141	155
Cross-country skiing	High	100	154	211	290	376	479
	Medium	100	133	161	200	241	280
	Low	100	118	134	151	172	190
Downhill skiing	High	100	162	227	318	416	538
	Medium	100	142	178	228	279	334
	Low	100	125	146	171	199	226
Snowmobiling	High	100	126	151	191	229	277
	Medium	100	109	120	141	161	181
	Low	100	107	114	122	133	141

[1] Keyed on anticipated population and economic projections.
[2] Medium = level projection rate.

Source: U.S. Department of Agriculture, Forest Service, *An Assessment of the Forest and Range Land Situation in the United States.* Washington, DC: Government Printing Office, 1980, pp. 100–101.

TABLE 8.3
Estimated Visitor Days of National Forest Recreation Use, By Activities, 1965 to 1982[1]

Activity	Thousands of Visitor Days					
	1965	1970	1975	1980	1981	1982
Camping	40065	46454	53092	57211	59628	57089
Snowmobiles	516	1950	3276	3448	3141	3328
Swimming/SCUBA	3273	3459	3930	5140	5334	5209
Climbing (hiking and mountain)	4086	5592	9059	12259	12791	12734
Horseback riding	2242	2288	2617	3346	3651	3671
Skiing (total)	4329	5515	7790	12211	9935	12772
Cross-country (snowshoe)				11000	8586	
Down-hill				1204	1349	
Self-propelled boats	1733	1405	2988	3965	4048	3868

[1] Visitor Day—12 person hours, or 12 people for one hour; or a combination.
Source: U. S. Department of Agriculture, Forest Service.

Aggregated projections, however, do not complete the picture. To fully understand the growth of outdoor adventure pursuits, Figure 8.1 illustrates participation rates of some selected outdoor activities, including adventure pursuits.

As can be seen from the preceding tables and figure, outdoor adventure pursuit activities are participated in by a substantial number of people. In addition, a recent study conducted for the President's Commission on Americans Outdoors (PCAO, 1986) reaffirms the above data that a substantial portion of the American public is interested in many forms of outdoor recreation. As shown in Figure 8.1, six of the eleven types of activities listed have potential aspects of outdoor adventure recreation. These activities include backpacking, canoeing, nordic skiing, mountain/rock climbing, and board sailing. Together, these activities account for 29.8 million out of a total reported number of 281.8 million participants (10.5 percent).

Of these six activities, four reported a relatively substantial percentage of high use participation. (See Figure 8.2). These four included sailing/windsurfing, backpacking, canoeing/kayaking, and cross-country skiing (nordic). High use participation for this data analysis was considered to be participation in the activity three or more times per month.

A different viewpoint is gained from Figure 8.3, in which the fastest growing sports are listed (adventure sports are shaded with diagonal lines). The activities growing fastest in popularity, according to these

FIGURE 8.1
Outdoor Activity Participation

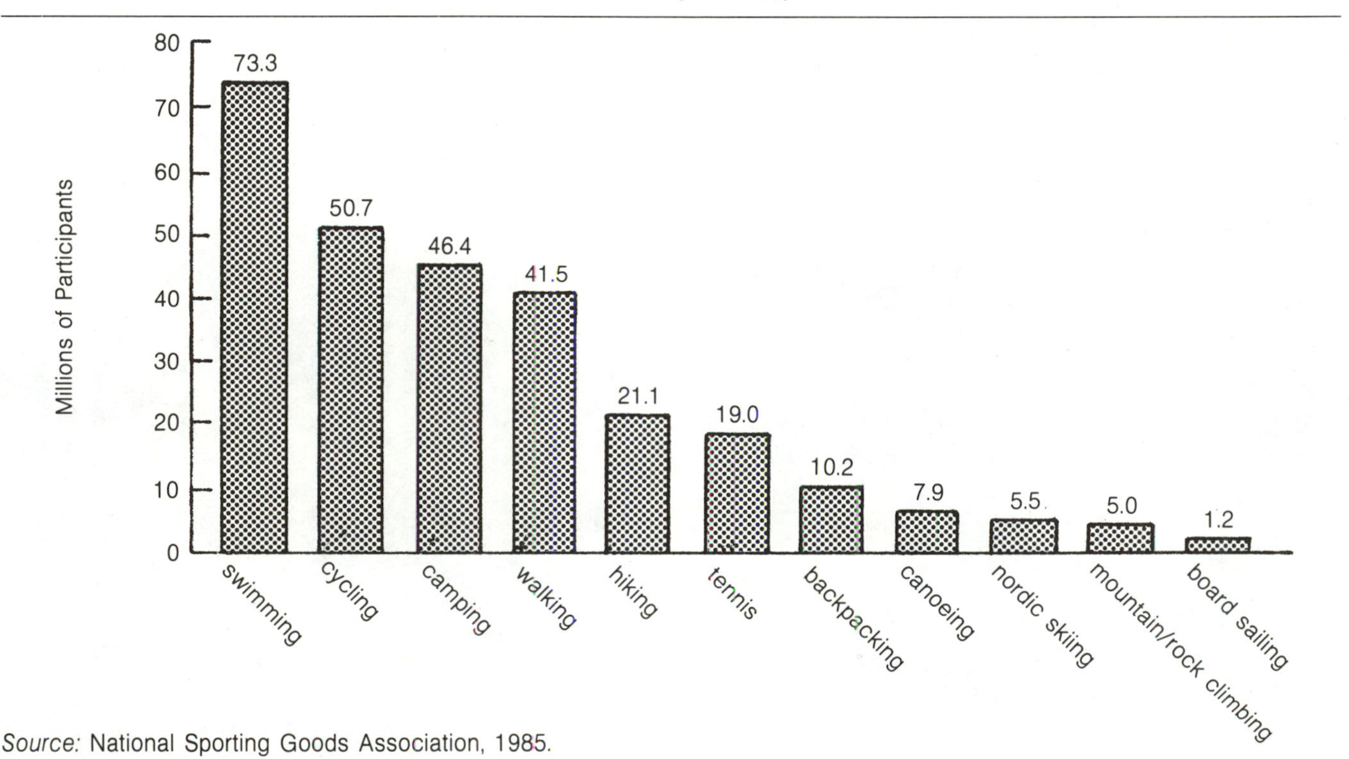

Source: National Sporting Goods Association, 1985.

FIGURE 8.2
High Use Participation Rates of Selected Activities

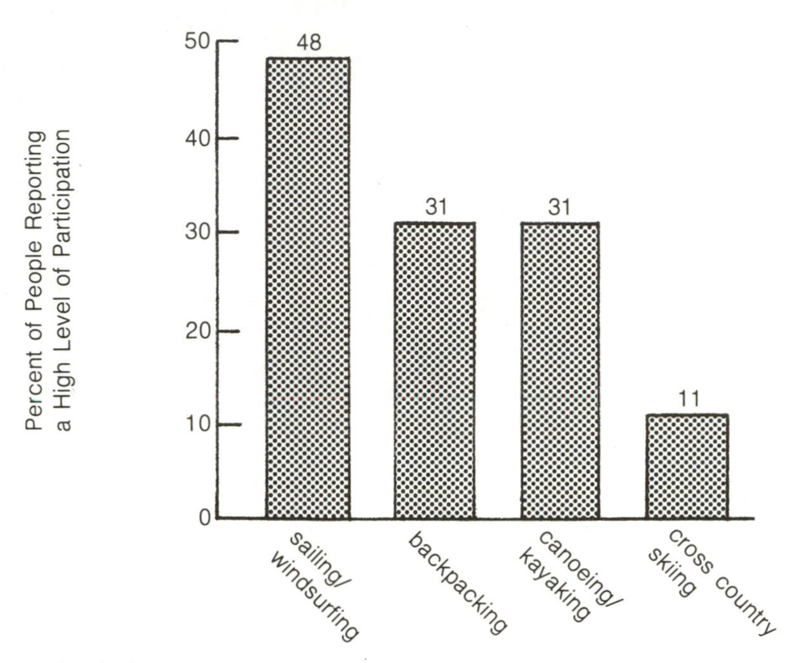

Source: Study by Market Opinion Research for the President's Commission on Americans Outdoors, 1986.

data, are boardsailing and boardsurfing, followed by mountain/rock climbing, horseback riding, and sailing.

The message in these recent studies is clear. Adventure recreation activities and their participants cannot be overlooked by the recreation programmer or resource manager. As shown in Figure 8.3, outdoor recreation activities comprise an important share of the American recreation scene, and adventure pursuits activities make up a substantial portion of that share. Similarly, these participation rates appear to be stabilized or increasing, although a note of caution is advised by Cordell and Hendee (1982) in their statement:

> National surveys contain expected errors in estimated participation rates (with) wide differences between survey results hampering demand forcasting and recreation planning based on them. (p. 44)

Using other methods to indicate change, Cordell and Hendee (1982) report the following sport goods sales between 1979 and 1980: Backpack

FIGURE 8.3
Fastest Growing Sports
(In percentage gain - 1985 vs. 1984)

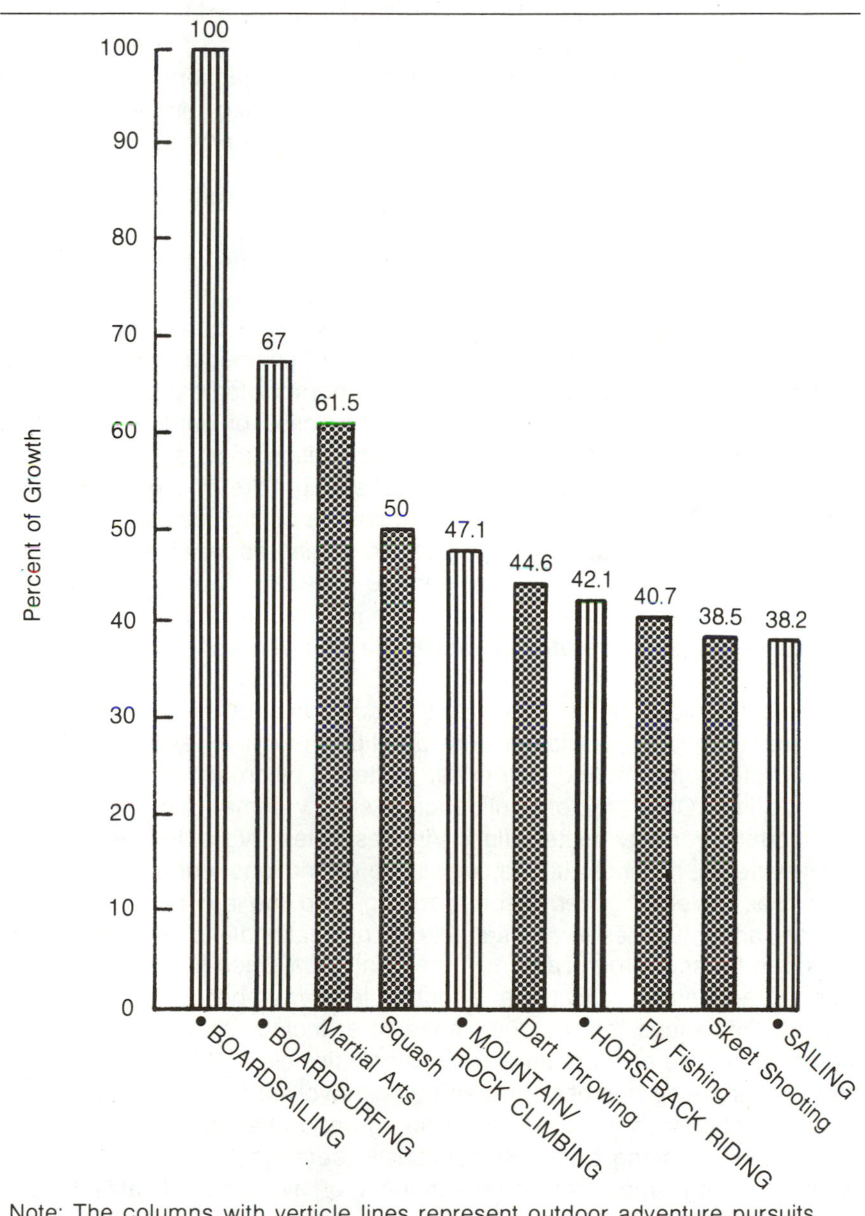

Note: The columns with verticle lines represent outdoor adventure pursuits.

Source: National Sporting Goods Association, Mount Prospect, Illinois, 1985.

sales up 11 percent, tent sales up 20 percent, sleeping bags down 30 percent, and hiking boots down 10 percent. The last two categories may reflect a technological change with synthetic sleeping bags replacing the more expensive down-filled bag. Likewise, cheaper, lighter tennis shoe-type boots have begun to rapidly replace the heavier, more expensive leather boots. Nevertheless, any discussion of projections or emerging trends in recreation or outdoor adventure must take into account the social and economic factors impacting upon future participation.

SOCIOECONOMIC FACTORS

Like many facets of recreation, participation in outdoor adventure activities will be impacted by a variety of factors. Any emerging trend in outdoor recreation will be determined by two main considerations: the contextual base of the activity and the ambient socioeconomic variables. *Contextual base* refers to the physical, psycho/sociological, and cognitive requirements surrounding the activity. In the case of outdoor adventure pursuits, many activities require a predisposition that is both psychologically and physically amenable to accepting risks in the recreational setting (Zuckerman, 1979). Other requirements include equipment or material and a geographically acceptable setting such as a white-water river or rock-climbing site. To engage in many outdoor adventure activities requires a certain level of outdoor and/or technical skills, either possessed by the recreator or made available through an instructor or guide.

Ambient socioeconomic variables that could impact the outdoor adventure scene include population considerations (such as age distribution), growth rates, mobility and distribution patterns, discretionary income, and composition. Other factors influencing supply/demand responses are transportation/energy costs, inflation/interest rates, available time, employment patterns, political attitude, legislative restrictions, competing uses of resources, level of government spending, and the amount of available outdoor adventure resources suitable for recreationalists (See Table 8.4).

As can be seen from Table 8.4, the contextual base surrounding each outdoor adventure activity is affected in a number of ways. Major positive influences on outdoor adventure include population growth, increases in discretionary time, increasingly flexible employment patterns, and an increasing number of organizations involved in outdoor adventure. Negative influences include increasing age and changing composition of the population; rising transportation costs; decreasing levels of government spending; and decreasing amounts of available, suitable natural resources.

These and other developing influences have created a situation in which outdoor adventure could go either way: toward greater public involvement or toward a lessening impact upon the society. To date, a

TABLE 8.4
Selected Factors Influencing the Supply and Demand of Outdoor Adventure Recreational Opportuniites, 1984–2000

		Effect on Contextual Base Surrounding Activity			
Social Economic Variable	Trend of Variable	Individual Predisposition and Motivation	Acceptable Setting	Equipment Material	Net Effect
Population:					
Growth	↑	++	–	O	+
Age	↑	––	O	O	––
Distribution	South/West	+	++	O	+++
Discretionary income	↑	+	O	O	++
Composition	Minority Represent	–	O	–	––
Transportation Energy costs	↑	––	–	–	––––
Inflation/interest rates	⟷/↑	+	O	+	++
Discretionary time	↗	++	O	O	++
Employment patterns	More Flexible	++	+	O	+++
Political attitude of public	Conservative Assertive	–	–	O	––
Legislative restrictions on users	↑	–	+	–	–
Competing uses of resources	↑	–	–	O	––
Level of gov't spending	↓	–	––	O	–––
Amount of available resources	↓	–	––	O	–––
Number of organizations in outdoor adventure	↑	+	+	++	++++
Technology	↑	++	O	++	++++
Overall effect		12+ 10–	5+ 8–	5+ 3–	21+ 19–

Notes: ↑ = increase, ↓ = decrease, ⟷ = stable, + = positive, – = negative.

number of organizations involved with outdoor adventure, such as Outward Bound, have experienced changes in enrollment patterns. In response to these and other changes, several trends have emerged in outdoor adventure. These trends are discussed in the following section.

EMERGING TRENDS IN OUTDOOR ADVENTURE PURSUITS

Individuals and organizations have responded to the aforementioned influences in a number of ways. A search for broader financial support through new audiences and funding sources has led to the development of shorter three- to nine-days, intensive outdoor experiences specifically aimed at attracting the affluent but time-pressed professional or business person. Past research (Ewert, 1982; Thomas, 1985) has suggested that, if shorter courses are to become the norm, a redirection of program goals may be necessary. For example, the improvement of self-concept is an often-cited benefit of participation in outdoor adventure. As suggested by Ewert (1982) and Thomas (1985), the shortened course format (three- to nine-days versus two- to five-weeks) may be less effective in creating a positive change in self-concept. Likewise, the professional adult participant, a likely candidate for a short course, may be less able or willing to change his or her self-concept (Ewert, 1982).

Group initiatives are important components in many outdoor adventure pursuits programs.

Other populations that are receiving increased attention are juniors (14 to 17 years old), women, youth at risk (a.k.a. juvenile delinquents), and senior adults (aged 50 and above). Many of the outdoor adventure programs are becoming prescriptive, in that they are specifically designed for a particular population's abilities and needs. Much of the research conducted to date has indicated that outdoor adventure activities can beneficially affect the participant (Meier et al. 1987, 1980; Ewert, 1983). Other populations which will receive wide attention from outdoor adventure programs in the future will be the physically and/or mentally disabled and the chemically dependent. A number of recent studies (Arthur, 1976; Black, 1983) have indicated that participation in outdoor adventure programs can be rehabilitative in terms of enhanced physical fitness, motor skills, increased self-esteem, and socialization.

To coincide with the developing educational trend of life-long learning (Rillo, 1984, p. 15), an increasing number of colleges, universities, and high schools will be offering credit for participation in outdoor adventure programs (Siedentop, 1980). Other concurrent themes will be cross-cultural adventure courses, outdoor instructor centers, and organizations that specifically cater to outdoor adventure workshops.

In addressing the problem of providing adventure in urbanized settings, the high-adventure course (i.e., ropes course) will become a widely used method. Being defined as an obstacle course of cables, ropes, swings, logs, and nets, and constructed in trees, rafters, or prearranged planted telephone poles (McBride, 1984, p. 16), the high-adventure course will become a primary focus in many programs (McAvoy, 1980).

Other emerging trends include a greater structuring and formalization of outdoor adventure programs, such as more sophisticated programming, improved marketing techniques, increased adherence to risk-management planning, diversification of programs, and more intensive program evaluation. Market saturation will eventually lead to a substantial failure rate of programs, but the survival of many larger organizations will exploit and develop existing or new markets. Organizations such as the Boy Scouts, Outward Bound, Project Adventure, and the National Outdoor Leadership School will continue to be widely emulated in both their models and programs. Many organizations will seek to broaden their financial bases by external grants, incorporating successful business operations into their financial picture, and emphasizing high-profit operations such as junior's courses or exotic cultural programs. In addition, successful programs involved in outdoor adventure pursuits and the allied fields of outdoor recreation, outdoor education, and environmental education will recognize the trend in society moving away from natural resource issues and focusing on environmentally related health issues (Siehl, 1985). For the field of outdoor pursuits, this will mean a deemphasis of wilderness skills training and a reemphasis of physical and emotional health and fitness.

From the perspective of the field instructor, a number of changes will impact outdoor programs. These changes revolve around both an increase in users and a change in field instructor training and background. These issues include the following:

PROGRAM ISSUES

The program issues will center on

- Greater emphasis on minimum impact camping and travel techniques.
- Increased use of outdoor adventure activities in camps and other educational settings.
- Increased use of outdoor adventure outfitters.
- Increased use of highly structured programming.
- Changes in clientele with respect to demographics (older). expectations (more demanding), and motivations (image, excitement).

INSTRUCTOR ISSUES

The instructor issues will focus on

- Greater reliance on technological improvements in fibers/clothing, sheltering systems, equipment, nutrition/fluid delivery systems, and position location/search and rescue.
- Diminished use and knowledge of traditional outdoor skills, such as natural shelter location and selection, natural navigation, food /water procurement, adaptation and improvisation techniques, and fire building.
- More sophisticated delivery of material.
- More specialization of expertise, i.e., instruction for business clients, youth, special groups, etc.

PERCEPTIONS OF OUTDOOR INSTRUCTORS

To provide empirical evidence of the preceding trends, a survey was conducted in 1986 to determine what trends practitioners in the field believed were emerging. There were two foundational assumptions underlying this research. First, it was believed that a survey of experts in the field, using the consensus as a forecast, would produce a more accurate analysis of future trends than relying on a few individual predictions (McCall and Simmons, 1969). Herkowitz (1985) reports that few experts or forecasters are more consistently accurate than a consensus of their peers.

Second, it was reasoned that individuals make trend predictions based on external and internal factors. These factors are related to the types and amounts of information available to the individual, often through the workplace. Based on the work of Mescon, Albert, and Khedouri (1981), internal factors are those items centered within the organization and include perceptions of available resources, ability of the organization to change, energy levels of the personnel, existing plans within the organization, and the visible impact of the organization upon the client. External factors are perceived as situations beyond immediate control, but which impact the organization. These factors include the economic, political, and legal environments; anticipated market conditions; and costs to the organization. Understanding these factors is important, as different pictures of the future may be held by people within the same field, depending upon the extent and quality of information they receive.

As with most organized movements, the direct service personnel, that is, instructors, may have a different perception of emerging trends in outdoor adventure recreation than do the administrators of their programs. To determine the most accurate set of predicted trends, the study's questionnaire was categorized by position, that is, instructor or administrator, rather than pooling both types of personnel into one group.

As can be seen from Figures 8.4 to 8.6, instructors were deemed to have the greatest potential for accuracy in the areas of emphasis on outdoor skills and the professionalization of the outdoor instructor/leader. With respect to program emphasis on outdoor skills, the internal factor of close contact with the participants suggests that the instructors have a better view of what adventure participants want from a course or program. Instructors may also be in a better position to see the emerging trend of professionalization within the field because this will have a direct impact upon their training and employment patterns. The data suggest that this is a trend most instructor-oriented respondents see coming.

Without exception, the administrators held a more conservative view of future increases. Because administrators may have greater knowledge in the areas of organizational plans and resources, actual program costs, current legal environment, and anticipated market conditions, this group was thought to have a more accurate perception of increases in disabled and female participants, aerial activities, and the growing emphasis on stress-reduction programs. In each case the administrators' group believed that increases in these areas would be less than did the instructors. Using the internal and external factors previously mentioned, Table 8.5 lists the values placed on each item by the groups and the hypothesized most accurate prediction.

To the extent that the professional staff in adventure programs can be relied upon to accurately forecast future trends, outdoor adventure recreation should experience a moderate growth rate in the next fourteen years. Programmatic trends include (1) an overall increase in the number of participants, particularly those from high-income households; (2) the use of ropes courses and counseling techniques; and (3) an increasing emphasis on the issues of accountability and evaluation.

FIGURE 8.4
Reported Trends in Outdoor Adventure Education

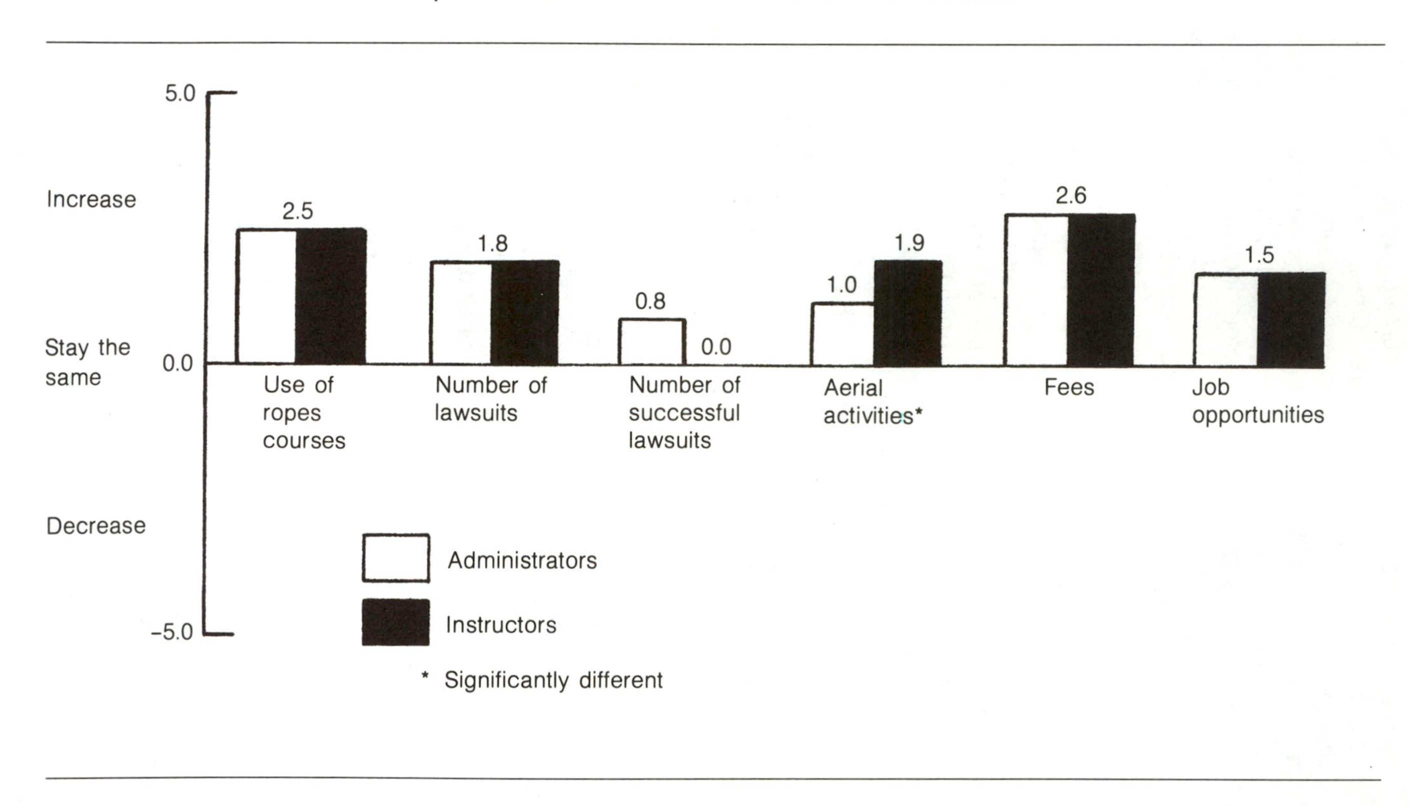

FIGURE 8.5

Reported Trends in Outdoor Adventure Education

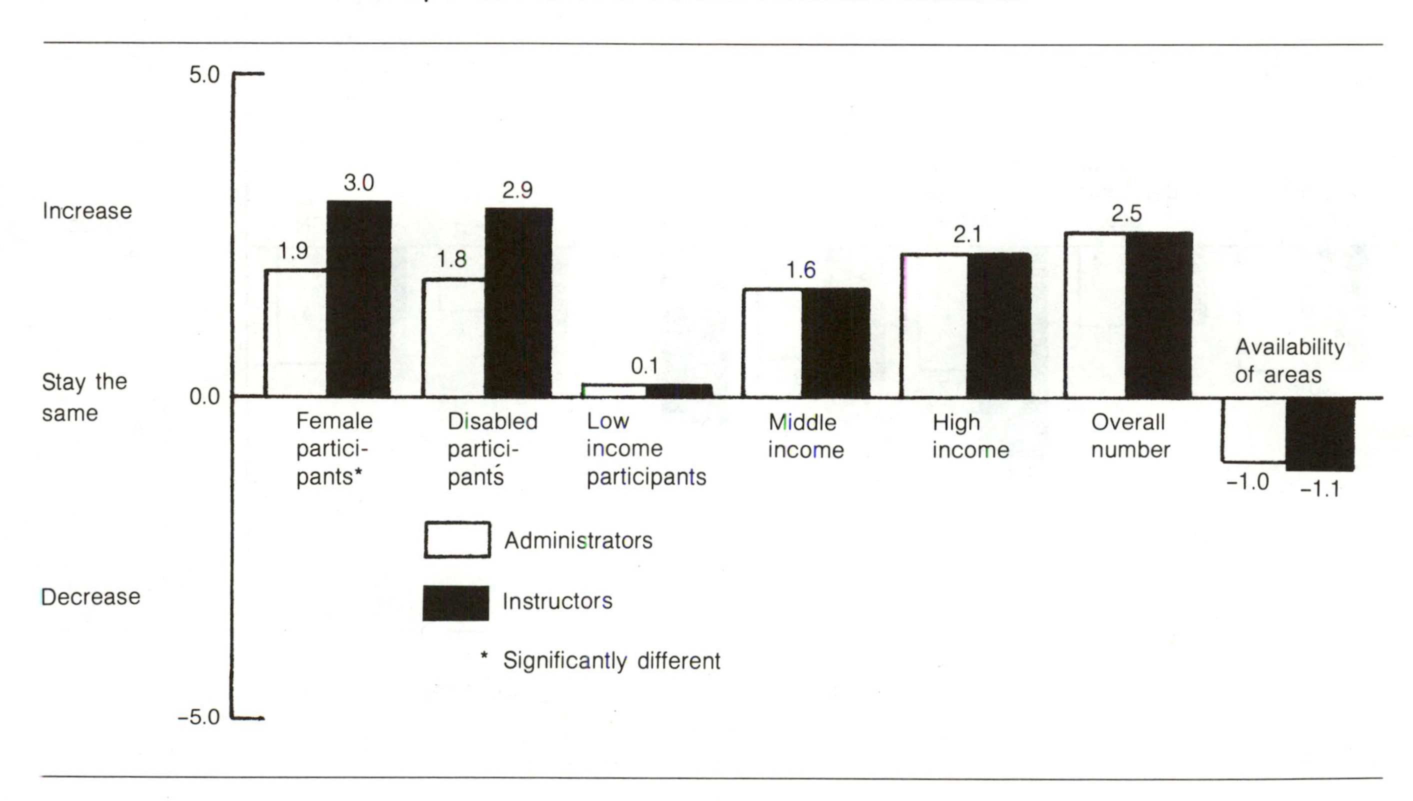

FIGURE 8.6
Reported Trends in Outdoor Adventure Education

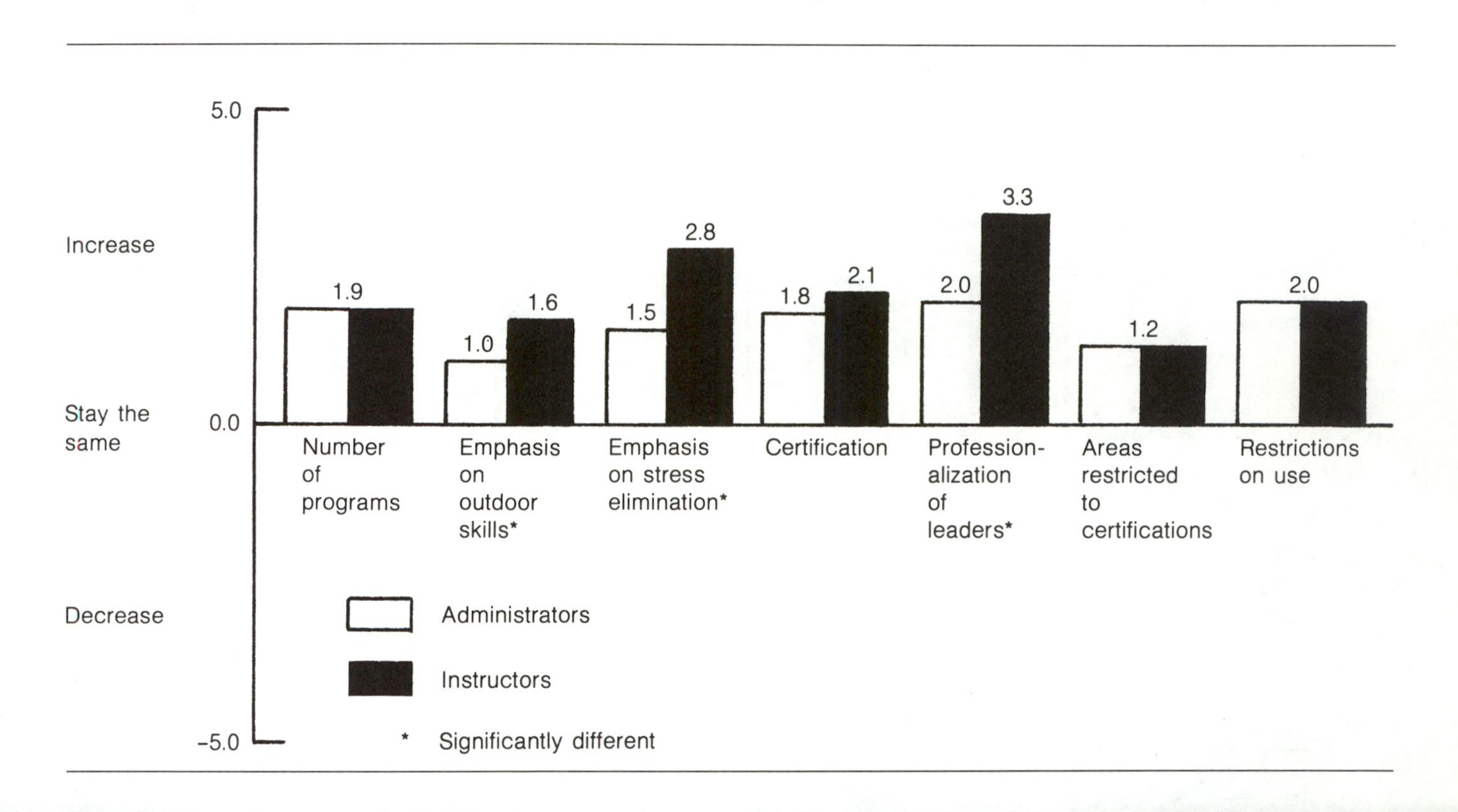

TABLE 8.5[1]
Item Values and Their Relative Accuracy

Item	Values[2]		
	Administrators	Instructors	Most Accurate
Emphasis on outdoor skills	1.0	1.6	Instructors
Professionalization of instructors/leaders	2.0	3.3	Instructors
Disabled participants	1.8	2.9	Administration
Female participants	1.9	3.0	Administration
Emphasis on stress reduction	1.5	2.8	Administration
Aerial activities	1.0	1.9	Administration

[1] Mean values range from 0.0 to 5.0. Higher values represent a belief in stronger increases in the future.
[2] Significant at 0.05 level, two-tailed.

Moreover, as restrictions on land/water areas become more pronounced and suitable course areas become more limited, the emphasis on ropes courses and qualified instructors to ensure minimized impact to the resource will increase. Overall, it appears that outdoor adventure recreation is becoming more sophisticated and mature as a profession. Increased efforts in evaluation and documentation will inevitably lead to more critical analyses of the benefits and outcomes accrued through participation. As these benefits are better delineated, outdoor adventure programming will continue to move from the realm of the daredevil to acceptance as a legitimate recreational pursuit.

The supply and demand of outdoor adventure recreational opportunities will reflect a variety of external and internal forces. A growing, more urbanized, mobile, and affluent population will create a greater demand for outdoor adventure. Inhibiting this demand will be rising transportation costs and competing interests for a decreasing supply of available resources. It appears that by the year 2000 the demand for outdoor adventure opportunities, as they currently exist, will exceed the supply of acceptable areas. In other words, the geographical locations needed to provide those opportunities will become fewer as development of urban areas continues.

COMMERCIAL TRENDS

From the commercial perspective, outdoor adventure pursuits offer an area that has experienced substantial and steady growth over the last fifteen years. In accordance with this growth, Christy (1980) offers five elements that could have an impact on this popularity. These elements

Many outdoor adventure sites have been developed into profitable commercial operations.

are the ease of participation, image associated with the activity, ability to identify with the activity, opportunities for demonstrating skills to others, and a perception of the activity being a legitimate use of leisure time. As most outdoor adventure activities require a higher degree of skill, commitment, and equipment, many of these recreational endeavors may never attract a mass following similar to downhill skiing or Disneyland. However, the specialized equipment and mystique of the outdoor environment (Progen, 1979), as well as affective feelings of accomplishment, well-being, and competence, all add to the powerful image surrounding these activities. In addition, the media has provided a highly desirable image of the outdoor person (Keyes, 1985, pp. 252–272). The desirability of these perceived images offsets the remoteness, risk potential, and higher level of skill usually needed to perform these outdoor activities.

Currently, much evidence points to outdoor adventure claiming a small but stable or increasing portion of the outdoor recreation market (Van Doren, 1985; Ewert, 1985a). Further supporting this claim is the 1985 National Outdoor Outfitters Market Report that showed increases in sales, profits, store expansions, and numbers of employees hired over the 1984 season (Bishoff, 1985), as reported by more than 500 retail and wholesale outlets throughout the United States.

Kelly (1985) reports that, with respect to the United States, the proportion of expenditures for recreation has remained fairly constant at 6.5 percent. This amounts to a total expenditure of over 320 billion in 1985 (Kelly, 1985). Bullaro and Edginton, (1986) provide a rough estimate of

TABLE 8.6
Organizations Offering Outdoor Adventure Opportunities

- American Alliance for Health, Physical Education and Recreation
- American Youth Hostels
- Appalachian Trail Conference
- Izaak Walton League of America
- National Recreation and Park Association
- Nature Conservancy
- American Camping Association
- American Canoeing Association
- Appalachian Mountain Club
- Council for National Cooperation in Aquatics
- National Campers and Hikers Association
- Sierra Club
- Audubon Society

95 billion or roughly 28 percent of the total amount being spent on outdoor recreation activities. Table 8.6 presents an abbreviated listing of various suppliers of outdoor adventure services.

While some have argued that the expenditure picture for outdoor recreation is varied, with numerous examples of slowing growth and even decreases in certain areas, such as equipment and travel, Bischoff (1987) contends that outdoor adventure activities are still a growth segment for the outdoor specialty retailer. Furthermore, based on the 1985 "Sports Participation Study" conducted by the National Sporting Goods Association (NSGA), it appears that Americans are still very much interested in outdoor recreation. Of the top ten participation categories, seven have a strong connection with the outdoors and two, camping and cycling, are often associated with outdoor adventure pursuits. A similar study in 1986 by the NSGA reported that the family camping trend has spurred strong sales in camping and backpacking equipment sales. Of the 1,837 stores responding, 51 percent reported increases in sales, 32 percent indicated "no change," and 16 percent reported that sales decreased.

Although it is apparent that outdoor adventure activities enjoy a high level of participation, most of these activities fall behind the more traditional forms of outdoor recreation such as baseball or tennis. Indeed, some forms of outdoor recreation, such as snowmobiling and off-road vehicle driving (ORV), appear to be declining in popularily (Van Horne, Szwak, and Randall, 1985) although these rates are subject to variability as a function of geography. With respect to outdoor adventure pursuits, five of the top ten fastest growing sports (in percentage gain, 1985 versus 1984) are boardsailing (100 percent), boardsurfing (67 percent), mountain/rock climbing (47 percent), horseback riding (42 percent), and sailing (38 percent).

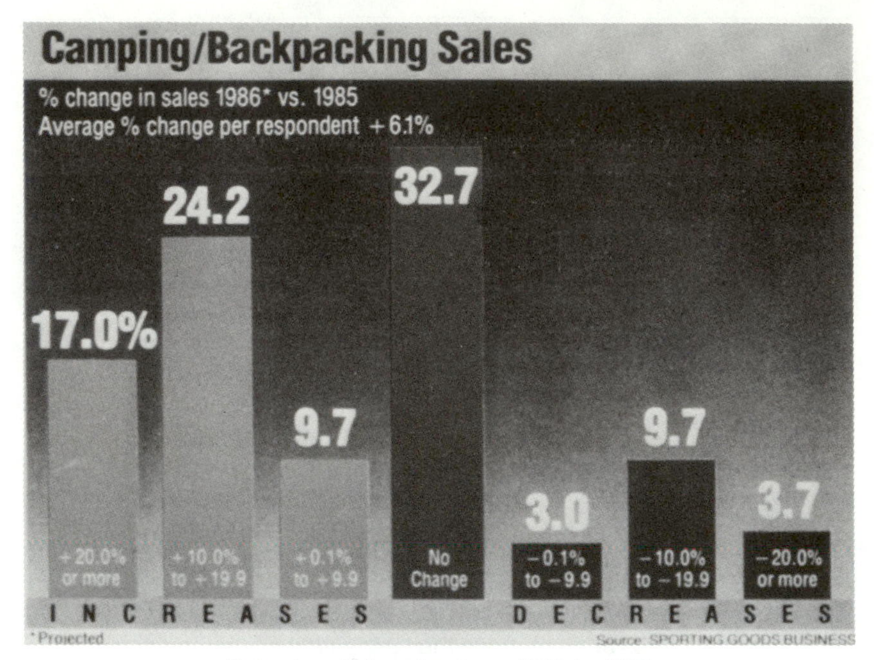

Sales trends in sales from 1985 to 1986.

Participation rates and trends do not complete the picture, however, since customer interest is also an important factor. According to the National Outdoor Outfitters Market Report (1985), outdoor adventure pursuits that have maintained a high degree of perceived customer interest over the past three years include backpacking, camping, and nordic skiing. Increased customer interest was noted for bicycle touring, mountaineering, nordic skiing, sailing, and SCUBA diving. Figures 8.7 and 8.8 illustrate these trends.

SALES TRENDS IN 1986

Related to the concept of different levels of participation in an activity, as briefly illustrated in Figure 8.8, are the actual trends in sales from 1986. According to recent trade publications such as *Sporting-Goods Business, Outside Magazine,* and *Outside Business,* the following sales trends in outdoor specialty retailing have occurred:

- Increased sales are expected in:
  - Family-sized camping tents
  - Internal frame backpacks, particularly daypacks
  - Hiking boots
  - Sleeping bags
  - Family outfitting
  - Stylish fitness-related apparel
  - High-tech fibers, such as "CoolMax (DuPont)" with vivid coloring patterns

FIGURE 8.7
Perceived Customer Interest by Activity
(1 of 2)

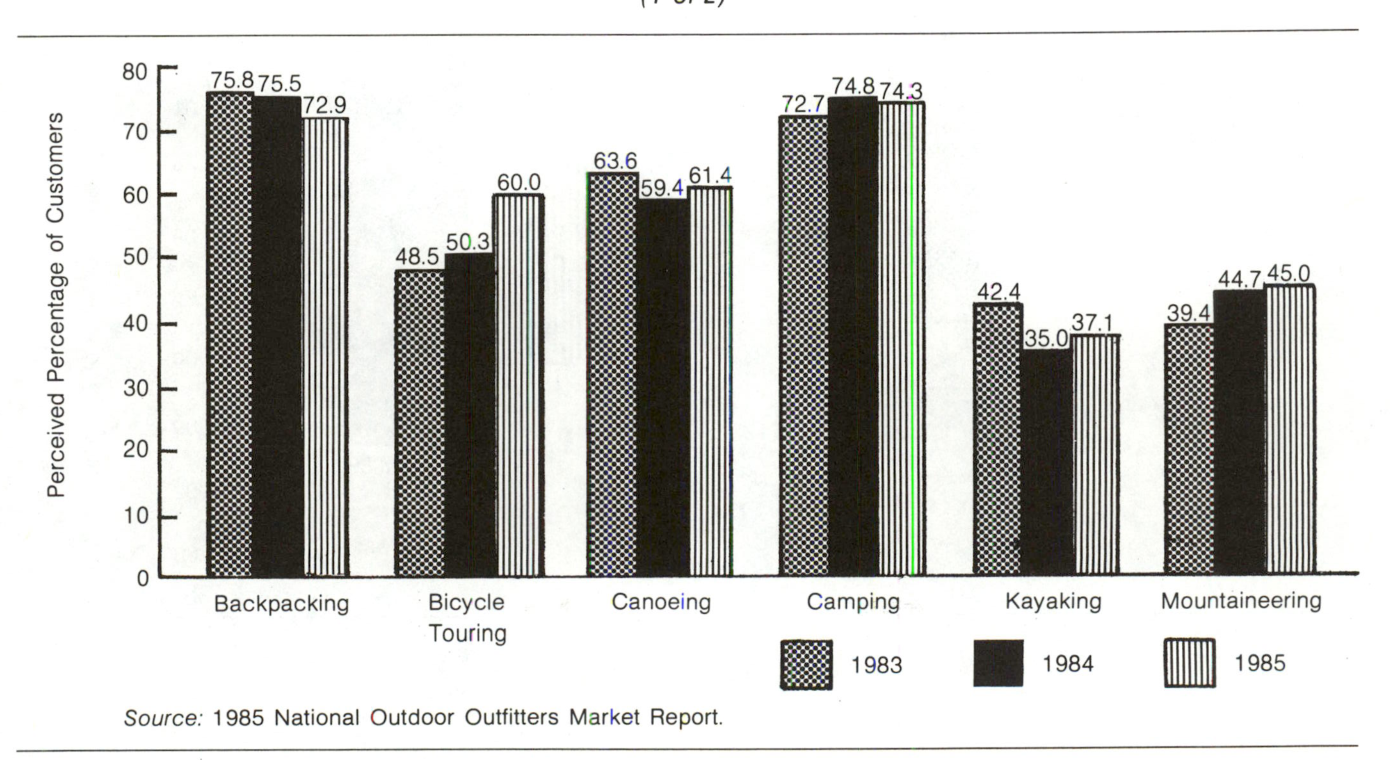

Source: 1985 National Outdoor Outfitters Market Report.

FIGURE 8.8
Perceived Customer Interest by Activity
(2 of 2)

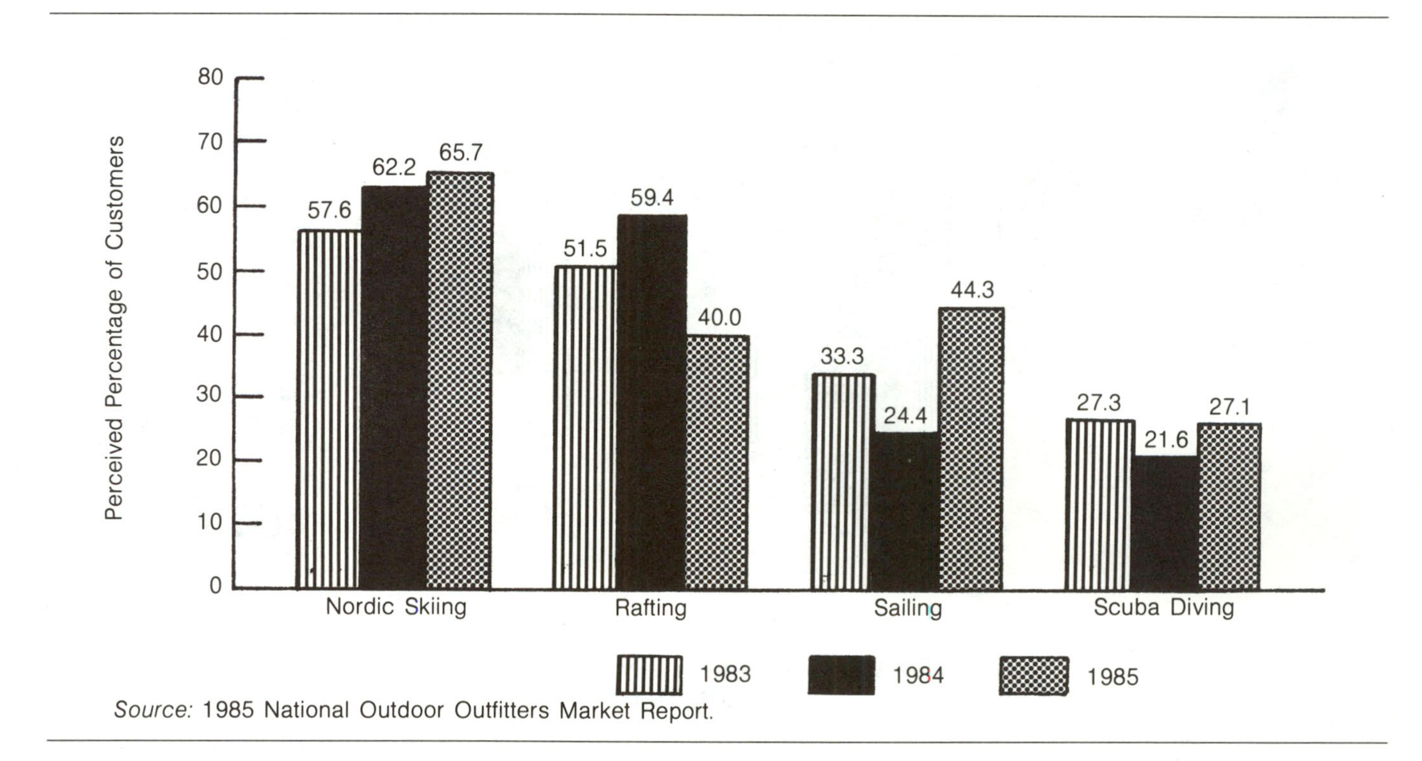

Source: 1985 National Outdoor Outfitters Market Report.

High-tech specialized equipment, such as mountain bikes
Outdoor items especially designed for families and women

- Decreased sales are expected in:
  Big-ticket items such as recreational vehicles (RVs)
  External frame packs
  Leather boots
  Nonsynthetic fiber items such as wool pants or down sleeping bags.

While the near future for outdoor specialty retailing appears to be stable and growing, there is an increasing level of competition, with other retailers and suppliers of services and equipment. Within the last ten years, there has been a substantial growth in organizations offering outdoor adventure activities, with a number of stores such as Recreational Equipment Incorporated (REI) now acting as outdoor adventure expedition and trip organizers as well as retail merchandizers. Moreover, there has been a dramatic increase in merchandise and suppliers both in North America and from foreign countries (Dockery, 1986). Companies such as Patagonia, Campmor, Wild Country, Forrest, Marmot, Sierra Designs, and North Face are examples of the multitude of organizations offering adventure-related equipment and apparel.

Another source of competition to the adventure-business entrepreneuer stems from other forms of recreation and leisure offerings. Bischoff (1986) reports that spending for nonoutdoor recreation categories substantially increased in a number of categories. Some of these categories include spectator sports (40 percent increase from 1980 to 1985), theater and motion pictures (66 percent), and, perhaps most disturbing of all (from the perspective of involvement in active, physical recreation), is the increase in cable television (246 percent).

Bischoff (1987) makes several suggestions for meeting this new set of challenges from a commercial perspective. These suggestions include identifying who are the customers and what are their needs, creating a specialty niche, understanding the customer's goals, and creating more opportunities for outdoor adventure involvement. Moreover, the perception of "quality" in both products and services can make the difference between success and failure for the adventure-related business.

CONCLUSION

In sum, the emerging trends in outdoor adventure pursuits have been discussed from three perspectives: (1) the social-economic factors which are exerting an influence on the field, (2) expected changes as perceived through the eyes of the professional, and (3) expected trends in the business of providing the means and opportunities for outdoor pursuits. In addition to the above trends, there are other factors affecting the availability and popularity of outdoor adventure endeavors. These factors include the costs associated with an activity, the accessibility of areas for outdoor pursuits (Brown, 1985), barriers which preclude participation, and the changing demands of the public. Moreover, the development of a national federal entity similar to the past Bureau of Outdoor Recreation, as has been recommended by the President's Commission on Americans Outdoors (PCAO, 1986), or the expansion of the Land and Water Conservation Fund (LWCF) are issues that will impact the future availability of suitable outdoor settings and opportunities. Table 8.7 lists these and other potential factors which could impact the future of both outdoor recreation and outdoor adventure pursuits.

TABLE 8.7
Future Impacting Variables for Outdoor Recreation

• PCAO/National entity	• Barriers to participation
• Potential trust fund	• Operation costs
• LWCF	• Operating concerns
• User pays concept	• Public expectations
• Decreasing rates of growth	• Greater sophistication
• Constraints on leisure time	

Currently, outdoor adventure pursuits command an image in the public's mind of exotic, adventurous activities that either border on the realm of the daredevil or are thought to provide recreational and educational opportunities that are both exciting and invigorating. How these images develop will be an important deciding factor in the continued development of outdoor adventure pursuits. If the public eventually concludes that these types of activities are only for the college-age person or those relatively affluent, with disposable income and expendable time, the popularity of outdoor adventure activities may become stagnant and eventually decline.

Conversely, if outdoor adventure pursuits continue to become more accepted and widespread as legitimate forms of recreation, the popularity of these activities will continue to grow, as will the potential to supply and service these types of demands. The supply and demand of outdoor adventure recreational opportunities will reflect a variety of forces. A growing, more urbanized, mobile, and affluent population will create a greater demand for risk recreation activities. Inhibiting this demand will be increases in transportation costs and competing interests for a decreasing supply of available resources. In a broader sense, changes in population, economics, and spending patterns announce major upcoming structural alterations within our society.

To meet this growing need, several steps must be implemented. Utilizing these steps would constitute an outdoor adventure management strategy, with the ultimate goal being the provision of outdoor adventure activities to all individuals who wish to pursue them. These steps include (1) inventorying the types and locations of organizations offering adventure recreation, (2) firmly establishing the benefits and costs realized through participation in adventure recreation, (3) providing information networks for the public concerning the availability and objectives of adventure recreation, and (4) initiating efforts to better understand the use of outdoor adventure pursuits. Other concerns focus on the standardization of risk-management procedures and the safeguarding of physical resources in which risk recreation activities take place.

It appears that by the year 2000 demand for outdoor adventure opportunities, as they currently exist, will exceed the supply of natural resources, for example, geographical locations needed to provide these opportunities. This demand might be partially met in ways such as the development of local man-made obstacle courses (e.g., ropes courses). Outdoor adventure pursuits can also become a vehicle for life-long learning while engaged in different cultures and pedagogic settings (e.g., the overseas SCUBA trip or family backpacking trip to another state or province). Whatever the future holds for outdoor adventure pursuits, it will become increasingly important for our professional and governmental organizations to provide high-quality, available outlets for adventure pursuits.

MAIN POINTS

1. There are a number of sociological variables, such as increased amounts of discretionary income, which increase the popularity of outdoor adventure pursuits.
2. While the growth rates of traditional outdoor recreation activities such as fishing and hunting appear to be flattening out, the popularity of outdoor adventure pursuits continues to increase.
3. There are a number of indices which reflect the popularity of outdoor adventure pursuit activities.
4. Greater emphasis on minimum-impact camping techniques is one example of programming components which will reflect changes in how outdoor adventure pursuit programs are conducted.
5. A number of trends, as indicated by instructors and administrators in outdoor pursuits, suggest some significant changes in the field.
6. Expenditures in outdoor pursuits activities suggest a modest but steady market for the retail specialty outlet.
7. A variety of subjects, such as the continuance of the Land and Water Conservation Fund and a growth in user fees, will serve as future impacting variables in outdoor adventure pursuits.

REFERENCES

Arthur, M. (1976). The Survival Experience as Therapy: An Appraisal. *Journal of Leisurability,* 3(3): pp. 3–10.

Bischoff, G. (ed.). (1985). National Outdoor Outfitters Market Report. *National Outdoor Outfitters News,* 10(8): pp. 10–13.

Bischoff, G. (1987). Today's Outdoor Retailing Opportunities. *Trends,* 24(3): pp. 33–39.

Black, B. (1983). The Effect of an Outdoor Experiential Adventure Program on the Development of Dynamic Balance and Spatial Veering for the Visually Impaired Adolescent. *Therapeutic Recreation Journal,* 17(3): pp. 39–49.

Brady, M. and Skjemstad, L. (1974). *Ski Cross-Country.* New York: Dial Press.

Brown, D. (1985). Eastern Whitewater: Opportunities for the Future. In J. Wood (ed.). *Proceedings: 1985 National Outdoor Recreation Trends Symposium II,* pp. 64–75. U.S. Department of the Interior, National Park Service, Southeast Regional Office, Atlanta, GA.

Bullaro, J. and Edginton, C. (1986). *Commercial Leisure Services.* New York: MacMillan.

Christy, F. (1970). Elements of Mass Demand for Outdoor Recreation Resources. *Elements of Outdoor Recreation Planning,* pp. 99–103. B. L. Driver (ed.). Ann Arbor, MI: University of Michigan Press.

Clawson, M. (1985). Trends in Use of Public Recreation Areas. *Proceedings: 1985 National Outdoor Recreation Trends Symposium II,* pp. 11–12. Atlanta, GA: National Park Service.

Clawson, M. and Van Doren, C. (1984). *Statistics on Outdoor Recreation.* Washington, DC: Resources for the Future, Inc.

Coffin, J. (ed.). (1985). *Federal Parks and Recreation,* 3(24). Washington, DC: Resources Publishing Company, 3.

Cordell, H.K. and Hartmann, L. (1983). "Aggregate Trends in Outdoor Recreation in the Two Decades Since ORRRC." Paper presented at the Southeastern Recreation Researcher's Conference, February 17–18, Ashville, NC.

Cordell, H. K. and Hendee, J. (1982). Renewable Resources Recreation in the United States: Supply, Demand, and Critical Policy Issues. Washington, DC: American Forestry Association.

Darst, P. and Armstrong, G. (1980). *Outdoor Adventure Activities for School and Recreation Programs.* Minneapolis, MN: Burgess Publishing Company.

Dockery, L. (1986). Off-Shore Manufacturing. *Outside Business,* 11(3): pp. 27–28.

Dunn, D. and Gulbis, J. (1976). The Risk Revolution. *Parks and Recreation,* 12.

Elsner, G. (1985). Recreation Use Trends: A Forest Service Perspective. In J. Wood (ed.). *Proceedings: 1985 National Outdoor Recreation Trends Symposium II,* pp. 143–147. U.S. Department of the Interior, National Park Service, Southeast Regional Office, Atlanta, GA.

Ewert, A. (1982). The Effect of Course Length on the Reported Self-Concepts of Selected Outward Bound Participants. Ph.D. Dissertation. University of Oregon.

Ewert, A. (1983). *Outdoor Adventure and Self-Concept: A Research Analysis.* Eugene, OR: Center of Leisure Studies, University of Oregon.

Ewert, A. (1985a). Emerging Trends in Outdoor Adventure Recreation. Paper presented at the Outdoor Recreation Trends Symposium II. Myrtle Beach, SC.

Ewert, A. (1985b). Emerging Trends in Outdoor Adventure Recreation. *Proceedings: 1985 National Outdoor Recreation Trends Symposium II,* pp. 155-165. Atlanta, GA: National Park Service.

Hale, A. (1978). *Directory: Programs in Outdoor Adventure Activities.* Mankato MN: Outdoor Experiences.

Herskowitz, D. (1985). Forecasting for Corporate Planning. *Business Quarterly.* London, Canada: University of Western Ontario, 50(1): pp. 32-35.

Hornback, K. (1985). Social Trends and Leisure Behavior. *Proceedings: 1985 National Outdoor Recreation Trends Symposium II,* pp. 37-48. Atlanta, GA: National Park Service.

Kelly, J. (1982). *Leisure.* Englewood Cliffs, NJ: Prentice-Hall.

Kelly, J. (1985). *Recreation Business.* New York: John Wiley and Sons.

Keyes, R. (1985). *Changing It.* Boston: Little, Brown, and Company.

McAvoy, L. (1980). The Experiential Components of a High Adventure Program. In J. Meier, T. Morash, and G. Welton (eds.). *High Adventure Outdoor Pursuits.* Columbus, OH: Publishing Horizons.

McBride, D. (1984). The Behaviors of Adolescent Boys in a Residential Treatment Center During High Ropes Course Experience. Ph.D. Dissertation. Columbus, OH: The Ohio State University.

McCall, G. and Simmons, J. (eds.). (1969). *Issues in Participant Observation: A Text and Reader.* Reading, MA: Addison-Wesley

McLellan, G. (1986). Outdoor Recreation: What the Trends Tell Us. *Parks and Recreation,* pp. 45-48, 63.

Meier, J.; Morash, T.; and Welton, G. (1987). *High Adventure Outdoor Pursuits.* Columbus, OH: Publishing Horizons.

Mescon, M.; Albert, M.; and Khedouri, F. (1981). *Management: Individual and Organizational Effectiveness.* Cambridge, MA: Harper and Row.

President's Commission on Americans Outdoors: A Literature Review. (1986). Washington, DC: U.S. Government Printing Office.

Petty, M. and Norton, E. (1987). The Dollars and Cents of Outdoor Recreation on the National Forest. *Trends,* 24(3): pp. 40-43.

Progen, J. (1979). Man, Nature and Sport. *Sport and the Body: A Philosophical Symposium,* 2nd ed. E. Gerber and W. Morgan (eds.). Philadelphia: Lea and Febiger.

Rillo, T. (1984). Megatrends in Outdoor Education: Past, Present and Future. *Journal of Outdoor Education,* p. 18.

Siedentop, D. (1980). *Physical Education: Introductory Analysis.* Dubuque, IA: Wm. C. Brown.

Siehl, G. (1985). "Federal Trends in Outdoor Recreation Policy." Paper presented at the Outdoor Recreation Trends Symposium II. Myrtle Beach, SC.

Thomas, S. (comp.). (1985). *Adventure Education: A Bibliography.* State University of New York at Buffalo, Department of Learning and Instruction, Amherst, NY.

Van Doren, C. (1984). State Park Systems. *Statistics on Outdoor Recreation,* pp. 235-244. M. Clawson and C. Van Doren (eds.). Washington, DC: Resources for the Future.

Van Doren, C. (1985). Social Trends and Social Indicators: The Private Sector. *Proceedings: 1985 National Outdoor Recreation Trends Symposium II,* pp. 13-23. Atlanta, GA: National Park Service.

Van Horne, M. J.; Szwak, L.; and Randall, S. (1985). "Outdoor Recreation Activity Trends—Insights from the 1983-84 Nationwide Recreation Survey." Paper presented at the Outdoor Recreation Trends Symposium II. Myrtle Beach, SC.

Wilson, W. (1977). Social Discontent and the Growth of Wilderness Sport in America: 1965-1974. *Quest,* 27, Winter 1977.

Zuckerman, M. (1979). *Sensation-Seeking: Beyond the Optimal Level of Arousal.* Hillsdale, NJ: John Wiley and Sons.

9

OUTDOOR ADVENTURE PURSUITS AND DIFFERENT POPULATIONS[1]

One of the most widespread uses of outdoor adventure activities for educational purposes involves special populations. Traditionally, outdoor adventure pursuits has been a class of activities engaged in by people who are white and belong in a middle or upper socioeconomic level. Moreover, while most participants continue to belong to the 20- to 40-year-old age group, these activities are increasingly becoming part of the repertoire of the older adult or younger student.

The issue of user groups revolves around the broader topic of participation. The concept of participation includes not only different user groups, but also nonparticipation and decision making regarding involvement in adventure types of activities. Indeed, from the commercial outdoor adventure perspective, understanding why people do not attend outdoor adventure activities can be as important as knowing who does come.

To better understand how outdoor adventure pursuits can meet the needs of different populations, this chapter is divided into a variety of sections. These sections include youth at risk, people with disabilities, older adults, and people engaging in adventure activities for special health and wellness reasons. In addition, the concepts of nonparticipation and decision making for engagement will be discussed.

YOUTH AT RISK

Since the 1960s, a substantial number of outdoor adventure programs have evolved that have been specifically designed to address the

[1]By Alan Ewert and Alison Voight, Ph.D.

problem of juvenile delinquency. Terminology used to describe these various programs includes youth in need, juvenile delinquents, hoods in the woods, troubled youth, and "alternatives [to incarceration] programming." A number of organizations have been involved with this type of programming, with various degrees of success, success usually being measured by a reduction in recidivism or in the number of antisocial behaviors observed. A partial listing of these types of organizations includes the Becket Academy, Outward Bound, Vision Quest, and Wilderness Inquiry. Essentially, what most of these programs attempt to do is use the components of outdoor adventuring (i.e., trusting, risk taking, compassion for others, and personal growth) to create feelings of personal worth and responsibility for one's life and actions. In turn, it is hoped that these new attitudes will modify or eliminate unsocial behavior or behavior which is destructive to the individual and/or others.

Golins (1979) outlines three principal characteristics that identify the delinquent:

- The delinquent often displays an unwillingness to assume any form of personal responsibility for his own actions or those of others.
- The delinquent is a limited learner in that information is collected without much evaluation, synthesis, or causal inferencing.
- The delinquent is usually lacking in self-confidence, both in physical and social situations. Moreover, this lack of self-confidence is augmented by defensive posturing and a distinct resistance to learning anything from anybody.

Golins also suggests that adventure activities allow delinquents an opportunity to integrate themselves into groups or other subsets of society in a manner which is consistent with their individual perceptions of their abilities and the "picture," they wish to portray. In other words, delinquents often wish to portray themselves as very physical individuals who like excitement and personal testing. Adventure activities can often provide outlets for these feelings but in a manner which is usually controllable and socially acceptable. Taking a risk by shoplifting is socially unacceptable but taking a chance by engaging in a rock climb is not.

Outdoor programs are widely utilized to provide an atmosphere for rehabilitation and behavioral change. These changes are precipitated through a number of mechanisms: a gamelike atmosphere; the organization of participants into primary peer groups; use of the outdoors as an objective, neutral source of information and challenge; the nature of these challenges; and the style of instruction (Golins, n.d.).

As most outdoor adventure activities are short-term and of a fixed duration, the delinquent can experiment with new forms of behavior without compromising his image back in a "normal" living environment (Golins, n.d.). This environment encourages responsibility, trust, and reflection on the part of the delinquent. Golins posits that the gamelike atmosphere of outdoor adventure activities becomes an entry point through which the delinquent can engage life.

Many agencies organize their participants into small groups, historically known as "ten groups." The small-group format is a useful tool for a variety of participants, including the delinquent. Through the small-group setting, a number of variables can be controlled or manipulated, including being physically able to observe the individual and the group, peer pressure, physical control, and ease in communication. In addition, the small-group context encourages the formation of community through commonality of experience. To accomplish the assigned tasks, participants in a number of outdoor adventure pursuits programs *must* work as a cohesive group. This often further enhances feelings of community, honest communication, and positive action.

Caving has become an adventure activity used by a number of different programs and with a variety of different populations.

The outdoor setting provides an environment which is unfamiliar, objectively neutral, and exceedingly complex. Delinquents, as well as most other participant types, respond to this environment by increased attention and sensual receptiveness. The outdoor setting also provides concrete rather than abstract problems. For example, getting to the top of a mountain involves action and doing, not just talking. Delinquents often respond more positively to concrete problems because they are more attuned to collecting and dealing with information which does not require a substantial amount of synthesis, analysis, or evaluation (Harmon and Templin, 1977). The behavioral aspects of outdoor adventure programs that participants have to perform emulate this "concreteness."

Golins indicates that the outdoors involves a tremendous potential for symbolic meaning. The often-used term "everything and everybody is important" is a classical example of how the outdoor environment can provide concrete examples for symbolic meaning. The "Figure Eight" is a small, metal device used in rope work which at first glance does not usually attract much attention. However, as a participant goes through a course or experience in which activities involving ropes are used, the lowly "Figure Eight" begins to assume an increasingly important position. This is particularly true since the delinquent often finds himself "hanging" from that "Figure Eight".

The nature of problems presented to the delinquents is another factor often employed in outdoor adventure pursuits programs. Not only are the problems very concrete but they are also structured in such a way as to help achieve the goals of the program and utilize the concept of progression. Progression implies movement from easy to difficult tasks, as well as utilizing different approaches. Roland et al. (1987) describe one program which uses progression in the establishment of five different levels of approach: goal setting, awareness, trust, group problem solving, and individual problem solving.

Another example of progression is illustrated in the seven sequential steps of a program adapted for children with behavioral disorders (Robb and Ewert, 1987). As illustrated in Figure 9.1, these steps are similar to that utilized by Roland et al. (1987) and involve goal setting, awareness of self and others, trust, cooperative activities, problem solving, group challenge, and adventure activities. Superimposed upon these steps are the operational aspects of the actual program model. These aspects are illustrated in Figure 9.2 and include an ignition experience, mobile experience, one-day inservice, 2- to 3-day inservice, residential experiences, post-residential experiences, and extended outdoor challenge education activities.

While traditional programs for rehabilitating youth in trouble have been concentrated on extended outdoor challenge experiences, it is appropriate to consider a more extensive course of offerings. For example, many programs which use adventure activities in a wilderness setting as the

FIGURE 9.1

The Seven Sequential Levels of the Challenge Education Model

Robb and Ewert (1987)

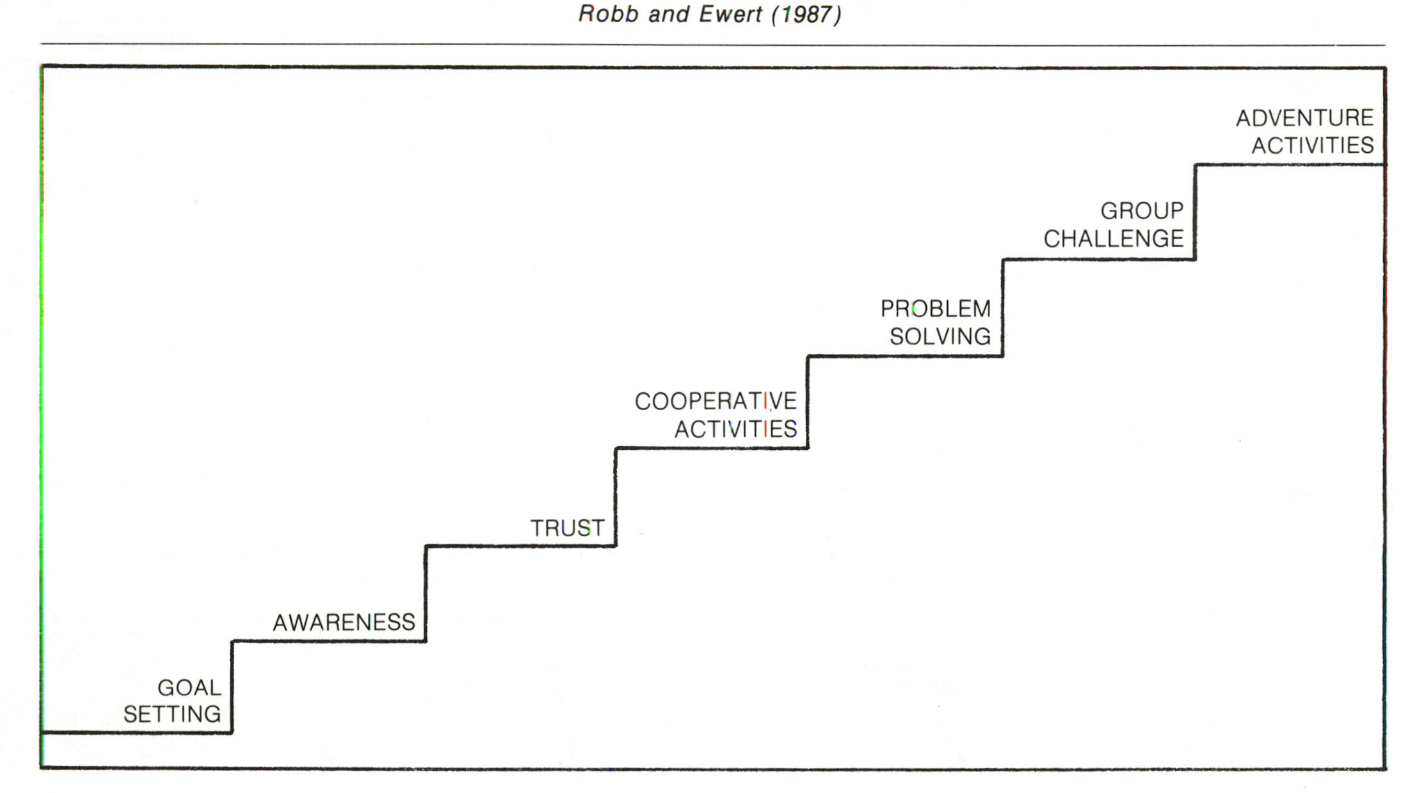

FIGURE 9.2

The Seven Sequential Levels of the Program Model

Robb and Ewert (1987)

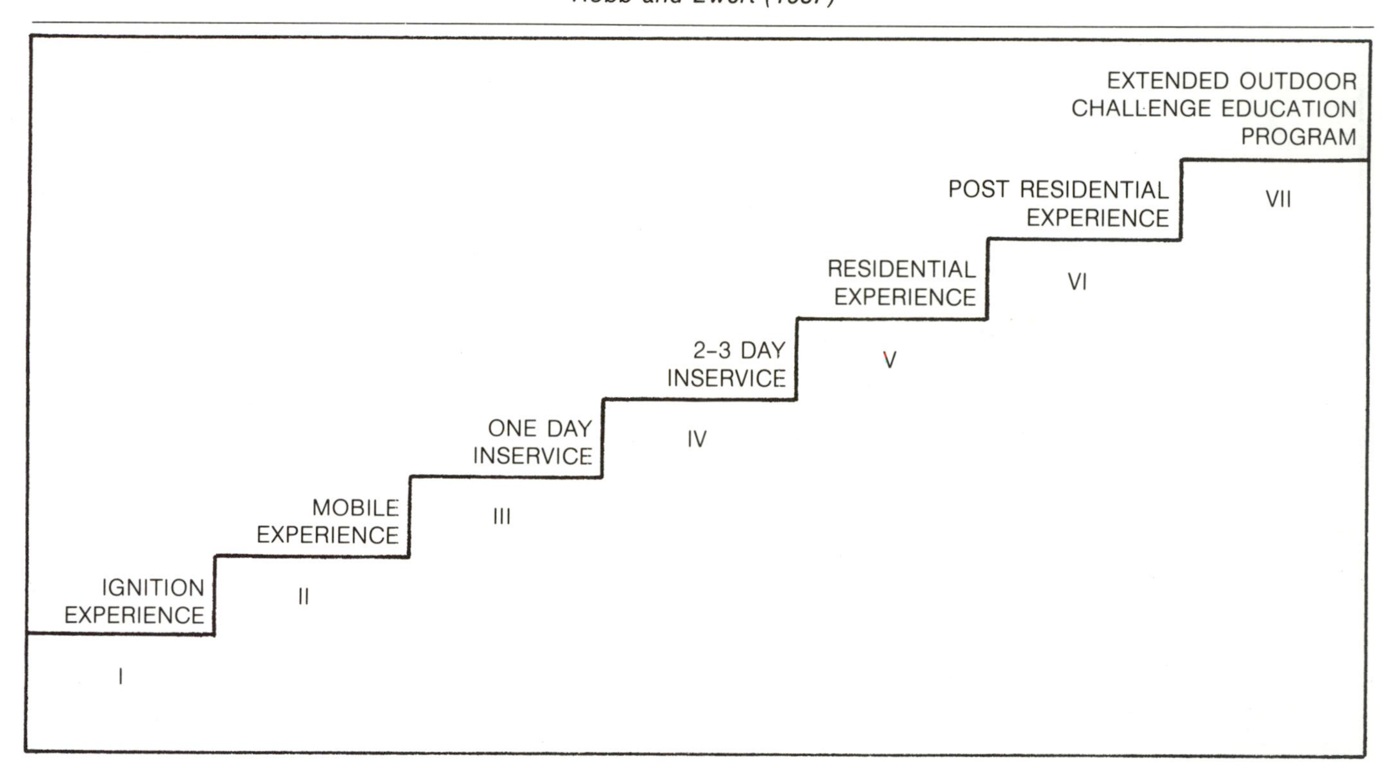

sole or primary source of intervention have been criticized for not being more useful to individuals after they return home.

Extending this discussion about the nature of the problems the delinquent faces in an adventure setting, the tasks posed often involve real threats to the individual's life and limb. Besides this realism, the problems presented (such as climbing a peak) necessitate the use of physical, mental, and emotional skills. If these skills are lacking, the delinquent must acquire them before the task can be successfully completed.

Whatever skills are needed to surmount the obstacles placed before him, the style of instruction inherent in the outdoor adventure pursuits setting is of primary importance in achieving successful rehabilitation of the delinquent. Many outdoor pursuits programs include an instructional format in which the instructor is with the participants twenty-four hours a day, for the duration of the course. This continuity enables the use of "teachable moments" and "time and opportunity teaching." In addition,

TABLE 9.1
Teaching Methods and Techniques When Dealing with Troubled Youth

1. Do not make presumptions about what students know, understand, or retain.
2. Keep activities practical and sequential—relate activities to those tasks and requirements coming up.
3. Be demonstrative as well as verbal.
4. Teach by example.
5. Avoid being judgmental.
6. Be congruent and straightforward.
7. Let people know what to expect from the course in terms of activities and requirements.
8. Let the participants know what is expected of them in terms of acceptable behaviors, communication patterns, and interaction with others.
9. Pace yourself.
10. Trust without trusting and care without "bleeding."
11. Discomfort is a difficult concept for delinquents to deal with responsibly.
12. Do not try to build your own personal support system from the students.
13. Look for the real messages behind the behavior.
14. Give feedback while focusing on the individual.
15. Use intervention and exhortation when necessary.
16. Delinquents live in and for the moment.
17. Have plans but have more options.

by being engaged in the same type of activities and physical tasks as the students, the instructor gains credibility with the students and is better able to bond with them.

In summary, a number of programs have evolved that seek to create behavior and affective change in the delinquent. From the widespread use of outdoor adventure programs there have emerged a number of techniques and teaching methods which have proved useful for working with troubled youth. These techniques and methods are listed in Table 9.1.

OUTDOOR ADVENTURE AND THE OLDER ADULT[2]

In recent years, outdoor adventure activities have mushroomed in both the public and private sectors. Unfortunately, the older adult (aged 45 to 65), confined to more sedentary and restricted activities, has been virtually excluded from this movement. Yet the U.S. population is becoming older and more urban (Knudson, 1980). Many of us reading this book will be in our 50s and 60s by the year 2000. Are we going to choose the sedentary, spectator activities which permeate the recreational scene, or will we demand different, more exciting recreation experiences?

While traditionally reserved for the teenager or young adult, outdoor adventure interests the older adult as well. Among these adventure interests might be mountaineering, scuba diving, white-water rafting, or backpacking. Organizations such as Outward Bound and the National Outdoor Leadership School (N.O.L.S.) offer courses for adults but their advertising schemes suggest that these programs are designed for young, vibrant individuals. If this perception is correct, many organizations are overlooking a growing segment of the participant market. Likewise, an increasingly large and politically powerful group of people are left unsatisfied by recreation services.

THE CHANGING OUTDOOR ADVENTURE SCENE FOR OLDER ADULTS

Our society is being shaped by a variety of forces. Among two of the more powerful are an aging population and the changing nature of work. By 1990, approximately one-third of our population will be over 50 (Underhill, 1981). The U.S. worker is increasingly white-collar in fields such as law, administration, finance, or tourism, with basic manufacturing accounting for less than 25 percent of the GNP (Byron, 1976).

These factors have produced an increasingly large number of older adults who have the time, energy, and wherewithal to pursue leisure interests. At the same time, a growing national interest in outdoor adven-

---

[2]A modified version of this section in Ewert (1983).

ture activities offers many leisure service delivery systems opportunities and demands from older adults (Dunn and Gulbis, 1976).

In outdoor adventure programming, the opportunities and demands from the older adult generally have been unmet. As individuals, older adults are faced with a battery of misconceptions concerning outdoor adventure activities. These misconceptions have created a number of formidable barriers to participation.

Older adults can enjoy a variety of outdoor pursuits including mountaineering.

BARRIERS TO PARTICIPATION

Participation in outdoor adventure activities by older adults is hindered by both internal and external factors. Internal factors include lack of time, feelings of inadequacy, expense, and a failure to see the activity as functional. Of these factors, feelings of inadequacy are the older adult's primary roadblock.

The reasons are both simple and complex, but self-image plays a decisive role in an individual's believing that tasks can be successfully accomplished. Will I be able to hike that distance? Negotiate those rapids? Deal with a strange group of people? These questions plague many potential participants.

As programmers, we can confront these problems by thoroughly explaining the activities and desired goals, proposing a conditioning regime which can strengthen the individual's physical and psychological preparedness, and structuring the program to maximize success without sacrificing goals. Intertwined with these techniques is the concept of "shifting control." By enabling the individual to help guide the program, we can shift some program structuring to where it belongs—the participant. For example, the programmer can assign a group of older adults a task such as rafting a particular set of rapids, while allowing the group to choose the route, emergency procedures, and strategy. Having a competent instructor check the group's ideas and abilities before the event protects participants from deficient or dangerous plans without taking away their control. After the activity, participants may rightly feel some pride; their abilities got them through!

External reasons for not attending can be as powerful as internal barriers. Peers may ridicule or denigrate the individual who wishes to participate in a "dangerous," "foolhardy" activity. The nearest program may be too far or the schedule may be inopportune. For their part, programmers may exclude the older adult simply because they have not marketed activities to make them known to this population. More seriously, many organizations do not offer outdoor adventure programs for the older adult at all. One cannot attend something that does not exist.

External barriers can and must be addressed. Peer pressure can be turned into a positive force if the participant returns healthier and happier. A decentralized approach (Sessoms, 1981) to providing services, coupled with dealing with groups of older adults through clubs, lodges, and organizations, enables the programmer to reach more people than does the traditional approach, in which an individual comes to the park and recreation building. For example, a library club could read books about the outdoors and then experience a weekend backpacking trip organized by the local leisure service delivery organization.

Redirected advertising schemes can reach market segments which are most likely to participate. Airline magazines, *The Wall Street Journal,* and professional journals are likely periodicals through which to attract a potential participant to an outdoor adventure program. An effective marketing scheme capitalizes on the excitement, physical and mental strengthening, and the lack of appreciable injury rates between older and younger populations (Meyer, 1979). Altering program length and timing can allow the older adult with a tight time schedule to attend.

The challenge lies in developing realistic program goals which make sense to them. Climbing a mountain can be pure drudgery if individuals don't know why they are doing it.

Combining socialization with family and friends, health building, and process orientation requires the development of a series of program components to produce an effective, quality outdoor adventure program for the older adult.

PROGRAM COMPONENTS

The programmer strives to create a positive experience for participants. Thus certain course components in the outdoor adventure setting need to be altered to enhance program safety and quality. Program components should be considered sequentially, as illustrated by Figure 9.3.

FIGURE 9.3
Program Components of an Outdoor Adventure Activity With Older Adult Participants

Time	Component	Reason
Before	Preactivity information	Marketing, information, allaying fears
Before	Proactivity training	Reduce likelihood of injury, build self-confidence, build physical and mental health
Immediately before	Activity orientation	Allay fears, inform participants of hazards, etc. Foster participants' abilities and strengths
During	Implement activity	Provide excitement and challenge. Allow for socializing, family/friends involvement, self-testing
Immediately after	Synthesis	Summarize event and conditions. Give input and feedback to group, allow group interaction
After	Reflection	Complete the self-building process. Create new perceptions. Dramatizes individual and group value(s)

The programmer needs to design programs that not only implement the activity but also enable the older participant to glean as many intrinsic values as possible from the experience, such as self-concept change, new perceptions, or personal enjoyment. This "buying the *experience*" rather than the *activity* must be addressed by using techniques appropriate for the older adult.

PROGRAMMING CHARACTERISTICS

Outdoor adventure programming for older adults operates under one basic assumption: The participants, who are there voluntarily, want to get something from the experience—pictures, their names on a summit register, or memories. Older adults generally place a high value on friends, family, and health (Levinson, 1978; Gould, 1975). Armed with this knowledge, the programmer can devise health-building adventure activities for groups of friends or families. Float trips, mountain walking, and snorkeling are activities with both a family and health orientation.

The older adult is process- rather than product-oriented. The value of an experience often lies in the socializing it provokes and the enjoyment it provides, rather than the attainment of a goal. One should not assume, however, that older adults won't or can't push themselves in physical and psychological terms; they can and do.

PROGRAM TECHNIQUES

Using techniques which complement the older adult's experience can finetune a program and ultimately determine its success or failure. In conducting an outdoor adventure program for older adults consider the following techniques.

Before the Program

1. Ensure an activity-specific medical clearance.
2. Explain the experience to avoid misconceptions or false expectations.
3. Tell about successful participants; the potential enrollee may question personal inabilities or inadequacies.
4. Provide mature, knowledgeable, and personable staff who can deal successfully with a variety of people.

Inplementing the Program

5. Discover participant expectations and fears and strive to make them manageable.
6. Be wary of hypothermic or hyperthermic reactions. Many older adults tolerate extremes in temperature with difficulty.
7. Sensory changes may create "awareness" gaps. Guard against safety problems which may result.
8. Employ staff that can not only implement an activity but can educate older adults about outdoor adventure as well.
9. Encourage the staff to be straightforward and encouraging. Avoid coyness, guessing games, and holier-than-thou attitudes.

10. Older adults generally have stable self-concepts and often resist obvious attempts at change. Staff should probe the participants' needs rather than implementing their own.

After the Program

11. Suggest ways in which participants may synthesize their experiences.
12. Program staff should strive to link the adventure experience with everyday living. These links can provide meaning and give function to the adventure experience.
13. The older participant often provides useful feedback to refine the program.
14. Provide materials, guidance, and opportunities for the older participant to promote the program. Whether past participants can attract or turn off potential participants depends on the input the participant received from the program staff.

The older adult represents a segment of our population which is also the most economically viable. Older adults can and will pay for leisure-time experiences. While adventure programmers can use the inherently powerful tools of excitement and the adventure mystique, they also compete with a growing armada of leisure alternatives. If outdoor adventure programs are to grow, programmers must recognize the varied, often divergent needs among persons. Whatever components and techniques an organization employs, the success or failure of a program will often depend on how well the older adult's adventure needs are met.

OUTDOOR RECREATION AND PEOPLE WITH DISABILITIES

PHYSICAL DISABILITIES

When considering the integration of physically disabled persons into an outdoor environment, an image of wheelchairs on trails, special equipment, and impossible situations comes to mind. These situations might include some activities that are simply perceived as unsuitable to the physically disabled (i.e., rock climbing, hiking, white-water trips, etc.). Most people assume that because of a physical impairment (i.e., paraplegia, amputation, cerebral palsy) the needs of the physically disabled are much greater or much different than nonphysically disabled persons. The fallacy in this type of thinking is that the physically disabled have the *same* needs or desires as those of the nondisabled. They have the same needs for socialization, self-esteem, self-confidence, and so on as anyone else.

Outdoor adventure pursuit activities can attract the physically disabled for the same reasons that it attracts the nondisabled. It offers challenge (physically and emotionally), group camaraderie and companionship, opportunities for solitude and serenity, excitement, and adventure. What may differ is the *way* in which physically disabled versus nondisabled persons become involved in the activities. In other words, special arrangements or special programming considerations may go into their involvement in outdoor recreation activities. But their needs for involvement are basically the same as those of anyone else. It is this misconception that their needs are so much different from those of the nondisabled that has greatly restricted their involvement in outdoor recreation activities.

Despite numerous misconceptions, people with disabilities can and should have access to outdoor pursuits activities.

BARRIERS TO INVOLVEMENT

Several barriers exist today that have continually excluded the physically disabled from participating in outdoor recreation activities. Social, emotional, financial, and physical barriers represent the major obstacles the physically disabled must overcome. Physical barriers may seem the greatest, but in reality it is usually the attitude of others that presents the single most daunting challenge to the disabled.

Taking a moment to differentiate terms that are often used to describe special populations, it may become apparent how society's attitudes "handicap" the disabled. Generally, the three terms: impaired, disabled, or handicapped have been used interchangeably in our society. But there is a difference in each term. *Impaired* implies that a body part is missing or dysfunctional (i.e., amputation, paralysis, fracture, infection, etc.). It may be a temporary or permanent impairment. *Disabled* indicates the degree to which one is restricted in performing certain skills because of an impairment. *Handicapped* represents an attitude or perception one has about himself or others have of him. It usually engenders a negative, helpless, or pitied perception. While many disabled feel that they are quite capable of performing the same skills as the nondisabled, society usually "handicaps" them with its perceptions of how helpless they are, how limited, and how sad the whole situation is. Society fails to give them a chance, and does indeed render the disabled "handicapped."

The denial to participate in outdoor recreation activities by the physically disabled may be attributable to several other specific barriers as well. A study by West (1981) cites that transportation is one of the major reasons that more disabled are not involved. Other specific barriers include architecture, inaccessibility to outdoor locations, fear on the part of parents, and the lack of qualified outdoor leaders who understand the needs and capabilities of persons with disabilities (Roland and Havens, 1983).

Although involvement among the physically disabled has increased a great deal in the last ten years, greater understanding on the part of families, outdoor professionals, and society in general is needed before their involvement can be considered "normal" and not "special" or different. At this point, "special" programs may be the only option to the physically disabled. Fear on the part of ski operators, national and state parks, administrators, and so on in terms of injuries and law suits, have held back participants' involvement. Several of the "special" programs that have, perhaps for the first time, allowed the physically disabled to experience outdoor adventure include Project Adventure (Massachusetts), Breckenridge Outdoor Education Center (Colorado), and S.O.A.R. (Oregon).

Despite involvement in outdoor adventure recreation activities, whether special programs or not, leaders, directors, and assistants may have to take into consideration several important points before they begin a program.

PROGRAMMING CONSIDERATIONS FOR THE PHYSICALLY DISABLED

Physical disabilities and the considerations for recreational involvement will vary according to each individual. No two disabled persons will be the same, or require identical care, regardless of a similar diagnosis. For example, two people with cerebral palsy could vary greatly in their physical capabilities: one might be ambulatory and the other confined to a wheelchair.

The important point for programmers and outdoor leaders is to allow all participants to use their capabilities to the fullest, within a safe and reasonable structure. The following areas should be carefully considered by leaders before any activity is implemented.

Transportation. Will disabled participants need any special assistance in getting to the outdoor activities/area or will they be able to come on their own?

Restrooms. Will indoor restrooms be available, accessible, or needed?

Staff/Assistance. Will more staff be needed to accommodate someone? Will one-to-one assistance be necessary?

Medical. Will any special medical problems need to be dealt with (e.g., medications, decubitus ulcers, emergency evacuations, etc.).

Activity/Group Objectives. What is the primary objective of the group regarding the outdoor activity? Will it be process- or goal-oriented?

THE MENTALLY RETARDED

One of the populations of people who have been traditionally overlooked

Pulk skiing is one example of how creativity and innovations have opened up the world of adventure to people with disabilities.

in outdoor recreation and outdoor adventuring has been the mentally retarded. The mentally retarded, or developmentally disabled, are those persons who have subaverage general intellectual functioning resulting from congenital, environmental, social, medical, or developmental factors. Learning disabilities, often considered synonymous with mental retardation, are now thought to be different, as those with learning disabilities usually have an average to above average I.Q. Unlike physical disabilities, mental retardation is essentially a social concern (Gunzberg, 1968). To date, the most serious barriers to participation in outdoor adventure activities are socially based. The social barriers of mental retardation involve social stigma, economic, family isolation, negative self-perceptions, and institutional barriers regarding recreational participation (West, 1981).

Social barriers associated with the mentally retarded often result from inappropriate behavior in social or public situations, which often lead to negative perceptions, feelings of avoidance, fear, and impatience on behalf of society. These negative feelings are then communicated to the mentally retarded, further contributing to their negative perception of inadequacy, low self-esteem, lack of confidence, low self-image, and inferior capabilities. While it is slowly being recognized that the mentally retarded can be a very functional and contributing group in our society, the stigma still exists. Perceptions of people who may look or act differently will often affect the way in which they are treated, and when persons are treated as being different—childlike or incapable—they will continue to act that way.

Recreational activities can provide an environment of growth and development for the mentally retarded. Recreation, and especially outdoor

TABLE 9.2
Considerations When Working with the Mentally Retarded

1. Consider mental age, environmental background, and previous activity experiences when selecting activities.
2. Progress from the known to the unknown and from the simple to the complex.
3. Be enthusiastic and participate with the clients.
4. Provide successful experiences and offer praise at appropriate times.
5. Provide greater challenges in each activity.
6. Encourage enjoyment of activities.
7. Give short, simple instructions.
8. Encourage participation by everyone.
9. Exercise firm discipline when appropriate.
10. Ensure that the activity is appropriate for the discipline of the group.
11. Do not frustrate the participant by teaching too much for extended periods of time.
12. Encourage good safety practices.

adventure recreation activities, can offer an opportunity for positive, successful experiences in a challenging and exciting setting. Not only does outdoor adventure promote group cooperation and socialization, but also allows for the development of more specific physical or motor skills in more unique, nontraditional circumstances. Outdoor activities can help visual-perceptual difficulties, body/spatial awareness, directionality, and overall, general physical fitness. Table 9.2 provides some program considerations when working with the mentally retarded.

THE MENTALLY ILL

The mentally ill and substance abusers differ from the physically disabled in that, for the most part, mental illness is an "invisible" disability. Several disorders associated with mental illness include personality, social, dissociative, affective, schizophrenic, and somatoform disorders. Although most mental illness is usually treated in hospital or clinical settings, some programs have begun to include outdoor recreation activities as a part of the rehabilitation process. Outdoor activities can provide important benefits to the mentally ill and, while there may appear to be no physical barriers to their participating, other considerations must be taken into account. Below are a list of programming considerations for inclusion of the mentally ill in outdoor adventure pursuits.

Adequate Staff. For certain types of mental illness, such as schizophrenia, psychoses, or social and personality disorders, more staff may be needed. Sometimes one-to-one ratios may be warranted for safety and control.

Nature of the Activity. Depending on the nature of the outdoor activity, some participants may be better suited to less threatening or stressful situations. For example, alcoholism, substance abuse, or depression are illnesses that may benefit well from the realities of completing tasks in order to fulfill or reach a goal in the outdoors. For psychotic participants, high-risk activities should be carefully monitored and supervised.

Medications. Mental illness is frequently treated with drugs, such as antidepressants, phenothiazines, and anti-E.P.S., which may cause difficulty in balance, energy level, memory, focus, and exposure to sunlight. Some outdoor activities may be better than others for the mentally ill, but careful monitoring of medication, regardless of the activity, is essential.

Doctor's Prescription. Most hospitalized psychiatric patients will require written orders by their physicians before they are able to leave the hospital and participate in certain activities. Nurses, doctors, and other staff can determine the type of supervision and activity involvement suitable for the participant.

SPECIAL HEALTH AND WELLNESS ISSUES

Similar to most of the topics discussed in this section, outdoor adventure pursuits are particularly well suited for people in transition. As previously mentioned, the progressive nature of the activities and challenging yet manageable tasks can provide insight for the participant. Moreover, these types of programs can offer adult participants a chance to experience novelty and a change in role. In an earlier work, Harmon and Templin (1977) described the problem of hypercoherence, in which adults often develop views of the world which are in accordance with their everyday "roles." For example, businessmen will often analyze events in terms of their businesses or positions in the company. Harmon and Templin suggest that for the participant to become a backpacker or mountan climber will often not help the person with an ingrained role structure. Rather, it is suggested that a number of other techniques be used to help the adult participant develop a new set of "roles." These techniques involve:

- Value clarification.
- Moral reasoning skills.
- Role-playing techniques.
- Symbolic learning responses.
- Human motivation.

While many of these techniques are also used in more "traditional" outdoor adventure programs, there are currently a number of innovative and relatively new types of programs concerned with a variety of health and wellness issues. A sample of these programs include:

- Substance abuse.
- Wilderness and outdoor therapy.
- Courses for cancer patients.
- Victims of violence.
- Professional development/managers courses.
- Women's courses.
- Couples under stress.
- Vietnam veterans.

Although little has been done in the way of research concerning the effects of participation in these types of courses, many programs will use outdoor activities as an adjunct to more-clinical therapeutic techniques. In addition, a professional counselor or therapist is often part of the instructional team. As with most other outdoor adventure programs, the primary objective of these courses is not to produce experienced rock climbers or river rafters but rather to provide opportunities to learn new behaviors and attitudes which are "transferable" to the individual's everyday or normal life-style.

THE CONCEPT OF PARTICIPATION

Despite the population or type of client served, one issue that consistently receives little attention is that of participation. Historically, many programs have simply considered numbers of participants as an adequate indicator of success of a program. Little attention has been given to motivations for engagement or reasons for nonparticipation. The concept of participation is complex in that it encompasses not only the reasons people choose to engage in an activity, such as outdoor adventure pursuits, but also includes the expectations or anticipated rewards that individuals have toward the activity and reasons for not attending. For this discussion, outdoor adventure pursuits will be assigned under the broader heading of outdoor recreation since the concept of participation is crucial and similar to both.

As stated previously, outdoor recreation can involve a mix of people, opportunities, and expected rewards. Within this taxonomy are a number of additional factors that affect participation, such as motivation, desired setting, and preferred activities. These factors ultimately influence an individual's decision as to whether or not to participate in outdoor adventure.

A MODEL OF NONPARTICIPATION

A growing body of research suggests that there are five major variables which contribute to nonparticipation or reduced participation in recreational activities. These variables include deficiencies in money, time, opportunities or facilities, skill, and interest (Godbey, 1985; Searle and Jackson, 1985; Schroeder and Wiens, 1986). Drawing from Godbey (1985), a model of nonparticipation was developed specifically for commercialized outdoor recreation. This model is illustrated in Figure 9.4.

Following this flow diagram, it can be seen that the paradigm provides both general and specific information from a marketing and programming perspective. Within a general context, nonparticipation should be as serious a concern as participation. As suggested by Howard and Crompton (1980), agency success must not only be measured by who and how many come, but also evaluated in the light of who doesn't participate. Lack of awareness of available opportunities can be considered a marketing and advertising problem. A deliberate decision not to engage in an outdoor recreation experience constitutes a type of problem which has programming implications. Past experience can play an important role in the decision-making process (Pride and Ferrell, 1985). A potential participant may have had a negative outdoor experience with respect to not having an enjoyable time or with aspects of the specific "setup" of the course. For example, the raft may have had a hole in it or the planned-for campsite was full, which necessitated moving to a less desirable location. In addition, these negative

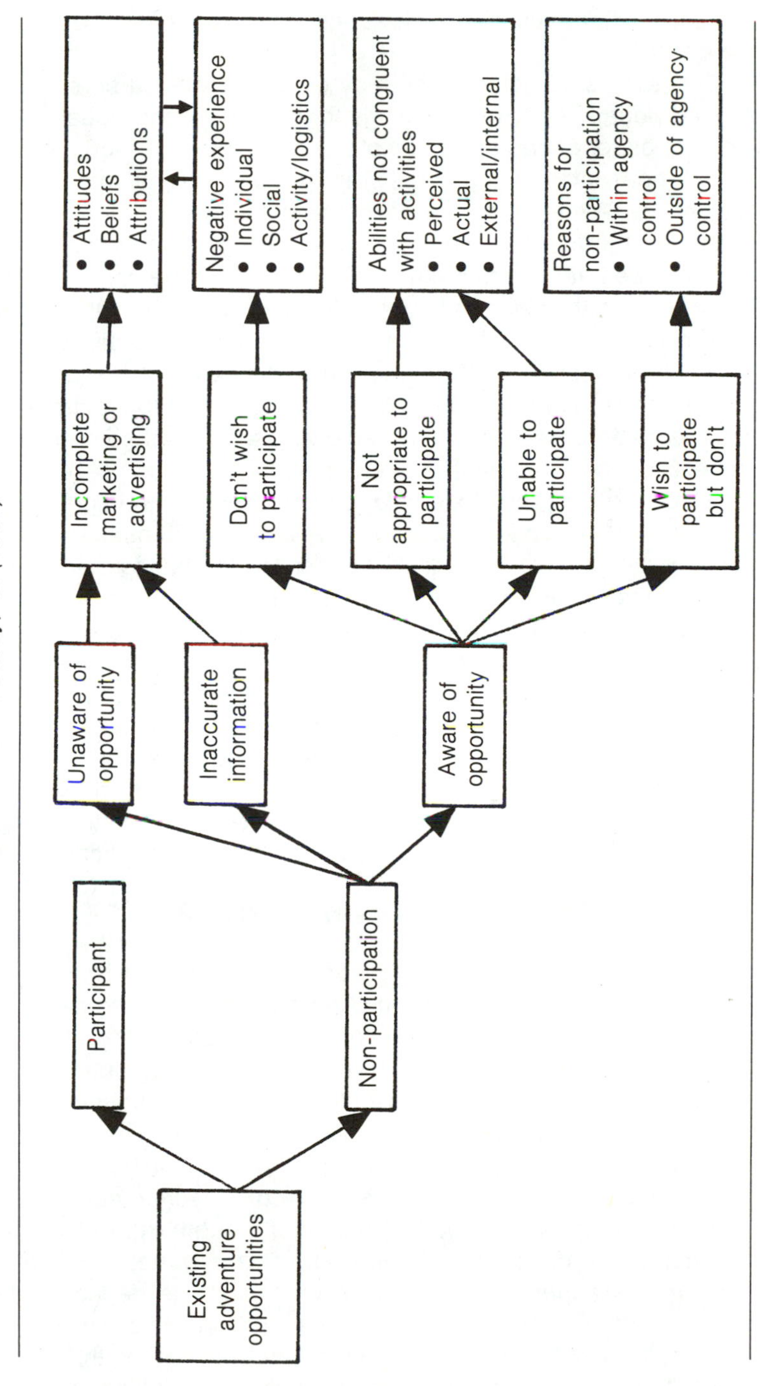

FIGURE 9.4

A Model of Nonparticipation in Outdoor Adventure Recreation

Modified from Godbey, G. (1986)

experiences may have contributed to the development of a series of beliefs, attitudes, or attributions which suggest that the activity is unenjoyable or dangerous.

Of even greater importance may be the perceived personal abilities of the individual. These ability ratings formed by the individual may be based on past experience but can also be perceived (not grounded in any past experience), internal (individual skills), or external (outcomes influenced by luck or fate). What is important from the outdoor recreation perspective is to realize that it does not matter if they [operators] know the potential client can succeed at the activity; what matters is that the *participant* knows that he or she has the skills and abilities to succeed. Without this knowledge the potential participant will have a natural inclination to disengage.

For those individuals who wish to participate but don't, the agency is faced with both internal (controllable) and external (uncontrollable) factors. Internal factors over which the agency usually has some control include scheduling, quality of staff and equipment used, cost, ease of application, and length of program. External factors over which the agency usually has little control involve items such as available locations that are suitable for the activity, cost, transportation facilities to the staging area, and individual events which ultimately preclude participation, such as an unanticipated expense. Kelly (1985) lists three other external factors which the outdoor recreation agency is dependent upon: climate/weather, the specific activity, and differences in the level of commitment or experience of the user.

In summary, knowing why people do not participate in an activity, whether it is due to age, disability, or the internal/external factors mentioned above, is as important as knowing who does come. Unfortunately, little effort has been directed toward a better understanding of the nonparticipant phenomenon, either from a market research or practitioner perspective.

THE DECISION-MAKING PROCESS

While understanding why people do not participate in outdoor recreational activities is of great use for the outdoor recreation agency, to complete the picture involves an exploration of the decision-making process by which consumers of any type, including outdoor users, make choices. Modifying work by Engle et al. (1986), a continuum is suggested of information collecting involving extended information gathering (EI), limited information gathering (LI), or routine information gathering (RI). This conceptualization is based on the theory of reasoned action advocated by Ajzen and Fishbein (1980), in which it is thought that people usually use information to make rational decisions. This information is often garnered through past experience, personal sources such as friends or relatives, and marketer-dominated sources such as advertising. In other words, choosing to engage in an outdoor recreational activity rather than watching the football game on television often involves an active decision-making process using expectations, personal relevancy, and the information an individual has about each potential choice. Howard (1985) reports that the consumer of public recreation services is not a highly involved information seeker and is often characterized by a high degree of spontaneity. In the case of outdoor adventure pursuits, this writer suggests that the consumers of outdoor adventure services and programs more likely fall into an extended information-gathering mode. This position is taken because of the very nature of many outdoor adventure endeavors, that is, leaving one's familiar surroundings and engaging in activities which require a substantial degree of personal involvement, skills, and commitment. In addition, factors such as unexpected storms, slips, or improperly negotiated rapids can involve serious consequences to the participant's health or welfare.

FIGURE 9.5

Decision-making Process for the Outdoor Adventure Consumer

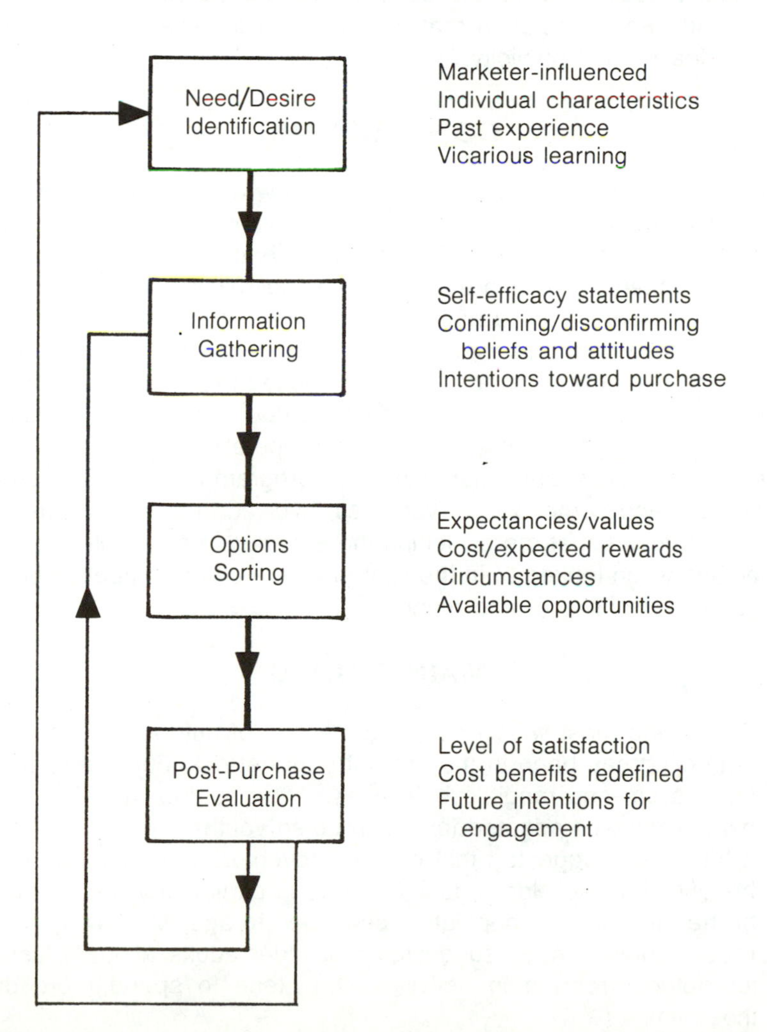

Information gathering is one part of the consumer decision-making process. Additional components of this process involve the variables of need or desire identification, evaluation of options, and purchase and postpurchase evaluation. The consumer decision-making process for outdoor adventure activities is illustrated in Figure 9.5.

Like consumers of other products and services, the potential outdoor adventure recreationalist follows a pattern of need identification, gathering information, choosing an option, and evaluating that choice after the experience. As illustrated in Figure 9.5, at each major point in this decision-making process there are a number of variables that can influence the individual. Operators of commercial outdoor recreation agencies might consider these variables, such as self-efficacy (ability) statements or predisposing beliefs held by the individual, in the development of marketing and programming plans. From a commercial standpoint, one of the primary goals is to create opportunities for satisfaction of the consumer, with the expectation that this will lead to repeat business or, at the very least, good publicity.

CONCLUSIONS

This brief treatise has provided an overview of the concept of participation in outdoor recreation and outdoor adventure pursuits. Integral to this understanding has been the outdoor recreation mix and the expectancy components which are inherent in the reward structure. Despite these rewards, there are a number of factors that contribute to nonparticipation. These variables include deliberate decisions not to engage or an unawareness of the opportunity. Juxtaposed to nonparticipation is the decision-making process of potential outdoor recreation consumers. From this paradigm it was posited that operators should consider a variety of factors in both marketing and programming plans. Moreover, the number and complexity of variables involved in the decision-making process suggests that merely letting the experience sell itself may not be efficacious when looked at in the light of all the other competing interests for the consumer's time and money.

MAIN POINTS

1. One of the most widely used adaptations of outdoor adventure programming has been in the area of youth at risk. For this population, the realism and tangible objectives of the outdoor adventure seem particularly well adapted for the troubled youth.
2. It has been suggested that outdoor adventure activities can also be beneficial to the older adult. This fact is particularly relevant in light of the fact that our population continues to age. Moreover, although recent surveys have suggested that older adults allocate less time for outdoor recreation activities, they tend to spend more during those times.

3. The physically impaired are attracted to outdoor adventure activities for the same reasons that attract the nondisabled. Indeed, the only real difference may be in the way the physically disabled engage in the activity when compared to the nondisabled.
4. In the case of the mentally retarded, it has been suggested that the main barriers to participation in outdoor adventure activities continue to be social. Of these, the largest impediment is a belief that the mentally retarded person will be unable to perform the activity safely. A growing amount of program experience suggests that this is not necessarily the case.
5. The mentally ill and substance abusers traditionally treated in hospital or treatment centers are now able to participate in more nontraditional rehabilitation programs, including outdoor adventure recreation.
6. A number of recent innovations in adventure programming has resulted in the development of special courses such as adventure opportunities for the person who has cancer, a victim of violence, or courses especially for women. One of the key ingredients of these types of offerings is the sense of empowerment the person gains from engaging in the adventure experience.
7. A model of nonparticipation was developed that can help explain the mechanism through which people do not engage in an outdoor adventure activity.
8. In addition, the decision-making process which explains the procedure through which a person buys an adventure experience suggests that there are four primary stages a consumer goes through: need identification, information gathering, sorting out options, and postpurchase evaluation of the service.

REFERENCES

Ajzen, I. and Fishbein, M. (1980). *Understanding Attitudes and Predicting Social Behavior.* Englewood Cliffs, NJ: Prentice-Hall.

Byron, C. (1976). Fighting the Paper Chase. *Time,* November 23, 1981, p. 66.

Dunn, D. R. and Gulbis, J. M. (1976). The Risk Revolution. *Parks and Recreation,* 11: p. 12.

Engel, J.; Blackwell, R.; and Miniard, P. (1986). *Consumer Behavior,* 5th ed. Chicago, IL: The Dryden Press.

Ewert, A. (1983). Adventure Programming for the Older Adult. *Journal of Physical Education, Recreation and Dance,* 54(3): pp. 64–66.

Godbey, G. (1985). Nonuse of Public Leisure Services: A Model. *Journal of Park and Recreation Administration,* 3(2): pp. 1–12.

Golins, G. (1979). *Utilizing Adventure Education to Rehabilitate Juvenile Delinquents.* Denver: Colorado Outward Bound.

Gould, R. (1975). Adult Life Stages: Growth Toward Self-Tolerance. *Psychology Today,* 8: pp. 74–78.

Gungberg, , H. C. (1968). *Social Competence and Mental Handicap: An Introduction to Social Education.* Baltimore, MD: Williams and Wilkins.

Howard, D. (1985). An Examination of the Decision-Making Process of Consumers of Public Recreation Agency Programs and Services. Paper presented at the 1985 NRPA Symposium on Leisure Research, October.

Howard, D. and Crompton, J. (1980). *Financing, Managing and Marketing Recreation and Park Resources.* Dubuque, IA: Wm. C. Brown.

Kelly, J. (1986). Investment Theory: Long-term Benefits. In R. Lucas (Comp.). *Proceedings— National Wilderness Research Conference: Current Research.* Fort Collins, CO: General Technical Report INT-212. Ogden, UT: Intermountain Research Station, pp. 393–397.

Knudson, D.M. (1980). *Outdoor Recreation,* pp. 60–62. New York: Macmillan.

Levinson, D.J. (with Darrow, C.N.; Klein, E.B.; Levinson, M.H.; and McKee, B.) (1978). *The Seasons of a Man's Life.* New York: Alfred A. Knopf.

Meyer, D. (1979). The Management of Risk. *Journal of Experiential Education,* 2(2): pp. 9–14.

Pride, W. and Ferrell, O. (1985). *Marketing: Basic Concepts and Decisions.* Boston: Houghton Mifflin Company.

Robb, G. and Ewert, A. (1987). Risk Recreation and Persons with Disabilities. *Therapeutic Recreation Journal,* 21(1): pp. 58–69.

Roland, C. and Havens, M. (1983). *Why Have Persons Who Have Disabilities Been Traditionally Excluded from Adventure Programs?* The Deluxe Check Printers Foundation.

Roland, C.; Summers, S.; Friedman, M.; Barton, G.; and McCarthy, K. (1987). Creation of an Experiential Challenge Program. *Therapeutic Recreation Journal,* 21(2): pp. 54–63.

Schroeder, T. and Wiens, M. (1986). The Nonuse of Public Park aand Recreation Facilities in Tulsa. *Journal of Park and Recreation Administration,* 4(3): pp. 75–87.

Searle, M. and Jackson, E. (1985). Recreation Non-Participation and Barriers to Participation: Considerations for the Management of Recreation Delivery Systems. *Journal of Park and Recreation Administration,* 3(2): pp. 23–35.

Underhill, A. H. (1981). Population Dynamics and Demography. *Journal of Physical Education and Recreation,* 52(8): p. 33.

West, P. (1981). Vestiges of a Cage. Natural Resources Sociology Research Lab. Monograph 1. Ann Arbor, MI: University of Michigan.

10

THE PROFESSIONALIZATION OF OUTDOOR ADVENTURE PURSUITS

Chapter 10 deals with an area of growing concern in the field of outdoor adventure pursuits, namely, that of professionalization. In a large measure, whether this field continues to become more like a profession will depend on the "vision" and importance of its role in society.

This vision needs to reflect the goals and aspirations of the individuals and organizations in outdoor pursuits. Moreover, this vision should provide guidelines and suggestions which can move agencies and individuals along in a progressive and forward fashion. Finally, this vision should provide a statement of inspiration from which outdoor adventure pursuits can evolve into an effective means of personal enjoyment and social good. Only organizations [and professions] which have a real sense of purpose and positive worth, which can be transferred through the practitioner to the participants or consumers, will form a positive image in the collective mind of society.

To accomplish these goals, this section is divided into the following categories: the distinction between discipline, field, and profession; outdoor adventure pursuits as a profession; philosophical-ethical issues facing the field; and the certification of outdoor professionals.

OUTDOOR ADVENTURE PURSUITS: DISCIPLINE, FIELD, OR PROFESSION?

Throughout this book, outdoor adventure pursuits has been consistently referred to as a type of activity usually occurring in a natural outdoor environment and involving elements of risk and uncertainty. When one moves past an activity orientation, however, a variety of terms attempt to encapsulate outdoor adventure pursuits as an entity.

One commonly used term is outdoor pursuits as a *field.* When properly used, field connotes an area or division of an activity. It follows then, that outdoor adventure pursuits is a field of outdoor recreation. As previously discussed (see chapter 1), the activities may occur in similar settings but the desired outcomes and participants are often different. Activities that have traditionally been considered outdoor recreational but also constitute adventure activities include wilderness tripping, flat-water canoeing, and sailing. The intuitive differences between the two fields can be seen in commonly thought of outdoor adventure activities such as white-water kayaking, rock climbing, skydiving, and spelunking.

In conclusion, outdoor adventure pursuits as a field refers to a collection of activities commonly associated with outdoor recreation. Both classifications follow a taxonomy of participants, opportunities, and expected rewards. This mix is illustrated in Figure 10.1.

In both outdoor recreation and outdoor adventure pursuits, a variety of people and opportunities interchange to provide a mix of rewards. In all

FIGURE 10.1
The Outdoor Adventure Pursuits Mix

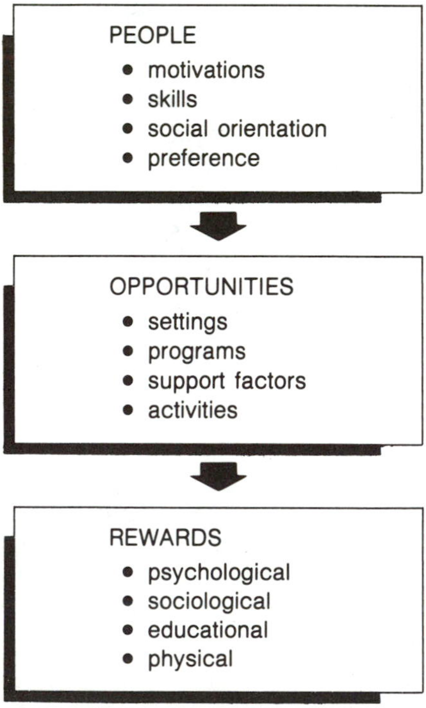

PEOPLE
- motivations
- skills
- social orientation
- preference

↓

OPPORTUNITIES
- settings
- programs
- support factors
- activities

↓

REWARDS
- psychological
- sociological
- educational
- physical

three cases (i.e., people, opportunities, and rewards) the differences can occur between outdoor recreation and outdoor adventure pursuits.

If outdoor adventure pursuits is discussed in the context of a *discipline,* the reference is made to a subject of study. More specifically, outdoor adventure pursuits can be considered as a course of study through a number of different approaches. Outdoor-related skills such as leadership, technical expertise, and environmentally sound behaviors are concepts taught in a variety of private and public institutions. From the private sector, institutions include the National Outdoor Leadership School (NOLS), Outward Bound (OB), the Wilderness Education Association (WEA), the Outdoor Leadership School (OLS), Scouting USA, and the Kurt Hahn Leadership Center. Institutions from a public perspective usually include colleges and universities. Examples of this type include Antioch College, Boston University, Earlham College, Eastern Washington University, Greenville Community College, and Prescott University. A more complete list of institutions and agencies is provided in Table 10.1.

TABLE 10.1
Selected Resources for Outdoor Leadership Training and Experience

Agencies and Organizations

Selected agencies and organizations offering Outdoor Programs and Outdoor Leadership training.

Acclimatization Experiences Institute
P.O. Box 288
Warrenville, IL 60555

Devises, demonstrates and distributes new environmental oriented educational techniques; training sessions, educational materials and publications.

Adirondack Mountain Club
172 Ridge Street
Glens Falls, NY 12801
(518) 793-7737

Programs, leadership training, skill workshops, publications, educational materials, facilities, membership and local chapters. Publishes: Membership Newsletter.

Adventurous Christians
Gunflint Star Route
Grand Marais, MN 55604
(218) 388-2286

Programs and leadership training in wilderness programs and experiences.

Alliance for Environmental Education
1619 Massachusetts Avenue, N.W.
Washington, DC 20036
(202) 465-3510

Conferences, technical assistance, publications and membership.

American Alliance for Health, Physical Education, Recreation and Dance (AAHPERD)
1900 Association Drive
Reston, VA 22091
(703) 476-3400

Professional membership, technical assistance, publications, conferences, workshops, job placement and Outdoor Education Council. Publishes: Journal of Physical Education, Recreation & Dance.

American Alpine Club, Inc., The
113 East 90th Street
New York, NY 10028

Table 10.1 *Continued . . .*

Membership, research, publications and technical training. Publishes: Accidents in North American Mountaineering.

American Camping Association
Bradford Woods
Martinsville, IN 46151
(317) 293-7070

Professional organization for organized camping: camping standards, workshops, research, conferences, publications, training workshops and technical assistance. Publishes: Camping Magazine.

American Canoe Association (ACA)
P.O. Box 24B
Lorton, VA 22079

Programs, training clinics, instructor standards, membership and publications. Publishes: American Canoeist.

American Nature Study Society
R.D. 1
Homer, NY 13077
(607) 749-3655

Conferences, workshops, publications and technical assistance. Publishes: Nature Study.

American Red Cross
National Headquarters
P.O. Box 37550
Washington, DC 20013

Training sessions, conferences, workshops, publications, audio-visual aids, aquatic schools, technical assistance and education packets.

American Youth Foundation
3460 Hampton Ave.
St. Louis, MO 63139
(314) 351-4456

Leadership training, program design and consulting services for Experiential Education programs.

American Youth Hostel, Inc.
Metropolitan New York Council
132 Spring Street
New York, NY 10012
(212) 431-7100

Publications, leadership training, membership, equipment, facilities and national and international travel programs in various outing sports, particularly bicycle touring in 27 national councils and 50 countries.

American Whitewater Affiliation
P.O. Box 1483
Hagerstown, MD 21740

Programs, training clinics, instructor training, membership and publications.

Appalachian Mountain Club
5 Joy Street
Boston, MA 02108
(617) 947-2220

Library, publications, technical assistance, education materials, conferences, training sessions, field study sites and public programs in Outdoor Recreation and Mountain Conservation. Publishes: Appalachia Bulletin & Appalachia Journal.

Association of Interpretative Naturalists
6700 Needwood Road
Derwood, MD 20855
(310) 948-8844

Conferences, workshops, technical assistance, membership, audio visual aids and publications. Publishes: Employment Opportunities.

Association for Environmental and Outdoor Education
915 West Dunne Avenue
Morgan Hill, CA 95037
(408) 779-6921

Workshops, technical assistance, conferences, and educational materials.

Association for Experiential Education
CU Box 249
Boulder, CO 80309
(303) 492-1547

Publications, regional and national conferences, workshops, membership, educational materials and employment information. Publishes: Journal of Experiential Education, Voyageur and Job Clearinghouse Newsletter.

Boys Scouts of America
1325 Walnut Hill Lane
Irving, TX 75062-12906

Outdoor opportunities for boys and young adults, resident camps, local troops, equipment and publications.

Christian Camping International
P.O. Box 646
Wheaton, IL 60187
(312) 462-0300

Membership, professional services, workshops, conferences and publications in Christian oriented organized camping. Publishes: Journal of Christian Camping.

Conservation Education Association
c/o Richard J. Myshak, President
Associate Director of Wildlife Resources
Fish and Wildlife Service
U.S. Department of the Interior
Washington, DC 20240

Conferences, membership, audiovisual aids and publications.

Christian High Adventure
2143 E. Locust
Montrose, CA 91401

Programs, services and leadership training in Outdoor Adventure Programs.

Conservation Foundation
1717 Massachusetts Avenue, N.W.
Washington, DC 20036
(202) 797-4326

Library, publications, conferences, workshops, internship program and technical assistance. Publishes: Conservation Foundation Newsletter.

Dynamy
57 Cedar Street
Worcester, MA

Educational programs, community service, outdoor activities, and field experience in Experiential Education.

Earthwatch
10 Juniper Road
P.O. Box 127
Belmont, MA 02178
(617) 489-3030

Conferences, workshops, technical assistance, publications, programs, and career training. Publishes: Earthwatch News.

Eastern Mountain Sports Climbing School, Inc.
Main Street
Conway, NH 03860
(603) 356-5433

Skill instruction in rock climbing, ice climbing, mountaineering and other outing sports.

Eastern Professional Ski Instructors of America (E.P.S.I.A.)
Plaza 7
Latham, NY 12110
(518) 783-1130

Training, certification, workshop, clinics, conferences; educational materials, research, public programs, publications and membership.

Educational Resource Information Center (ERIC)
Clearinghouse for Science, Math and Environmental Education
Ohio State University
1200 Chambers Road, Room 310
Columbus, OH 43212

Publications, research materials and audio visual aids.

Encounter Four
Butler County Community College
Butler, PA 16001
(414) 287-8711

Programs, services, leadership training and college credit for training in outdoor related activities.

Table 10-1 *Continued . . .*

Environmental Action
1346 Connecticut Avenue
Suite 731
Washington, DC 20036
(202) 833-1845

Publications, technical assistance, and educational materials. Publishes: Environmental Action.

Forest Service
U.S. Department of Agriculture
South Building, Room 3233
12th and Independence Avenue, S.W.
Washington, DC 2050
(202) 447-6605

Publications, conferences, workshops, audiovisual aids, regional offices, land management, recreational planning and technical assistance.

Foxfire Fund, Inc., The
Rabun, GA 30568

Programs, educational services, publications, technical assistance, funding and training in cultural journalism.

Friends of the Earth
530 7th Street, S.E.
Washington, DC 20003
(202) 543-4312

Publications, conferences, technical assistance and local action programs in national and international environmental conservation. Publishes: Not Man Apart Environmental News.

Greenpeace
Building E
Fort Mason
San Francisco, CA 94123
(415) 474-6767

Workshops, educational materials, publications and audiovisual aids on marine ecosystems.

Green Mountain Club, Inc.
P.O. Box 94
27 Center Street
Rutland, VT 05701
(802) 775-0495

Trail maintenance, training programs, consultation, facilities and publications.

Girl Scouts of America
830 Third Avenue
New York, NY 10022
(212) 940-7500

Outdoor and community opportunities for girls 6-16; resident camps, local troops, publications and equipment.

Hardscrabble Hill
Castine Road, Box 130
Orland, ME 04472
(207) 469-7112

A residential retreat and workshop center for women, special outdoor activities.

Hemlocks Outdoor Education Center
Jones Street
Amston, CT 06231
(203) 228-9496

Programs, services, workshops, and internships for participations, college students and professionals working with the handicapped.

Intercollegiate Outing Club Association (IOCA)
P.O. Box 101X Newcomb Hall
Charlottesville, VA 22903

Association of college and university outing clubs. Publications, research, technical assistance, membership and advocacy. Publishes: IOCA News.

International Mountain Climbing School, Inc.
P.O. Box 239
Conway, NH 03818
(603) 356-5287

Skill courses and leadership training in rock climbing, winter mountaineering, hiking and ice climbing.

Institute for Environmental Awareness
George Williams College
555-31st Street
Downers Grove, IL 60156

Programs, facilities, publications and leadership training in environmental awareness programs.

Institute for Environmental Awareness, Inc.
P.O. Box 821
Greenfield, MA 01302

Publications, workshops, residents facilities, programs and leadership training.

Institute for Environmental Education
8911 Euclid Avenue
Cleveland, OH 44106
(216) 791-1775

Workshops, seminars, training programs, publications and education materials.

Junior Maine Guide
North High Street
Bridgton, ME 04009
(207) 647-5278

Outdoor training, skill workshops and leadership training sponsored by the Maine Camp Directors Association.

Mountaineers, The
715 Pike Street
Seattle, WA 98101

Instructional course, workshops, publications, research, membership and technical assistance in outdoor pursuits, particularly backcountry medicine and safety. Publishes: Medicine for Mountaineering.

Mountain Safety Research, Inc.
South 96th at 8th Avenue South
Seattle, WA 98108

Outdoor equipment research and production, technical assistance, workshops, equipment and publications. Publishes: NSR Newsletter.

Mountain Rescue Association
P.O. Box 396
Akadena, CA 91001

Organization for the support and improvement of mountain rescue and safety. Membership, publications and tecnical assistance.

Mountain Rescue Council
P.O. Box 696
Tacoma, WA

Skill training workshops, consultation, educational materials, and publications in backcountry oriented safety and rescue.

Nantahala Outdoor Center, Inc.
Star Route, P.O. Box 68
Bryston City, NC 28713
(704) 488-2175

Outdoor adventure programs and services, equipment outfitters, leadership training, skill instruction, publications and women's skill courses.

National Association for Environmental Education
P.O. Box 4000
Troy, OH 45373
(513) 698-6493

Publications, conferences and workshops.

National Audubon Society Expedition
950 3rd Avenue
New York, NY 10022

Full academic year of field study and research; credits toward BA, BS or MA Degree.

National Center for Service Learning
806 Connecticut Avenue, N.W.
Room kk06-AE
Washington, DC 20525
(800) 424-8580

Programs and services for educators who coordinate student volunteers in community service projects. Publishes: Synergist.

National Commission on Resources for Youth
36 West 44th Street
New York, NY 10036
(212) 840-2844

Table 10.1 *Continued . . .*

Clearinghouse for youth participation programs in community service. Publishes: Resources For Youth.

National Humanistic Education Center
110 Spring Street
Saratoga Springs, NY 12866
(518) 946-2206

Programs, services, resource center, publications, facilities, workshops and technical assistance.

National Marine Education Association, Inc.
c/o Great Neck Public Schools
Great Neck, NY 11020

Publications, technical assistance, audiovisual aids, workshops and conferences in marine education and research.

National Organization for River Sports (NORS)
P.O. Box 6847
Colorado Springs, CO 80934
(303) 473-2466

Membership, publications, conventions, river festivals, lobby and advocacy work, research discount at equipment outfitters. Publishes: Currents.

National Parks and Conservation Association
1701 18th Street, N.W.
Washington, DC 20009
(202) 265-1717

Publications, conferences, workshops, technical assistance, facilities, conferences, workshops and professional training: National Environmental Education Development (NEED).

National Outdoor Leadership School (NOLS)
Box AA
Lander, WY 82520
(307) 332-4381

Outdoor adventure programs, leadership training, college credit and field sites.

National Recreation and Parks Association
3101 Park Center Drive
Alexandria, VA 22302
(703) 820-4940

Publications, conferences, workshops, memberships, training and technical assistance in local, county and state recreation services. Publishes: Parks & Recreation.

National Society for Internships and Experiential Education (NSIEE)
810 18th Street, N.W., Suite 307
Washington, DC 20006
(202) 331-1516

Publications, conferences, workshops, technical assistance consultation, membership and research. Publishes: Experiential Education.

National Ski Patrol System
National Nordic Advisor
2901 Sheridan Boulevard
Denver, CO 80214

Service organization for the promotion of safe nordic skiing. Nordic ski clinics, First Aid and emergency care, publications and membership. Publishes: The Ski Patroller's Manual.

National Wildlife Federation
1412 16th Street, N.W.
Washington, DC 20036
(202) 797-6800

Outdoor Education Programs, publications, internships, field study centers and educational materials. Publishes: National Wildlife: Conservation Directory.

New England Orienteering Club, Inc.
Garrison House
Sudbury, MA 01776
(617) 443-8502

Organization and support of the orienteering: clinics, workshops, equipment and publications.

New Games Foundation
P.O. Box 7901
San Francisco, CA 94120
(415) 664-6900

Training programs, conferences, programs, consultation, presentation, leadership training and publications and play sessions.

Northfield Mountain Environmental Center
RR 1 P.O. Box 377
Northfield, MA 01360
(413) 659-3713

Environmental interpretation programs, skills workshops, educational programs, facilities (ski touring center), and publications.

Nova Scotia Outdoor Leadership Development Program
c/o Nova Scotia Department of Culture, Recreation and Fitness
P.O. Box 864
Halifax, Nova Scotia, Canada B3J 2V2

Outdoor leadership training in the skills and abilities of outdoor programs.

Office of Environmental Education
U.S. Department of Education
110 Donohoe Building
400 Sixth Street, S.W.
Washington, DC 20202
(202) 245-9231

Funding, workshops, educational materials, career information and publications.

Outdoor Center of New England, Inc.
8 Pleasant Street
Millers Falls, MA 01349
(413) 659-3926

Skill workshops, training clinics, leadership training, publications, audiovisual aids, public programs, consultation and equipment outfitter, specialists in white-water canoeing.

Publishes: Recreational Whitewater Canoeing.

Outdoor Leadership Training Seminars
2220 Birch Street
Denver, CO 80207
(303)333-7831

Workshops and graduate level credit in outdoor leadership.

Outdoor Women's School, The
2519 Cedar Street
Berkeley, CA 94708
(415) 848-5189

Wilderness programs, and skill instruction for women.

Outward Bound Canada
P.O. Box 550
Winona, Ontario, Canada L0R 2L0

Outward Bound programs, professional training, college credit programs and community services. Two schools: The Canadian Outward Bound Mountain School and the Canadian Outward Bound Wilderness School.

Outward Bound, Inc.
384 Field Point Road
Greenwich, CT 06830
(203) 661-0797

Programs, services, publications, research, leadership training, teachers practicum, college credit, and regional OB schools.

Outward Bound Schools
Dartmouth Outward Bound Center
P.O. Box 50
Hanover, NH 87501

Hurricane Island Outward Bound School
P.O. Box 429
Rockland, ME 04841

Colorado Outward Bound School
945 Pennsylvania Street
Denver, CO 80203

Minnesota Outward Bound School
308 Walker Avenue
Wayzata, MN 55391

Table 10.1 *Continued . . .*

North Carolina Outward Bound School
P.O. Box 817
Morgantown, NC 28655

Pacific Crest Outward Bound School
1001 S.W. Bancroft
Portland, OR 97201

Project Adventure, Inc.
P.O. Box 157
Hamilton, MA 01936

Training workshops, publications, design and construction of adventure facilities, educational materials, and consultation. Publishes: Cowstails and Cobras: Project Adventure Guide.

Sargent Camp Environmental Studies Center
Boston University
Peterborough, NH 03458

Adventure programs, resident facilities, staff training, internship program and consultation.

School of Field Studies
50 Western Avenue
Cambridge, MA 02139
(617) 497-9000

International research and field study programs in environmental studies: college credit available.

SEA Education Association (SEA)
P.O. Box 6
Woods Hole, MA 02543

Undergraduate credits and training workshops in ocean related study and research.

Sierra Club
530 Bush Street
San Francisco, CA 94118
(415) 981-8634

Publications, conferences, workshops, exhibits, membership, educational programs, audiovisual aids, and career information for protection of nation's forests, waters, wildlife and wilderness. Publishes: Sierra Club Books.

Solo—Stonehearth Open Learning Opportunities
RFD 1, P.O. Box 163
Tasker Hill
Conway, NH 03818
(603) 447-6711

Skill workshops and leadership training in backcountry activities, focus upon emergency medicine and rescue procedures.

Student Conservation Association
P.O. Box 550
Charleston, NH 03603
(603) 826-5206

Publications, internships, work projects and educational programs in conservation and forestry.

Touch of Nature Environmental Center
Southern Illinois University
Carbondale, IL 62901
(618) 457-0348

Supervised internships, leadership training and programs in Outdoor and Experiential Education.

Treeline, Inc.
P.O. Box 488
Middleton, MA 01949
(617) 774-6536

Programs, skill workshops, leadership training, adventure facilities design and construction, technical assistance and consultation.

United Nations Environment Programme
United Nations
Room A-3630
New York, NY 10017
(212) 754-8093

Publications, audiovisual aids, conferences, workshops and educational packets in international environmental education. Publishes: Connect: UNESCO-UNEP Environmental Education Newsletter.

United States Canoe Association
6338 Homer Road
Indianapolis, IN 46260

Programs, training clinics, membership and publications.

Urban Adventures
331 West 25th Street
New York, NY

Programs, services, skill training in urban Experiential Education and outing sports.

Wilderness Society
1901 Pennsylvania Avenue, N.W.
Washington, DC 20006
(202) 828-6600

Publications, conferences, workshops, membership, educational materials, programs, technical assistance. Publishers: Wilderness Report.

Wilderness Use Education Association
P.O. Box 1121
Lander, WY
(800) 443-4040

Leadership training, wilderness programs and technical assistance and workshops.

Women in the Wilderness, Inc.
Building 201 Fort Mason
San Francisco, CA 94123
(415) 556-0560

Outings, expeditions, publications, skills training, educational programs and membership for women. Publishes: Woman in the Wilderness Quarterly.

Women Outdoors, Inc.
474 Boston Avenue
Medford, MA 02155
(617) 628-2525

Network of environmentally concerned women; wilderness activities, membership, workshops, and technical assistance. Publishes: Women Outdoors Magazine.

Woodswomen
3716 Fourth Avenue South
Minneapolis, MN 55409
(612) 823-1900

Outdoor skill workshops, courses, trips and programs for women of all ages and experience.

Colleges and Universities

Selected colleges and universities offering advanced degrees and special programs related to Outdoor Program Leadership.

Antioch/New England
Graduate School
Roxbury Street
Keene, NH 03431

MS Environmental Studies and Resource Management and Administration.

Arizona State University
Dept. of Leisure Services
204 Dixie Gammage Hall
Tempe, AZ 85281

BS, MS Recreation; Outdoor Recreation option.

Bemidji State University
Center for Environmental and Outdoor Education
P.O. Box 44 Memorial Hall
Bemidji, MN 56601

BS Community Service; Environmental/Outdoor Education emphasis. BS Communication Media; Environmental Interpretation emphasis. MA Environmental Studies; MS Environmental and Outdoor Education.

Boston University
Leisure Studies Program
School of Education
Boston, MA 02215

BS, MS, Cert. of Ad. Graduate Study, DEd in Education; Environmential/Outdoor Education option.

California State University-Northridge
Dept. of Rec. and Leisure Studies
Darby Annex 107
Northridge, CA 91330

BS, MS Recreation and Leisure Studies; Outdoor Recreation Resources with camping and outdoor recreation emphasis.

Table 10.1 *Continued . . .*

Central Michigan University
Dept. of Recreation and Park Admin.
Mt. Pleasant, MI 48859

BS, BA Recreation and Parks; MS Outdoor Recreation and Field Biology; Outdoor and Environmental Recreation emphasis.

Central Missouri State University
Dept. of Recreation
Room 201, Education Bldg.
Warrensburg, MO 64093

BS, MS Recreation and Leisure Services; Outdoor Education and Recreation options.

College of Notre Dame
Office of Graduate Studies
1500 Ralston Avenue
Belmont, CA 94002

MEd Outdoor Education and Environmental Education

Clemson University
Dept. of Recreation and Park Administration
263 Lehotsky Hall
Clemson, SC 29631

MRPA (Masters of Rec. and Park Admin.): Environmental Interpretation emphasis.

Drake University
Recreation and Leisure Studies
Bell Center
Des Moines, IA 50311

BSE, MS Physical Education and Recreation; Outdoor Education and Camp Administration emphasis.

Earlham College
P.O. Box 87
Richmond, IN 47374

BA Independent major in Outdoor Education.

Evergreen State College, The
LAB 1
Olympia, WA 98505

BA Degree; Experiential Education emphasis.

Eastern Washington University
Dept. of Recreation
Cheney, WA 99004

MS College Instruction; Outdoor Recreation Education emphasis.

George Williams College
Department of Recreation
555 31st Street
Downers Grove, IL 60515

MA, MS Recreation; Outdoor, Environmental Education emphasis.

Greenfield Community College
Outdoor Leadership Program
Greenfield, MA 01301

AA Recreation Leadership and Leisure Services; Outdoor Recreation emphasis. Year-long competency-based Outdoor Leadership certification program.

Indiana University
Alternative Schools Teacher Education Program
School of Education 337
Bloomington, IN 47401

MS Education; Secondary or Elementary; Resident Teacher option.

Indiana University
Dept of Recreation and Park Admin.

BS, MS, Re. Dir., Re. D (Doctorate) Recreation; Outdoor Recreation and Camping emphasis.

Keene State College
Operation L.I.V.E.
Keene, NH 03431

BS, BA, BSEd; Modified Outward Bound programs and experiential learning emphasis.

Kent State University
Recreation Unit
Memorial Gym Annex
Kent, OH 44242

BS Recreation and Leisure Services; MS Physical Education (Rec. emphasis); Recreation option.

Lewis and Clark College
Director of Graduate Studies
Portland, OR 97219

MA Teaching-Secondary and Elementary; experiential learning options.

Michigan State University
Learning and Evaluation Services
1 Morrill Hall
East Lansing, MI 48824

Credit for out-of-class experiential learning.

Murray State University
Center for Environmental Education
Murray, KY 42071

MEd Environmental Education emphasis.

Murray State University
Dept. of Recreation and Physical Education
Murray, KY 42071

BS, MS Recreation and Leisure Services; Outdoor Recreation and Education emphasis.

Mankato State University
P.O. Box 52 Armstrong Hall
Mankato, MN 56001

MA Experiential Education; outdoor oriented practicums and workshops.

Michigan State University
Dept. of Park and Recreation Resources
131 Natural Resources Building
East Lansing, MI 48824

BS, MS, PhD Park and Recreation Resources; Interpretation emphasis.

North Carolina State University
Dept. of Recreation Resources Admin.
4008 Biltmore Hall
Raleigh, NC 27650

BS, MS Interpretation.

North Country Community College
29 Winona Avenue
Saranac Lake, NY 12983

AA Wilderness Recreation Leadership.

North Dakota University
HPERA, Leisure Services and Community Recreational Services
Fargo, ND 58105

BS, BA Leisure Studies and Community Recreational Services; MS MEd Education; Outdoor Recreation emphasis.

Northeastern University
Dept. of Recreation and Leisure Studies
Boston-Bouve College, 3-Dockser Hall
360 Huntington Avenue
Boston, MA 02115

*BS, MS Recreation and Leisure Studies; Outdoor Recreation/*Environmental Education concentration.

Northern Illinois University
Outdoor Teacher Education
Taft Field Campus, Box 299
Oregon, IL 61061

MS, MA, EdD Outdoor Education.

Oklahoma State University
Dept. of Leisure Services
Colvin Center
Stillwater, OK 74078

BS Recreation; MS Health, Physical Education and Leisure; EdD Higher Education; Outdoor Recreation option.

Ohio State University
Larkins Hall
Columbus, OH 43210

MS, MA Outdoor Education specialization.

Oregon State University
Resource Recreation Management
108 Peavy Hall
Corvallis, OR 97331

BS Resource Recreation Management; Outdoor Recreation and Interpretation option; MS Outdoor Recreation Management.

Table 10.1 *Continued . . .*

Prescott Center College
220 Grove Avenue
Prescott, AZ 86301

BA, Experiential Education option.

Pennsylvania State University, The
Recreation and Parks Dept.
University Park, PA 16802

BS, MS, PhD Recreation Service; Outdoor Education and Interpretive Services emphasis.

Radford University
Dept. of Recreation and Leisure Services
Box 5736
Radford, VA 24142

BS, BA, MS Recreation Administration; Outdoor Education/Recreation option.

San Francisco State University
School of Education
1600 Holloway Avenue
San Francisco, CA 94132

MA Education; ECO Education concentration.

Slippery Rock College
Dept. of Parks and Recreation
101 Elsenberg Classroom Building
Slippery Rock, PA 16057

BS, Environmental Education; MEd Environmental Education Administration.

Southern Connecticut State College
Dept. of Rec. and Leisure Studies
501 Crescent Street
New Haven, CT 06515

MS, Recreation and Leisure Studies; Outdoor Education emphasis.

Southern Illinois University at Carbondale
Dept. of Recreation
408 West Miller Street
Carbondale, IL 62901

BS, MS Education with major in Recreation; Outdoor Recreation option.

Springfield College
Recreation and Leisure Services Dept.
Springfield, MA 01109

BS, MEd Recreation and Leisure Services; Resource Management option.

St. Louis University
Department of Education
DuBourg Hall
221 N. Grand Blvd.
St. Louis, MO 63103

BS, BA Undergraduate Teacher Education; Outdoor Adventure and Experiential Education components.

State University of New York at Buffalo
Department of Instruction
582 Baldy Hall
SUNY at Buffalo
Amherst, NY 14260

MEd Urban Education; Outdoor /Experiential Education emphasis.

University of Colorado
School of Education, Room 116
Boulder, CO 80309

MA Education; Experiential Education Program.

University of Georgia, The
Dept. of Recreation and Leisure Studies
No. Peabody Hall
Athens, GA 30602

BS, MEd, MS, EdS, EdD Recreation and Leisure Services; Outdoor Recreation emphasis.

University of Illinois at
Urbana-Campaign
Dept. of Leisure Studies
104 Huff Gym, 1206 S. Fourth St.
Campaign, IL

BS, MS, PhD Leisure Studies; Outdoor Recreation option.

University of Illinois-Chicago
College of Education
Box 4348
Chicago, IL 60680

BA, Experiential Education focus.

University of Maryland
Dept. of Recreation
College Park, MD 20742

BS, MA and PhD Recreation; Outdoor Recreation and Interpretative Services options.

University of Minnesota
Recreation, Park and Leisure Studies
203 Cooke Hall
1900 University Ave., S.W.
Minneapolis, MN 55455

MA, MEd Recreation, Park and Leisure Studies, PhD Education; Outdoor Recreation option.

University of Montana
Recreation Management
Science Complex 412
Missoula, MO 59812

BS, MS Recreation Management; Outdoor Recreation Program Services and Resources Management options.

University of New Hampshire
Department of Education, Morrill Hall
Durham, NH 03824

MAT, MEd Education; Internship and Experiential Education components.

University of Northern Colorado
Recreation Dept.
Gunter Hall
Greely, CO 80639

BS, MA EdD Recreation; Outdoor Recreation emphasis.

University of Oregon
Dept. of Recreation and Park Management
Eugene, OR 97403

BS, BA, MS, MA, EdD, PhD Recreation and Park Management; Outdoor Recreation and Education graduate option.

University of Southern Alabama
Dept. of HPERLS
307 University Blvd.
Mobile, AL 36688

BS, MS Leisure Services; Outdoor Recreation Resource Management option.

University of Utah, The
College of HPER, Division of Leisure Studies
Salt Lake City, UT 84112

BS, MS Leisure Studies; EdD, PhD Health, Physical Education and Recreation with Leisure emphasis.

University of Vermont
Recreation Management Program
16 Colchester Ave.
Burlington, VT 05401

BS Recreation Management; MS Natural Resource Planning; Public and Private Outdoor Recreation options.

University of Wyoming, The
Dept. of Recreation and Park Administration
Box 3402 University Station
Laramie, WY 82071

BS, MS Recreation and Leisure Studies; Outdoor Recreation Management option.

Wayne State University
Dept. of Recreation and Park Services
259 Matthaei Bldg.
Detroit, MI 48202

BS, MS Recreation and Park Service; Outdoor Recreation option.

Webster College
Education Department
470 E. Lockwood
St. Louis, MO 63119

MAT Education; Outdoor Adventure and Experiential Education components.

Western Kentucky University
Dept. of Physical Education and Recreation
Bowling Green, KY 42101

BS, MS Recreation; Outdoor Recreation emphasis.

William Penn College
Human Relations and Psychology
Oskaloosa, IA 52577

BA Human Relations and Psychology; minor in Environmental studies or Recreation.

Non-Traditional Programs

Selected non-traditional, self-directed degree and training programs.

Beacon College
Academic Office
14 Beacon Street
Boston, MA 02108

AA, BA, MA self-directed degree program; Outdoor Leadership Education and Experiential Education options.

Friends College
Plover Lane
Huntington, NY 11743

BA Interdisciplinary Liberal Arts; Experiential in nature, world-wide in scope.

Florida International University
External Degree Program
Miami, FL 33199

BA, BS School of Education, Arts and Sciences, Public Affairs and Services.

Goddard College
1757 S. Street N.W.
Washington, DC 20009

MA Human Services; self-directed study projects.

Governor's State University
BOG Degree Program, G.S.U.
Park Forest, IL 60466

Board of Governor's BA Degree

Hispanic International University
900 Lovett Suite 103
Houston, TX 77006

BA, BS in various fields of the Liberal Arts, self-directed learning.

Metropolitan State University
Metro Square Building
7th and Robert Street
St. Paul, MN 55101

BA Competency-based program for adult community.

Nova University
3301 College Avenue
Fort Lauderdale, FL 33314

National External Master's program for Child Care Administrators.

Union Graduate School
The Union for Experimenting Colleges and Universities
2331 Victory Parkway
Cincinnati, OH 45206

PhD, Individually designed program.

University of Alabama
New College External Degree Program
P.O. Drawer CD
University, AL 35486

BA, BS, Interdisciplinary Degree for persons over 21 years.

University of Massachusetts
Amherst, MA 01002

BS, BA University Without Walls (UWW) and Baccalaureate Degree in Individual Concentration (BDIC) Environmental Education option.

University Without Walls
Union of Experimenting Colleges and Universities.
2331 Victory Parkway
Cincinnati, OH 45206

BS, BA Consortium of colleges and universities offering individualized degree programs. Check your region for institutions with UWW options. Experiential Leadership options have been used.

A typical curriculum with an outdoor adventure pursuits orientation would include courses in outdoor skills (e.g., rock-climbing, orienteering, or camping), leadership training (including first-aid, decision making, and group dynamics) and outdoor recreation management. With respect to outdoor recreation management, emphasis is often placed on land management agencies such as the Forest Service or National Park Service, trail maintenance, and visitor management. Hendee and Roggenbuck (1984) have reported that 642 courses in universities or colleges within the United States offer curricula with a wilderness-based orientation. As illustrated in Table 6.1, the majority of these courses are based in physical education, recreation, or education departments. These data do not even represent the substantial number of courses that are labeled outdoor education or other similar terms. Clearly, as a primary or complementary subject, outdoor adventure pursuits draw the interest of a substantial number of students with activities based in a number of college departments and programs. In sum, as a discipline, outdoor adventure pursuits becomes an arrangement of the facts and understandings related to a specialized body of knowledge (O'Morrow, 1980).

Development of a discipline is not enough, however; to remain a viable benefit to society there must be an organized effort to train new members, discover new knowledge in the discipline, and promote leaders. It is at this point that a field becomes a discipline and a discipline develops into a profession.

Recently, outdoor adventure pursuits has been likened to a profession. For many, this has been a desirable trend, with Ewert (1987) reporting that a selected number of outdoor instructors and administrators of outdoor programs indicated that several components constituting a profession will increase. These components include certification of the instructors, accountability of programs, and the professionalization of the instructor corps. Even if the practitioners of a field, such as outdoor adventure pursuits, predict a growing trend toward professionalization, a profession will not develop unless there is a critical need or value perceived by society. Typical values that have evolved in this society are related to health, justice, or spiritual issues. The critical values which can be addressed by outdoor pursuits are the health, welfare, education, and personal development of the individual user. While professions are but one way to control a critical function, they are best suited to protecting society from incompetent persons or those deficient in character or integrity (Wenker, 1984). A number of criteria which can be used to define a profession are listed in Table 10.2. Many of these criteria for a profession can be applied to outdoor adventure pursuits. Those applicable to this field are discussed below.

TABLE 10.2
Criteria for a Profession

- A profession must satisfy an indispensable social need and be based upon a well-established and socially accepted scientific principle. Many of these principles were discussed in the previous section on models and theories of outdoor adventure pursuits.
- It must provide a guarantee of competence through training, extended educational preparation, and a demonstration of predetermined level of ability and/or judgment.
- It must utilize a body of specialized knowledge and skills which are systematically collected and not possessed by the public.
- It must have developed a body of literature and tested information.
- It should have the responsibility for establishing its own goals and responsibilities in relationship to meeting its commitment toward the needs of society and the roles of other professions.
- It must have a culture which promotes an organization that maintains an autonomy of judgment over its members and develops a set of ethical standards and practices.

INDISPENSABLE SOCIAL NEED

As mentioned previously, these indispensable social needs include the health and welfare of the users. Just as the airline industry has a professional pilots association to safeguard the public, a profession in outdoor pursuits could be formed around the principles of providing effective and safe leaders for the outdoor user. In addition, the provision of enjoyable and socially acceptable forms of recreation is an increasingly important need felt by our highly urbanized population. The growing importance of this recreational "need" was recently documented in the findings of the recently completed President's Commission on Americans Outdoors (1987). This report stated that while the vast majority of Americans are now urban dwellers, almost 80 percent of the American public consider themselves to be outdoors people (PCAO, 1987).

GUARANTEE OF COMPETENCE

With the advent of the Wilderness Education Association in the 1970s, the issue of competency assessment became a heated topic in outdoor adventure pursuits. The issue has revolved around who will certify, what will they certify, and what will a certification actually do. While certification of competence will be covered in greater depth later in this section, it should be noted that it (certification) is but one of a number of avenues available for guaranteeing competency. Toward this end, conferences, entry requirements, ongoing research activities and training programs, journals, and more informal controls such as reputation and a personal exchange of information, serve as gatekeeping devices in any profession, including outdoor adventure pursuits. While the concept of certification of either the outdoor user or the outdoor instructor/leader has continued to be bogged down in controversy, there are currently a wide variety of training programs (e.g., SOLO, Wilderness First-Responder, NOLS, National Training Institute for Outward Bound, WEA) in outdoor adventure pursuits. In addition, conferences such as those of the Association of Experiential Education, American Camping Association, Canadian Alliance of Health, Physical Education, Recreation and Dance (CAHPERD), and New York State Outdoor Education Association (NYOEA) serve as meeting places for the sharing of information. Table 10.3 presents a partial listing of the salient organizations and journals/periodicals which distribute information relative to competencies in the field of outdoor adventure pursuits.

TABLE 10.3
Representative Institutions and Periodicals Featuring Outdoor Adventure Pursuits

Institutions	Periodicals/Journals
Association of Experiential Education	Journal of Experiential Education
American Alliance of Health, Physical Education, Recreation and Dance	Camping Magazine
American Camping Association	Journal of Physical Education and Recreation
American Alpine Club	Parks and Recreation
Canadian Alliance of Health, Physical Education, Recreation and Dance	Therapeutic Recreation Journal
National Outdoor Leadership School	Journal of Leisure Research
Outward Bound	Leisure Sciences
Project Adventure	Adventure Education Journal
Scouting USA	Bradford Papers Annual
National Association of Recreation and Parks	Journal of Forestry
	Adventure Education and Outdoor Leadership

BODY OF SPECIALIZED KNOWLEDGE AND SKILLS

Closely aligned with a guarantee of competence is the presence of a body of specialized knowledge and skills relative to that profession. Wenker (1984) reports that, because the average layperson does not have the knowledge to recognize competence, the laws of the marketplace or political process are too slow to preclude the potential for serious harm before the incompetent person can be removed or trained. Accordingly, the knowledge held by a profession involves those related to specific skills, theoretical information, and societal awareness. What distinguishes professions from trades is that professional skills and knowledge arise from an organized and systematically developed body of information which is built around theories and models rather than simply past experience. Moreover, societal awareness implies a cognizance of how and when specific skills should be provided and what role that profession plays in the broader context of the society it serves.

Kalisch (1979) suggests that the outdoor instructor assumes a variety of roles including skills trainer, program designer, translator, group facilitator, and counselor. Desired skills and competencies of outdoor instructors/leaders has been a topic of a number of recent research studies. Several competencies have emerged, which are listed in Table 10.4.

TABLE 10.4
Reported Competencies of Outdoor Leaders

An Outdoor Leader Should Be Competent In:					
McAvoy 1978	Green 1981	Swiderski 1981	Buell 1983	Ewert/ Johnson 1983	Priest 1987
Decision making	Analyzing risks	Outdoor techniques	Evaluation	Judgment	Judgment
Judgment	Judgment	Navigation	Outdoor skills	Outdoor skills	Awareness empathy
Outdoor skills	Risk management	Shelter construction	Human development	Human resource management	Teaching
Group interaction	Minimum impact	Clothing/ equipment	Safety	Medical skills	Group management
Safety administrative skills	First-aid		Program planning	Personality	Problem solving
			Environmental ethics		
			Instructorship		
			Philosophical foundations		

As can be seen, the "ideal" outdoor instructor/leader must possess a wide and often divergent collection of skills and knowledge to do his or her job. In addition, corresponding to this specialized body of knowledge is a developing jargon specific to the field of outdoor adventure pursuits. This jargon or language has evolved around the activities in outdoor adventure pursuits; examples are provided in Table 10.5.

TABLE 10.5
Terms Specific to Outdoor Adventure Pursuits

"Friends"	Tri-cam	RURP
Hero loop	Munter hitch	Bachman knot
Smearing	Equalizing anchor	Arete
Gendarme	Adiabatic	Lenticular
Jumar	Adze	Thinsulate
Positive clearance	Quallofill	Koflach
HAPE	HACE	"Zipper"
Placement	Slidders	FIRES
Hexcentric	Front-pointing	French pointing
Couloir	Tether line	Footfangs
K-1	C-1	Throwbag
"Chicken loop"	Sweep	Sweeper
Keeper	Ferry	High Brace
Eskimo roll	"Z" pulley	Hypothermia
Cold-water immersion	"J" stroke	Keeper
Hydraulic	Strainer	Declination
Antidipticum	Positive error	Lensatic
Lava tube	Living cave	Drag bag
100-miler	Pannier	"Sentry"
Ripcord	Ram-Air	Opening shock
Transderivational search	Isomorphic	Transfer
Waxing theory	Telemark	Double poling
Destructive metamorphism	Fall line	Deposition zone
Ensolite	Thermarest	PTFE
A-frame	PIEPS	Quincy
Priorities of life	Rule of Three	Spinning
Ankling	Eddy out	Duffek
River right/left	Brake bar	Figure Eight
Initiative games	New Games	Traverse
Lie-back	Belay	Kernmantle
Counseling theories	Group dynamics	"Risky shift"
At-Pac	Downproofing	"J" Valve
Emergency swimming ascent	Nitrogen narcosis	Power fin
Solar still	Survival swimming	Line of sight
Tautline hitch	Wilderness first-aid	Guardia
Bollard	Environmental impact	No-impact camp
Naisbett's rule	Bearing	Slab avalanche
Prussik knot	"J" line	Lock step
One-third/Two-thirds Rule	Triangulation	Duffersitz

Just as terms used in law or medicine are, at best, esoteric to the layperson but very meaningful to the attorney or physician, the phrases provided in Table 10.5 are examples of an extensive list of terms that have relevance and meaning to the professional in outdoor adventure pursuits. At the very least, they represent a growing body of skills and knowledge that the professional outdoor adventurer needs to possess and use.

BODY OF LITERATURE AND TESTED INFORMATION

As can be seen in the previous example, the outdoor adventure pursuits professional is expected to possess a wide variety of skills and knowledge. Even greater importance is placed on these expectations and responsibilities when one considers that the health and welfare of the client, as for many other professions, is often at stake. This concern alone has created the need for even greater emphasis on the training and subsequent systematic sharing of information, as well as a heightened concern for proper risk-management systems.

While still in an early development stage, there is a growing body of literature that addresses the field of outdoor adventure pursuits on either a periodic or continuing basis. Periodicals for a general readership include *Backpacker, Back Country Wilderness Camping, Bike World, Cycling, Mountain, Outside, Underseas Journal, Outdoor Life, Nordic World, Response,* and *Ultra-Sport.* Academic and research-oriented journals which feature articles on outdoor adventure recreation include *Environmental Education, Experiential Education, Journal of Forestry, Leisure Science, Adventure Education, Leisure Research, Outdoor Education, Outdoor Recreation Research Journal, Park and Recreation Administration, Bradford Papers Annual,* and *Physical Education and Recreation.* Other similar periodicals are *Camping Magazine,* the *Outdoor Communicator, Recreation Research Review,* and *Trends.*

Textbooks and research collections currently used for outdoor adventure recreation consist of *Adventure Education: A Bibliography* (Thomas, 1986), *High Adventure Outdoor Pursuits* (Meier, Morash, and Welton, 1987), *Outdoor Adventure Activities for School and Recreation Programs* (Darst and Armstrong, 1980), *Outdoor Adventure and Self-Concept: A Research Analysis* (Ewert, 1983), *Outward Bound: A Reference Volume* (Shore, 1977), *Principles and Practices of Outdoor Environmental Education* (Ford, 1981), and *Administration of Outdoor Pursuits Programs* (Ford and Blanchard, 1985).

Consistent with this growing body of literature is a developing source of information which has been empirically tested and subjected to replication. While an overview of the research component of outdoor adventure pursuits has been presented in another chapter, there are currently a number of topics in outdoor adventure pursuits that have received research attention that has resulted in a growing body of knowledge within the profession. For example, the construct of self-concept has been a widely used and investigated issue. From this work, professionals in this field now know that a participant's self-concept is multidimensional in that a number of components such as past experience and feelings of self-efficacy are involved. In addition, research in outdoor adventure pursuits has suggested that the self-concept is resistant to change. Any changes from participating in a program or course are often short-lived unless there is a follow-up intervention and people come to outdoor adventure pursuits courses such as Outward Bound ready to change and indeed, expecting to change (Borstelman, 1970).

There are a number of other topics in which the outdoor adventure pursuits profession can now claim a body of tested knowledge. An example of these topics and what is known is illustrated in Table 10.6.

TABLE 10.6
Topics of Information Subjected to Empirical Investigation in Outdoor Pursuits

Topic	Status of Information[1]	Additional Comments
Self-concept	Substantial (7)	Most widely studied
Self-efficacy	Substantial (6)	Concept on which many programs are based
Experiential learning	Substantial (6)	A cornerstone when offering outdoor pursuits programs as part of education
Behavior modification	Moderate (5)	Often employed in juvenile delinquent and special population programs and courses
Processing experiences	Moderate (5)	Integral to achieving many other program goals such as self-concept development
Development of groups and the individual	Moderate (5)	Includes a variety of variables such as trust, compassion, and confidence
Sequencing/progression	Low-to-moderate (4)	Leads to effective course design
Transfer/generalization	Low (3)	High intuitive belief that experiences carry over to other life experiences but little empirical support at this time
Stress	Low(3)	Widely used program component but still needs further study

[1] Based on scale from 1 to 10, with 10 being highly developed and sophisticated and 1 implying a rudimentary understanding.

As can be seen, while still in a developmental state, there is a growing body of specialized and tested knowledge. With the increasingly sophisticated input of both practitoners and scholars of outdoor adventure pursuits, this body of knowledge will continue to grow in complexity and effectiveness.

PROFESSIONAL GOALS AND RESPONSIBILITIES

A profession is not just a collection of skilled, trained individuals performing services for society but also acts as an autonomous entity with a collective view toward those services and responsibilities. Indeed, many professions develop a culture that, in part, attempts to achieve commonality in both acceptance and practice by utilizing a code of ethics and accepted values. Documents such as the *Common Practices in Adventure Programming* (Johanson, 1984) provide examples of this trend. There are numerous related professions and concomitant organizations that have generated similar statements concerning standards of conduct, goals, and objectives of the profession and philosophies. Listed below are some examples of these statements.

> The NRPA [National Recreation and Park Association] serves as a powerful 'balance wheel' in the current environmental movement, with a strong commitment to people, NRPA is in a position of national leadership to define the policies that help assure the preservation of parks for people, not simply their preservation from people. NRPA's strong people-perspective is unique in this regard. (National Recreation and Park Association Membership Statement, 1986)

Objectives of the American Alliance for Health, Physical Education, Recreation and Dance

1. Professional growth and development—to support, encourage and provide guidance in the development and conduct of programs in health, leisure and movement-related activities which are based on the needs, interests and inherent capacities of the individual in today's society.
2. Communication—to facilitate public and professional understanding and appreciation of health, leisure and movement-related activities as they contribute toward human well-being.
3. Standards and guidelines—to further the continuous development and evaluation of standards within the profession for personnel and programs in health, leisure and movement-related activities.

In most cases, stated objectives and goals revolve around either a written or unwritten statement of philosophy concerning that particular profession. From this philosophical position flows the objectives, principles, strategies, and tactics of the profession. This concept is illustrated in the following diagram.

Selecting a Philosophical Position

PRINCIPLES

▼

FORMULATION OF OBJECTIVES

Long range (5 + years) Short range (immediate)

▼ ▼

STRATEGIES TACTICS

In this example, principles refer to matters of primary importance. Strategies suggest broad decisions for action and resource allocation. Tactics are plans for achieving immediate plans or goals.

Principles that can be considered appropriate for outdoor adventure pursuits include the following:

- People and the natural environment have intrinsic worth.
- That worth is independent of the evaluation by others.
- People can experience positive benefits from an interaction with the natural environment.
- Activities which occur in the natural environment utilizing direct experience and a variety of senses can be both educational and recreational.
- Success in outdoor adventure pursuits programs is measured by the satisfaction of the participant and the protection of the environment.
- Effective programs and experiences in outdoor adventure pursuits lead to positively affected individuals who will ultimately contribute to a better society.

Concomitant with these principles are the goals of outdoor adventure pursuits. While, in part, dependent on the setting (i.e., education-oriented program, purely a recreational endeavor, or a combination of both), a number of goals and expected outcomes have emerged which are common to most activities or programs. These outcomes and goals include the following.

1. To have intrinsically satisfying and rewarding educational or recreational experiences.
2. To increase one's self-image with respect to beliefs, attitudes, intentions toward behavior, and actual behaviors. In other words, one of the goals of outdoor adventure pursuits is to create opportunities in

which the participants feel good about themselves (i.e., more confident or capable) and turn those beliefs about self into positive actions toward others and the environment.

3. Related to the previous goal (number 2) is the development of sound environmental ethics and actions.
4. A heightened awareness and ability to conduct one's self safely in a new or different environment such as the outdoors.
5. The development of leisure skills which can be used throughout one's lifetime.
6. The provision of socially acceptable opportunities for personal testing, challenge, and risk taking.

From these goals and outcomes, a code of professional conduct can be developed which provides guidelines for professional behavior. The key word here is guidelines, since no effort is made or intended to regulate the behavior of the outdoor adventure pursuits professional. The code of professional conduct is based on the belief that there is intrinsic value and worth in both the environment and people which should be safeguarded.

CODE OF PROFESSIONAL CONDUCT IN OUTDOOR ADVENTURE PURSUITS

1. The principal objective of the outdoor adventure pursuit professional is to assist in the development of the individual, both educationally and with respect to the quality of his or her life, while promoting the environmentally sound use of the natural resources.
2. Professionals in outdoor adventure pursuits should strive to provide activities which are within the capabilities of both the participant and the staff and that are congruent with the stated objectives of the specific program.
3. Programs and activities should reflect accepted standards or practices currently in use within the field of outdoor adventure pursuits.
4. The professional should seek to protect against occurrences or impacts which are adversive or damaging to the participant, program, or environment.
5. The professional should conduct his or herself in a manner which reflects a high level of quality without abuse to the student/instructor relationship, particularly while engaged in a field setting.

Moving beyond this code of conduct, professional behaviors need to take into account a number of ethical and procedural issues. Hunt (1984, AEE Meeting) suggests that there are situational, relational, virtuous, and regulatory issues which should be considered by the outdoor pursuits professional. In turn, these issues impact individuals, groups, organizations, and the environment. These impacts and issues are illustrated in Figure 10.2.

FIGURE 10.2
Ethical/Procedural Issues

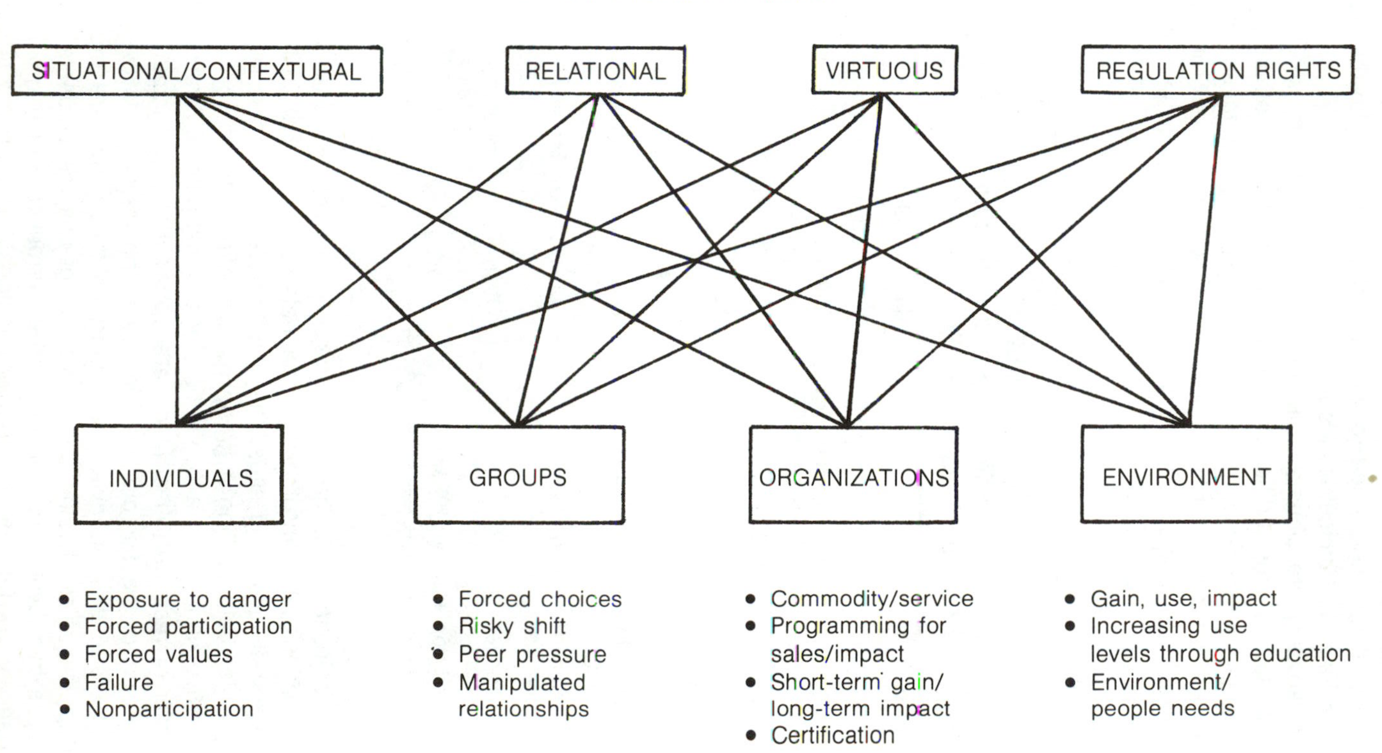

As can be seen from Figure 10.2, there are a number of issues that can impact the outdoor adventure situation. Both organizations and individual staff members need to assess each situation with respect to the professional and ethical issues involved.

Moreover, professionals in outdoor adventure pursuits are faced with a substantial number of differences in job settings when compared to more traditional occupations. Havens (1985) reports that these differences involve a number of variables, including time, ambient environment, level of supervision, and job longevity. These differences in job settings are illustrated in Table 10.7.

TABLE 10.7
Differences in Job Settings Between Outdoor and Traditional Professions[1]

Outdoor	Traditional
24-hour day	Usually 8:00 to 5:00 PM
Participants faced with environmental and risk-related circumstances	Clients usually in a controlled environment
Short term/little evaluation	Long term/formal evaluation
Remote setting—high, direct, and often solo responsibility	Team approach with accessible aid
Direct supervision limited	Direct supervision often available
Low pay with few fringe benefits	Higher pay, often with attractive benefits
Intermittent, often long absences from a home environment	Stable work/home environment
High turnover	Often life-long careers

[1] Modified from Havens (1985).

The point to this is not that outdoor professionals have an easier or more difficult job than other professionals but rather that their profession entails knowledge and situations that can be very demanding. Contrary to popular belief, taking a group on a backpacking trip or rafting down some river is not "fun and games" for the instructor but rather entails a number of responsibilities which are both serious and important for the well-being of the participants. Moreover, the instructor is usually faced with the same set of environmental circumstances that are impacting the group. If it rains, it rains on everyone, not just the students or clients. Despite this level of responsibility, the current rate of reimbursement is abysmally low for most outdoor professionals. In part, this is due to the public's level of understanding concerning what happens on an outdoor trip (e.g., people just going on a camping trip). The scholars and researchers in outdoor adventure pursuits have to assume some of the responsibility for this situation, as well, by not adequately identifying the benefits accrued to the public through participation in adventure activities.

Another factor creating this situation is the relative lack of systematic training regimes which are both visible to the public and rigorous. Toward this end, the issue of certification of the outdoor instructor/leader has emerged. The following section deals with that issue.

CERTIFICATION OF THE OUTDOOR PROFESSIONAL[1]

One does not have to look far to see the extent to which certification has developed in civilizations. Even without formalized diplomas, most civilizations have required certification, as exemplified by the ancient helmsman or soothsayer. More recently, the broader field of education has dealt with certification of primary and secondary teachers within the school systems. The American tradition of the outdoor camp has been subject to accreditation and, not ironically, greater scrutiny from both outside and within the camping movement (Mason, 1978).

With few exceptions, every profession maintains standards which must be met in order for an individual to practice that profession. Certification is one type of credentialing by which those standards have been upheld. Other forms of credentialing include licensure, registration, and accreditation. While similar in outcome, these methods differ in procedures and audience. More specifically, these terms can be defined as the following:

- *Certification*—recognition of an individual who has met certain predetermined qualifications specified by an agency or organization.
- *Licensure*—granting of permission to persons meeting certain requirements to engage in a given occupation.
- *Registration*—the process by which qualified individuals are listed on an official roster.
- *Accreditation*—recognition of a program or institution as meeting certain predetermined qualifications. (O'Morrow, 1980, p. 79)

As can be seen, certification is but one way in which established standards in the field of outdoor leadership can be maintained.

THE FORM OF OUTDOOR LEADERSHIP CERTIFICATION

Before examining what form certification of outdoor leaders will take, a few words on the concept of outdoor leadership may be in order. While

---

[1]This section has been adapted from an article that originally appeared as Certification of the Outdoor Leader: Analyzing the Possibilities. *Camping Magazine,* 57(6): pp. 16–19 (1985).

defined in several ways, the term "outdoor leadership" generally revolves around the areas of purposefully taking individuals/groups into the outdoors for recreation or education; teaching skills; problem solving; ensuring group/individual safety; judgment making; and facilitating the philosophical, ethical, and esthetic growth of participants (Ewert and Johnson, 1983). Other components of outdoor leadership include assisting the individual or group identify goals and objectives; utilizing specific action to achieve these goals; creating the opportunities for learning (Buell, 1983); and training new or less experienced outdoor instructors and leaders.

The literature surrounding outdoor "competencies" appears to be both cohesive and distinct. Various studies have suggested the existence of required competencies for effective outdoor leadership. These competencies were listed in Table 10.4.

Being able to both define outdoor leadership and dissect it into its various components elicits the question of which "form" certification should take. The concept of "form" is really what the certification controversy is all about. Many individuals may concede that certification is inevitable, but *how* that process will be accomplished is what is perceived as threatening.

Certification usually revolves around the components of programs and people. For example, a program can be stamped "qualified," implying that the staff within the program will deliver a safe, quality experience to the participants. The second approach, certifying individuals, carries the implication that whatever the program makeup, participants will receive a safe, quality experience because of the individual staff member. Merely looking at the potential method of certification does not complete the picture, as there is also a need to explore the possible pathways of each method. Credentialing programs (and their staff) might entail instituting certain training requirements with the organization coupled with periodic peer reviews and specific hiring requirements. Certifying individuals could be accomplished by attending a designated course(s), possessing certain experiential and educational backgrounds, an examination, or a combination of the above.[2] A certification scheme could include both programs and staffs.

Regardless of the format, the primary purpose will continue to be one of "quality control." Stated another way:

> Certification, in whatever form, is a means to ensure that only qualified people may systematically engage in the formal teaching and/or leading of individuals in the outdoor adventure situation.

Given that raison d'etre, the effectiveness of *any* certification plan must be judged by how effectively that screening takes place.

---

[2] For a brief treatise on this topic, see Green (1982).

A CURRENT ASSESSMENT

Having discussed the development and possibilities of certification, a look at some recent research studies may reveal how the profession actually *feels* about the certifying of its outdoor leaders. Today's answers to the questions of what, where, and how, and to what extent certification should be employed, will help shape the certification schemes of the future. While the literature is still scarce in this area, some studies have focused upon these issues and are listed in Table 10.8.

TABLE 10.8
Results of Studies in the Certification of Outdoor Leaders[1]

	Senosk 1977	Cousineau 1977	Ewert/ Johnson 1983	Priest 1987
Certification Support				
• YES	37.20	76.20	71.00	
• NO	48.60	13.80	20.00	
Reasons For Certification				
• Fewer accidents	7.00	Agreed[2]	34.00	• Positive experience
• Higher quality of leadership	46.00	Agreed	34.00	• Teaching skills
• Participant satisfaction	40.00	Agreed	23.00	• Reduce accidents
• Reduced insurance premiums		Disagreed	29.00	• Reduce environ mental damage
Acceptable Certifying Body				
• Governmental agency	19.60	Disagreed	9.00	• Program trainers
• Private organizations	48.00	Agreed	52.00	• Self
• Individual's agency		Agreed	14.00	• Outside experts
				• Peer leaders
Who Should Be Certified				
• Organizations		Disagreed	20.00	• Individuals
• Individuals		Agreed	20.00	
• Individuals for each specific subject/location	41.20	Agreed	17.00	
How Should Certification Be Accomplished?				
• Workshops/clinics	62.80	Agreed		• Field trips
• Life/field experience	62.80	Agreed	46.00	• Discussions
• University/college		Disagreed	46.00	• Lectures
• Private organizations	48.00	Disagreed	34.00	• Simulations
• Standardized exam	22.30	Agreed		• Role playing

[1] Percentage of respondents. For a more detailed account of each study, see individual document.
[2] The majority of respondents indicated this preference.

While much could be written about the validity of the studies cited in Table 10.8, some trends are discernible: support for certification, acceptable certifying bodies, and how certification should be accomplished. Obviously, more research in this area needs to be done; what is important is the fact that no one agency speaks for the area of outdoor leader certification.

SOME ADDITIONAL CONCERNS ABOUT CERTIFICATION

Before proposing a certification scheme for the future, some additional concerns surrounding certification need to be mentioned. Whatever method is eventually employed to certify outdoor leaders, a particularly vexing issue is that of the distance between the scheme, the consumer, and the candidate. This ultimately becomes a question of quality and usefulness. A certification scheme in outdoor leadership will suffer the same malady as other similar methods—a lengthening distance between the certification and the people using or benefiting from it. Hefferlin (1969), epitomizes this by his statement, "The evidence of history all points to the near inevitability of institutional inertia." What is needed is a systematic and reoccurring process through which the participants and staffs engaged in outdoor adventure can give input back into the certification process. Without this feedback, certification will become a one-way gate proclaiming quality but becoming ever more isolated from the public it serves.

A second item of concern is the very essence of certification. Will it be used to allow passage to the pastures of outdoor adventure on the basis of ability to lead or completion of a leadership course? Using Lierheimer's (1970) example, if there are two candidates, who should be allowed to lead an outdoor adventure group: the uncertified but highly capable instructor or the certified but less qualified individual? Certification must not become a constraining device that precludes all but those passing a prescribed sequence of courses or experiences regardless of competence or ability.

The third area of concern is that of delinking the separate functions of training and certification. If objectivity and credibility are to be maintained, it is ludicrous to have an agency involved in the training of outdoor leaders and also be involved in their certification (Cousineau, 1977). Delinking the two functions helps avoid the aura of self-serving interests, profiteering, and the "good ole boy" syndrome.

A WORKABLE MODEL

Having examined the myriad of possibilities and problems associated with certification, what are some solutions to the certification issue? Obviously, what we want as a profession is to avoid linking the outdoor student with an incompetent, unqualified outdoor leader. What is desired is an individual who is capable of working effectively with students; has enough outdoor, medical, and safety skills to meet the program's needs; displays good judgment; is environmentally astute; and is capable of working within the organization (administration skills). Some of these attributes can be objectively tested, for example, environmental ethics, safety procedures, and many outdoor skills. The *Accepted Peer Practices in Adventure Programming* (Johanson, 1984) and *Camp Staff Training Series* (Vinton and Farley, 1979) are examples of possible reference points from which exams could be constructed. The areas of student interaction and working within organizations could be determined by prior work experience. If work experience is lacking, then a probationary certification could be issued with the purpose of encouraging employment and the gaining of needed experience. The areas of judgment and decision making are more difficult to quantify but certainly not impossible. The military and emergency service organizations have been doing it for years. What is needed is to give a candidate an opportunity to display his or her judgment-making skills before a jury of selected observers. Sources such as Buell (1983) and Kalisch (1979) can be utilized as reference points from which to develop judgment-making and instructorship criteria. Ultimately, some body comprised of individuals representing a *variety* of outdoor adventure programs such as the A.E.E., N.O.L.S., O.B., Scouts USA, and so on, must serve as the summative evaluation point to issue, deny, or postpone certification of an individual. Figure 10.3 represents how this model might appear in graphic form.

As depicted in Figure 10.3, a candidate for outdoor leader certification would begin the process with or without a variety of attributes. These attributes would be looked at in three ways, that is, examination, experience, and/or a selected jury. Performance input from these three sources would then be used by the certifying body (supported through fees charged to participating individuals and agencies) to determine eligibility for certification. Periodic input would be sought from the public to ensure that the certification process is benefiting the consumer.[3] The comprehensive nature of the certifying board would help ensure that the certification process is responsive to the needs of the various agencies.

SOME FINAL COMMENTS

While we seem to be heading down the track toward certification, it is uncertain when we will arrive and what the station will look like. There are some who fear overregulation through certification, and feel some structuring now will probably lead to an overall reduction in restrictions later (Dustin and McAvoy, 1984). Similar to teacher certification (Dorros,

---

[3] See comments by Ray Smutek in Senosk (1977, p. 21).

FIGURE 10.3
Proposed Certification Model for Outdoor Leaders

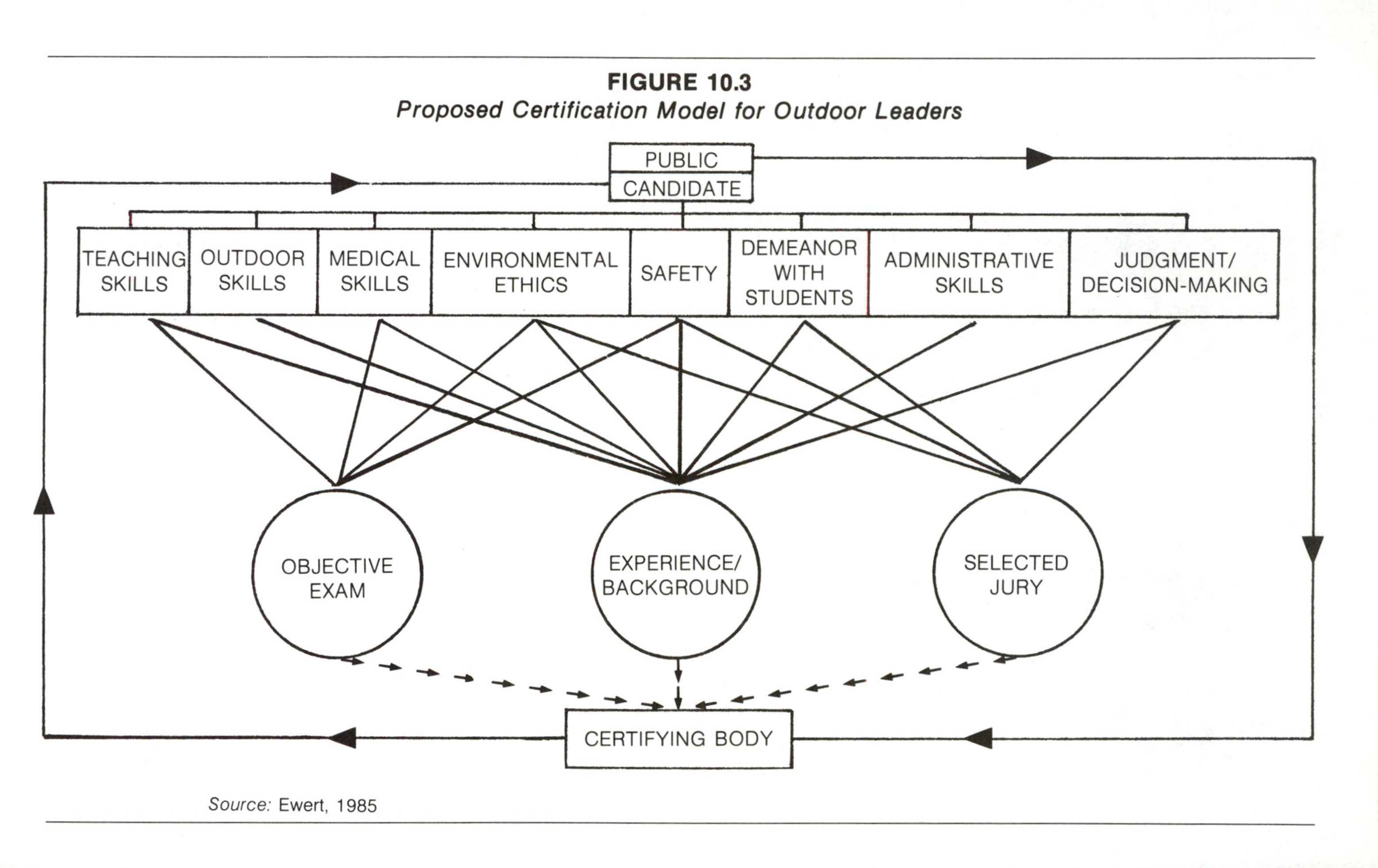

Source: Ewert, 1985

1968), the field of outdoor leadership must come to grips with the questions of control, quantity versus quality for required experiences, courses, and so on, and the issue of differing needs between agencies. With any certification scheme, procedures must be established to decertify incompetent leaders. The challenges surrounding the certification of outdoor leaders will be difficult to surmount. The process will be as important as the ultimate product. It may be true that whether and how we deal with this issue will be one way of measuring the vitality of the emerging profession of outdoor education.

In sum, we have examined the concept of professionalization in outdoor adventure pursuits from a variety of vewpoints. These viewpoints have included the distinction of a discipline, field, and profession; identified a number of outdoor leadership training centers; discussed the criteria for professionalization; and constructed a code for professional conduct. In addition, differences between the outdoor professional and other professions were discussed. Finally, the issue of certification of the outdoor instructor/leader was examined with a possible solution to the problem.

Because of the importance of conducting safe and rewarding programs in the outdoor environment, the field of outdoor pursuits can ill afford to hesitate much longer in more *effectively* establishing itself as a profession, the keyword being *effective* rather than *formal*. Formal professions such as the American Medical Association have been subject to much criticism for being more concerned with the profession than with the patient. Professionalizing involves setting guidelines, rules of conduct, and accepted procedures, all of which necessitate the formation of a bureaucracy. As it stands, organizations involved in outdoor adventure pursuits may not have the underpinning of a guiding professional institution but neither has a professional structure gotten in the way of meeting the needs and expectations of the participants. It is hoped that by examining where this field is in relation to becoming a profession, some of the pitfalls can be avoided with service to the individual participant always being a primary goal.

MAIN POINTS

1. Outdoor adventure pursuits can be considered a discipline, field, or profession.
2. Outdoor adventure consists of a mix of people, opportunities, and rewards.
3. There are a number of organizations and agencies that provide outdoor adventure activities.
4. There are a number of criteria which serve to define a profession, including satisfying an indispensable social need, a guarantee of competence, and utilizing a body of specialized knowledge.
5. Recently, there has evolved a growing body of literature and infor-

mation that has been subjected to empirical testing.

6. There are a number of principles that are appropriate for outdoor adventure pursuits. In addition, there are a number of goals for the outdoor adventure profession.
7. These goals and principles have led to the establishment of a code of conduct for the outdoor adventure professional.
8. Currently, there are a number of job-related differences between the outdoor and traditional professional.
9. Because of the big level of expertise demanded of the outdoor professional, certification of the outdoor leader has emerged as a widely discussed topic.
10. While certification is not likely to become a mandated provision in many outdoor areas, the discussion and emerging techniques directed toward this end will likely elevate the standards and expertise of the outdoor professionals.

REFERENCES

Borstelmann, L. (1970). Psychological Readiness for and Change Associated with the Outward Bound programs. North Carolina Outward Bound School. Morganton, NC: (Mimeographed).

Buell, L. (1983). *Outdoor Leadership Competency.* Greenfield, MA: Environmental Awareness Publications.

Cousineau, C. (1977). "A Delphi Consensus on a Set of Principles for the Development of a Certification System for Educators in Outdoor Adventure." Ph.D. Dissertation. Greeley, CO: University of Northern Colorado.

Darst, P. and Armstrong, G. (1980). *Outdoor Adventure Activities for School and Recreation Programs.* Minneapolis, MN: Burgess Publishing Company.

Dorros, S. (1968). *Teaching as a Profession.* pp. 48–56. Columbus, OH: Charles E. Merrill Publishing.

Dustin, D. and McAvoy, L. (1984). The Limitation of the Traffic Light. *Journal of Park and Recreation Administration,* 2(3): pp. 28–32.

Ewert, A. (1983). Outdoor Adventure and Self-Concept: A Research Analysis. Eugene, OR: Center of Leisure Studies, University of Oregon.

Ewert, A. (1987). Outdoor Adventure Recreation: A Trend Analysis. *Journal of Park and Recreation Administration,* 5(2): pp. 57–67.

Ewert, A. and Johnson, W. (1983). Outdoor Adventure Leadership: A Study of Current Issues Facing the Profession. *Proceedings: Intermountan Leisure Symposium,* pp. 53–56. Provo, UT: Brigham Young University.

Ford, P. (1981). *Principles and Practices of Outdoor/*Environmental Education. New York: John Wiley and Sons.

Ford, P. and Blanchard, J. (1985). *Leadership and Administration of Outdoor Pursuits.* State College, PA: Venture Publishing.

Green, P. (1981). The Content of a College-Level Outdoor Leadership Course for Land-Based Outdoor Pursuits in the Pacific Northwest: A Delphi Consensus. Ph.D. Dissertation. Eugene, OR: University of Oregon.

Green, P. (1982). *The Outdoor Leadership Handbook.* Tacoma, WA: The Emergency Response Handbook, pp. 25–28.

Havens, M. (1985). Ethical Challenges in the Outdoor Setting. *Therapeutic Recreation Journal.* 29(4): pp. 75–80.

Hefferlin, M.E. (1969). *Dynamics of Academic Reform.* San Francisco, CA: Jossey-Bass.

Hendee, J. and Roggenback, J. (1984). Wilderness-Related Education as a Factor Increasing Demand for Wilderness. Paper presented at the International Forest Congress Convention. Quebec City, CANADA.

Hunt, J. (1986). *Ethical Issues in Experiential Education.* Boulder, CO: Association for Experiential Education.

Johanson, K. M. (Comp.). (1984). *Accepted Peer Practices in Adventure Programming.* Boulder, CO: Association of Experiential Education.

Kalisch, K. (1979). *The Role of the Instructor.* Three Lakes, WI: Wheaton College.

Lierheimer, A. P. (1970). Changing the Palace Guard. *Phi Delta Kappan,* pp. 20–25.

Mason, J. (1978). Uncertain Outposts: The Future of Camping and the Challenge of Its Past. Bradford Woods, Martinsville, ID: American Camping Association.

McAvoy, L. (1978). Outdoor Leadership Training. *Journal of Physical Education and Recreation,* 49(4): pp. 42–43.

Meier, J.; Morash, J.; and Welton, G. (1987). *High Adventure Outdoor Pursuits,* 2d ed. Columbus, Ohio: Publishing Horizons, Inc.

O'Morrow, G. (1980). *Therapeutic Recreation: A Helping Profession,* p. 79. Reston, VA: Reston Publishing Company.

President's Commission on Americans Outdoors. (1987). *Americans and the Outdoors.* Washington, DC: Superintendent of Documents.

Priest, S. (1987). Preparing the Effective Outdoor Pursuits Leader. *Journal of Experiential Education* (in press).

Swiderski, M. (1981). Outdoor Leadership Competencies Identified by Outdoor Leaders in Five Western Regions. Ph.D. Dissertation. Eugene, OR: University of Oregon.

Senosk, M. E. (1977). An Examination of Outdoor Pursuit Leader Certification and Licensing within the United States in 1976. Master's Thesis. Eugene, OR: University of Oregon.

Shore, A. (1977). Outward Bound: A Reference Volume. Greenwich, CT: Topp Litho.

Thomas, S. (1986) *Adventure Education: A Bibliography.* Amherst, NY: Institute of Classroom Management and School Discipline at State University of New York at Buffalo.

Vinton, D. and Farley, E. (eds.). (1979). *Camp Staff Training Series.* Bradford Woods, Martinsville, ID: American Camping Association.

Wenker, K. (1984). *Foundations of Professional Morality.* Colorado Springs, CO: United States Air Force Academy.

BIBLIOGRAPHY

Abraham, H. (1970). *Psychological Aspects of Stress.* Springfield, IL: Charles C. Thomas.

Adams, W. (1970). Survival Training: Its Effects on the Self-Concept and Selected Personality Factors of Emotionally Disturbed Adolescents. *Dissertation Abstracts International, 1970–71,* 31, 388B.

Ajzen, I. and Fishbein, M. (1980). *Understanding Attitudes and Predicting Social Behavior.* Englewood Cliffs, NJ: Prentice-Hall.

Allen, S. (1980a). *Risk Recreation: Some Psychological Bases of Attraction.* Ph.D. Dissertation. University of Montana.

———. (1980b). Risk Recreation: A Literature Review and Conceptual Model. In J. Meier, T. Morash, and G. Welton (eds.). *High Adventure Outdoor Pursuits,* pp. 52–81. Columbus, OH: Publishing Horizons.

Arthur, M. (1976). The Survival Experience as Therapy: An Appraisal. *Journal of Leisurability,* 3(3): pp. 3–10.

Bacon, S. (1983). *The Conscious Use of Metaphor in Outward Bound.* Denver, CO: Colorado Outward Bound.

———. (1988). *Outward Bound and Troubled Youth.* Greenwich, CT: Outward Bound.

Bandura, A. (1977a). Self-Efficacy: Toward a Unifying Theory of Behavior Change. *Psychologist,* 37: pp. 122–147.

———. (1977b). Self-efficacy: Toward a Unifing Theory of Behavioral Change. *Psychological Review,* 84: pp. 191–215.

Barcus, C. and Bergeson, R. (1972). Survival Training and Mental Health: A Review. *Therapeutic Recreation Journal,* 6(1): pp. 3–8.

Bechtel, A. (1972). A Behavioral Comparison of Urban and Small Town Environments. In A. Berstein. Wilderness as a Therapeutic Behavior Setting. *Therapeutic Recreation Journal,* 4: p. 160.

Berlyne, D. (1960). *Conflict, Arousal, and Curiosity.* New York: McGraw-Hill.

Bertolami, C. (1981). *Effects of a Wilderness Program on Self-Esteem and Locus of Control Orientations of Young Adults.* ERIC Report No. 266 928.

Bischoff, G. (ed.). (1985). National Outdoor Outfitters Market Report. *National Outdoor Outfitters News,* 10(8): pp. 10–13.

———. (1987). Today's Outdoor Retailing Opportunities. *Trends,* 24(3): pp. 33–39.

Black, B. (1983). The Effect of an Outdoor Experiential Adventure Program on the Development of Dynamic Balance and Spatial Veering for the Visually Impaired Adolescent. *Therapeutic Recreation Journal,* 17(3): pp. 39–49.

Borstelmann, L. (1970). Psychological Readiness for and Change Associated with the Outward Bound Programs. North Carolina Outward Bound School. Morganton, NC: (Mimeographed).

Bowley, C. (1979). Motives, Management, Preferences of Crowding of Backcountry Hiking Trail Users in the Allegheny National Forest of Pennsylvania. Master's Thesis. Pennsylvania State University.

Brady, M. and Skjemstad, L. (1974). *Ski Cross-Country.* New York: Dial Press.

Brown, D. (1985). Eastern Whitewater: Opportunities for the Future. In J. Woods (ed.). *Proceedings: 1985 National Outdoor Recreation Trends Symposium II,* pp. 64–75. U.S. Department of the Interior, National Park Service, Southeast Regional Office, Atlanta, GA.

Bryan, H. (1979). *Conflict in the Great Outdoors.* Bureau of Public Administration, Sociological Studies No. 4. University, AL: University of Alabama.

Bucher, C. and Koenig, C. (1974). *Secondary School Physical Education.* St. Louis: C.V. Mosby Company.

Buell, L. (1983). *Outdoor Leadership Competency.* Greenfield, MA: Environmental Awareness Publications.

Bullaro, J. and Edginton, C. (1986). *Commercial Leisure Services.* New York: MacMillan.

Burke, J. (1985). *The Day the Universe Changed.* Boston: Little, Brown and Company.

Burton, L. (1981). A Critical Analysis and Review of the Research on Outward Bound and Related Programs. *Dissertation Abstracts International,* 42, 1581 B.

Byron, C. (1976). Fighting the Paper Chase. *Time,* November 23, p. 66 (1981).

Carney, R. (1971). *Risk-Taking Behavior.* Springfield, IL: Charles C. Thomas.

Cattel, R. (1968). Trait-View Theory of Perturbations in Ratings and Self-Ratings [L(BR)- and Q-data]: Its Application to Obtaining Pure Trait Score Estimates in Questionnaires. *Psychological Review,* 75: pp. 95–113.

Cave, S. and Rapoport, E. (1977). *The Wilderness Experience: A Conceptual and Theoretical Understanding.* Santa Fe, NM: New Mexico Department of Hospitals and Institutes.

Christy, F. (1970). Elements of Mass Demand for Outdoor Recreation Resources. In B. L. Driver (ed.). *Elements of Outdoor Recreation Planning,* pp. 99–103. Ann Arbor, MI: University of Michigan Press.

Clawson, M. (1985). Trends in Use of Public Recreation Areas. In *Proceedings: 1985 National Outdoor Recreation Trends Symposium II,* pp. 1–12. Atlanta, GA: National Park Service.

——— and Van Doren, C. (1984). *Statistics on Outdoor Recreation.* Washington, DC: Resources for the Future, Inc.

Clifford, E. and Clifford, M. (1967). Self-Concepts before and after Survival Training. *British Journal of Social and Clinical Psychology,* 6: pp. 241–248.

Cober, L. (1972). A Personality Factor Study of Participants in High Risk Sports. Master's Thesis. The Pennsylvania State University.

Coffin, J. (ed.). (1985). *Federal Parks and Recreation,* 3(24): p. 3. Washington, DC: Resources Publishing Company.

Colan, N. (1986). *Outward Bound: An Annotated Bibliography, 1976–1985.* Denver, CO: Colorado Outward Bound.

Cordell, B. (1985). Fitness as a Life-Style: The Trend toward Commitment. In *Proceedings: 1985 National Outdoor Recreation Trends Symposium II,* pp. 171–181. Atlanta, GA: National Park Service.

Cordell, K. and Hartmann, L. (1983). Aggregate Trends in Outdoor Recreation in the Two Decades since ORRRC. Paper presented at the Southeastern Recreation Researcher's Conference. February 17–18. Ashville, NC.

——— and Hendee, J. (1982). *Renewable Recreation Resources in the United States: Supply, Demand, and Critical Policy Issues.* Washington, DC: American Forestry Association.

Costilow, A. (1982). *The Leisure Diagnostic Battery: Background, Conceptualization, Structure, Theoretical and Empirical Structure, Remediation and User's Guide.* Denton, TX: Division of Recreation and Leisure Studies, North Texas State University, Office of Special Education, Grant No. G008902257.

Cousineau, C. (1977). *A Delphi Consensus on the Set of Principles for the Development of a Certification System for Educators in Outdoor Adventure.* Ph.D. Dissertation. University of Northern Colorado.

Craik, K. (1986). Personality Research Methods: An Historical Perspective. *Journal of Personality,* 54(1): pp. 18–51.

Crandall, R. (1980). Motivations for Leisure. *Journal of Leisure Research,* 12(1): pp. 45–54.

Crompton, J. and Sellar, C. (1981). A Review of the Literature: Do Outdoor Education Experiences Contribute to Positive Development in the Affective Domain? *Journal of Environmental Education,* 12(4): pp. 21–29.

Crume, C. (1983). *A Study of the Effect of Group Outdoor Activities on the Self-Concept of Physical Education and Recreation Majors.* Ph.D. Dissertation. University of Kentucky.

Csikszentmihalyi, M. (1975). *Beyond Boredom and Anxiety.* San Francisco: Jossey-Bass.

Cullingford, C. (1979). *The Philosophy of Adventure Education. Outdoors,* 10: pp. 4–5.

Cytrynbaum, S. and Ken, K. (1975). The Connecticut Wilderness Program: A Preliminary Evaluation Report. Report submitted to the State of Connecticut Council on Human Services, Hartford, CT.

Darst, P. and Armstrong, G. (1980). *Outdoor Adventure Activites for School and Recreation Programs.* Minneapolis, MN: Burgess Publishing Company.

Davis, R. (1973). Selected Motivational Determinants of Recreational Use of Belle Isle in Detroit. Master's Thesis. University of Michigan.

DeCharms, R. (1968). *Personal Causation: The Internal Affective Determinants of Behavior.* New York: Academic Press.

Deci, E. (1975). *Intrinsic Motivation.* New York: Plenum.

Deep-River Jim. (1923). *Wilderness Trail Book.* Boston: Open Road Publishing Company.

de Grazia, S. (1962). *Of Time, Work, and Leisure.* New York: The Twentieth Century Fund.

DiRenzo, G. (ed.). (1967a). *Concepts, Theory, and Explanation in the Behavioral Sciences.* New York: Random House.

———. (1967b). Conceptual Definition in the Behavioral Sciences. In G. DiRenzo (ed.). *Concepts, Theory, and Explanation in the Behavioral Sciences.* New York: Random House.

Dockery, L. (1986). Off-Shore Manufacturing. *Outside Business,* 11(3): pp. 27–28.

Dorros, S. (1968). *Teaching as a Profession.* Columbus, OH: Charles E. Merrill Publishing Company.

Driver, B. and Brown, P. (1984). Contributions of Behavioral Scientists to Recreation Resource Management. In I. Altman and R. Wohlwill (eds.). *Behavior and the Natural Environment,* pp. 307–339. New York: Plenum.

——— and ———. (1987). Probable Personal Benefits of Outdoor Recreation. In *Proceedings: President's Commission on Americans Outdoors,* pp. 63–70. Washington, DC: Superintendent of Documents.

——— and Rosenthal, D. (1982). *Measuring and Improving Effectiveness of Public Outdoor Recreation Programs.* USDA Forest Service, USDI Bureau of Land Management, and George Washington University.

——— and Tocher, R. (1970). Toward a Behavioral Interpretation of Recreational Engagements, with Implications for Planning. In B. Driver (ed.). *Elements of Outdoor Recreation,* pp. 9–31. Ann Arbor, MI: University of Michigan Press.

Duffy, E. (1957). The Psychological Significance of the Concept of Arousal or Activation. *Psychological Review,* 64: pp. 265–275.

Dunn, D. and Gulbis, J. (1976). The Risk Revolution. *Parks and Recreation,* 11(8): pp. 12–16.

Dustin, D. and McAvoy, L. (1982). The Decline and Fall of Quality Recreation Opportunities and Environments? *Environmental Ethics,* 4: pp. 49–57.

——— and ———. (1984). The Limitation of the Traffic Light. *Journal of Park and Recreation Administration,* 2(3): pp. 28–32.

Ellis, M. (1973). *Why People Play?* Englewood Cliffs, NJ: Prentice-Hall.

Elsnser, G. (1985). Recreation Use Trends: A Forest Service Perspective. In J. Wood (ed.). *Proceedings: 1985 National Outdoor Recreation Trends Symposium II,* pp. 143–147. U.S. Department of the Interior, National Park Service, Southeast Regional Office, Atlanta, GA.

Emerson, R. (1966). Mount Everest: A Case Study in Communication Feedback and Sustained Group Goal Striving. *Sociometry,* 29(3): p. 213.

Emerson, L. and Golins, G. (ed.). (n.d.). *Workbook on Adventure-Based Education.* Denver, CO: Colorado Outward Bound.

Engel, J.; Blackwell, R.; and Miniard, P. (1986). *Consumer Behavior,* 5th ed. Chicago, IL: The Dryden Press.

Epstein, S. (1976). Anxiety, Arousal and the Self-Concept. In I. Sarason and C. Spielberger (eds.). *Stress and Anxiety,* Vol. 3. Washington, DC: Hemisphere Publishing Corporation.

Ewert, A. (1982). *The Effect of Course Length on the Reported Self-Concepts of Selected Outward Bound Participants.* Ph.D. Dissertation, University of Oregon.

———. (1983) Adventure Programming for the Older Adult. *Journal of Physical Education, Recreation and Dance,* 54(3): pp. 64–66.

———. (1983). *Outdoor Adventure and Self-Concept: A Research Analysis.* Eugene, OR: Center of Leisure Studies, University of Oregon.

———. (1985). Why People Climb: The Relationship of Participant Motives and Experience Level to Mountaineering. *Journal of Leisure Research,* 17(3): pp. 241–250.

———. (1985a). Emerging Trends in Outdoor Adventure Recreation. Paper presented at the Outdoor Recreation Trends Symposium II. Myrtle Beach, SC.

———. (1985b). Emerging Trends in Outdoor Adventure Recreation. *Proceedings: 1985 National Outdoor Recreation Trends Symposium II,* pp. 155–165. Atlanta, GA: National Park Service, II.

———. (1985). Risk Recreation: Trends and Issues. *Trends,* 22(3): pp. 4–9.

———. (1985). Identifying Fears in the Outdoor Environment. In *Proceedings: Southeastern Recreation Research.* Athens, GA. Institute for Behavioral Research, University of Georgia.

———. (1986). The Therapeutic Modification of Fear Through Outdoor Adventure Recreation Activities. *Bradford Papers Annual,* 1: pp. 1–10.

———. (1987). Outdoor Adventure Recreation: A Trend Analysis. *Journal of Park and Recreation Administration,* 5(2): pp. 57–67.

———. (1987). Models and Theories in Outdoor Adventure Recreation. *Journal of Outdoor Recreation Research,* 2: pp. 3–16.

———. (1987). Values, Benefits and Consequences in Outdoor Adventure Recreation. In *Proceedings: President's Commission on Americans Outdoors,* pp. 71–80. Washington, DC: U.S. Government of Documents.

———. (1987). Research in Outdoor Adventure Recreation: Analysis and Overview. *The Bradford Papers,* 2: pp. 15–28.

———. (1987). Risk Recreation Poses New Management Problems. *Park Science,* 8(1): pp. 7–8.

Farley, F. (1986). The Big T Personality. *Psychology Today,* pp. 44–52.

Fishbein, M. and Ajzen, J. (1975). *Belief, Attitude, Intention and Behavior: An Introduction to Theory and Practice.* Reading, MA: Addison-Wesley.

Fitzgerald, R. (Trans.) (1963). *The Odyssey.* New York: Doubleday Anchor Books.

Ford, P. (1981). *Principles and Practices of Outdoor/Environmental Education.* New York: John Wiley and Sons.

——— and Blanchard, J. (1985). *Leadership and Administration of Outdoor Pursuits.* State College, PA: Venture Publishing.

Fornader, G. (1973). Report on Mitchell Senior Seminar. Master of Education Report. Boulder, CO: University of Colorado.

Fowler, H. (1966). *Curiosity and Behavior.* New York: MacMillan.

Frant, R.; Roland, C.; and Schempp, P. (1982). Learning Through Outdoor Adventure Education. *Teaching Exceptional Children,* 2: pp. 146–151.

Frigden, J. and Hinkelman, B. (1977). Recreation Behavior and Environment Congruence. Paper presented at the NRPA Research Symposium, National Recreation and Park Association. Las Vegas, NV.

Gass, M. (1987). The Effects of a Wilderness Orientation Program on College Students. *Journal of Experiential Education,* 10(2): pp. 30–33.

Gaston, D.; Plouffe, M.; and Chinsky, J. (1978). *An Empirical Investigation of a Wilderness Adventure Program for Teenagers: The Connecticut Wilderness*

School. ERIC Report No. 178 250.

George, R. (1979). Learning Survival Self-Sufficiency Skills and Participating in a Solo Camping Experience Related to Self-Concept. *Dissertation Abstracts International,* 40: 106A.

———. (1984). Learning Survival Skills, Solo Camping and Improvements in Self-Image: Is There a Relationship? *Psychological Reports,* 55: pp. 168–170.

Gibbons, M. (1974). Walkabout: Searching for the Right Passage from Childhood and School. *Phi Delta Kappan,* 55(9): pp. 596–602.

Glancy, M. (1976). Participant Observation in the Recreation Setting. *Journal of Leisure Research,* 18(2): pp. 55–80.

Godbey, G. (1985). Nonuse of Public Leisure Services: A Model. *Journal of Park and Recreation Administration,* 3(2): pp. 1–12.

Godfrey, R. (1972). *Outward Bound: A Model for Educational Change and Development.* Ph.D. Dissertation. Greely, CO: University of Northern Colorado.

Goldstein, K. (1939). *The Organism.* New York: American Book Company.

Golins, G. (1979). *Utilizing Adventure Education to Rehabilitate Juvenile Delinquents.* Denver, CO: Colorado Outward Bound.

Gould, R. (1975). Adult Life Stages: Growth toward Self-Tolerance. *Psychology Today,* 8: pp. 74–78.

Graber, L. (1976). *Wilderness as Sacred Space.* Washington, DC: Association of American Geographers.

Gray, D. and Ibrahim, H. (eds.). (1985). Recreation Experience—the Human Dimension. *Leisure Today.* In *Journal of Physical Education, Recreation and Dance,* 56(8): pp. 28–58.

Gray, J. (1974). *The Psychology of Fear and Stress.* New York: McGraw-Hill.

Green, P. (1981). *The Content of a College-Level Outdoor Leadership Course for Land-Based Outdoor Pursuits in the Pacific Northwest: A Delphi Consensus.* Ph.D. Dissertation. Eugene, OR: University of Oregon.

———. (1982). *The Outdoor Leadership Handbook.* Tacoma, WA: The Emergency Response Handbook.

Gungberg, H. (1968). *Social Competence and Mental Handicap: An Introduction to Social Education.* Baltimore, MD: Williams and Wilkins.

Haas, G.; Driver, B.; and Brown, P. (1980). Measuring Wilderness Recreation Experiences. *Proceedings of the Wilderness Psychology Group Annual Conference,* pp. 20–40. Durham, NH: University of New Hampshire.

Hackensmith, C. (1966). *History of Physical Education.* New York: Harper and Row.

Hackman, J. (1970). Tasks and Task Performance in Research on Stress. In *Social and Psychological Factors in Stress,* pp. 202–237. Joseph McGraph (ed.). New York: Holt, Rinehart and Winston.

Hale, A. (1978). *Directory: Programs in Outdoor Adventure Activities.* Mankato, MN: Outdoor Experiences.

Hamilton, L. (1981). The Changing Face of American Mountaineering. *Review of Sport and Leisure,* 6(1): pp. 15–36.

Hammerman, D. (1978). Outdoor Education. *Journal of Physical Education and Recreation,* 1: p. 28.

Hammerton, M. and Tickner, A. (1968). An Investigation into the Effects of Stress upon Skilled Performance. *Ergonomics,* 12: pp. 851–855.

Hammitt, W. (1982). Psychological Dimensions and Functions of Wilderness Solitude. pp. 50–60. In F. Boteler (ed.). *Wilderness Psychology Group,*

Morgantown, WV: West Virginia University.

Hamrick, M. and D. Anspaugh. (1983). *Activities for Health Decisions.* Winston-Salem, NC.: Hunter Textbooks, Inc.

Harmon, P. (1974). *The Measurement of Affective Education: A Report of Recent Work by Outward Bound Prepared for the Conference on Outdoor Pursuits in Higher Education.* Denver: Colorado Outward Bound.

——— and Templin, G. (1987). Conceptualizing Experiential Education. In J. Meier, T. Morash, and G. Welton, (eds.). *High Adventure Outdoor Pursuits, 2nd Edition,* pp. 69–77. Columbus, OH: Publishing Horizons.

Hauck, P. (1975). *Overcoming Worry and Fear.* Philadelphia: Westminster Press.

Havens, M. (1985). Ethical Challenges in the Outdoor Setting. *Therapeutic Recreation Journal.* 19(4): pp. 75–80.

Heaps, R. and Thorstenson, C. (1974). Self-Concept Changes Immediately and One Year after Survival Training. *Therapeutic Recreation Journal,* 8(2): pp. 60–63.

Hefferlin, M. (1969). *Dynamics of Academics Reform.* San Francisco: Jossey-Bass.

Heider, F. (1958). *The Psychology of Interpersonal Relations.* New York: John Wiley and Sons.

Hendee, J. and Roggenbuck, J. (1984). Wilderness-Related Education as a Factor Increasing Demand for Wilderness. Paper presented at the International Forest Congress Convention, Quebec City, Canada, August 5, 1984.

Herskowitz, D. (1985). Forecasting for Corporate Planning. *Business Quarterly,* 50(1): pp. 32–35. London, Canada: University of Western Ontario.

Hollenhorst, S. (1986). Towards an Understanding of Adventure and Adventure Education. Unpublished manuscript.

Hornback, K. (1985). Social Trends and Leisure Behavior. *Proceedings: 1985 National Outdoor Recreation Trends Symposium II,* pp. 37–48. Atlanta, GA: National Park Service.

Houston, C. (1968). The Last Blue Mountain. In S. Klausner (ed.). *Why Men Take Chances,* pp. 49–58. New York: Doubleday and Company.

Howard, D. (1985). An Examination of the Decision-Making Process of Consumers of Public Recreation Agency Programs and Services. Paper presented at the 1985 National Recreation and Park Association Symposium on Leisure Research, October.

——— and Crompton, J. (1980). *Financing, Managing, and Marketing Recreation and Park Resources.* Dubuque, IA: Wm. C. Brown.

Howard, G.; Heapes, R.; and Thorstenson, C. (1972). Self-Concept Changes Following Outdoor Survival Training. Provo, UT: Brigham Young Academic Standards Office (Mimeographed).

Huberman, J. (1968). *A Psychological Study of Participants in High Risk Sports.* Ph.D. Dissertation. University of British Columbia.

Hunt, J. (1986). *Ethical Issues in Experiential Education.* Boulder, CO: Association of Experiential Education.

Hunter, R. (1984). The Impact of Voluntary Selection Procedures on the Reported Success of Outdoor Rehabilitation Programs. *Therapeutic Recreation Journal,* 3: pp. 38–44.

Iida, M. (1975). Adventure Oriented Programs: A Review of Research. In *Research in Camping and Environmental Education.* Proceedings from the National Research Workshop, Pennsylvania State University.

Iso-Ahola, S. (1976). On the Theoretical Link between Personality and Leisure.

Psychological Reports, 39: pp. 3–10.

———. (1980). *The Social Psychology of Leisure and Recreation.* Dubuque, IA: Wm. C. Brown.

James, T. (1980). *Education at the Edge.* Denver, CO: Colorado Outward Bound.

Johanson, K. M. (Comp.). (1984). *Accepted Peer Practices in Adventure Programming.* Boulder, CO: Association of Experiential Education.

Johnson, D. and Johnson, R. (1983). The Socialization and Achievement Crises: Are Cooperative Learning Experiences the Solution? In L. Brickman (ed.). *Applied Social Psychology Annual,* Vol. 4. Beverly Hills, CA: Sage Publications.

Johnson, R.; Johnson, D.; and Tauer, M. (1979). The Effects of Cooperative, Competitive and Individualistic Goal Structures on Students' Attitudes and Achievement. *Journal of Psychology,* 102: pp. 191–198.

Jones, C. (1978). *An Evaluation of the Effects of an Outward Bound Type of Program upon the Self-Concepts and Academic Achievement of High School Students.* Ph.D. Dissertation. Boston: Boston University School of Education.

Jones, G. (1964). *A History of the Vikings.* Cambridge: Oxford University Press.

Kalisch, K. (1979). *The Role of the Instructor.* Three Lakes, WI: Wheaton College.

Kaplan, J. (1974). Cognitive Learning in the Out-of-Doors. Master's Thesis. The Pennsylvania State University.

Kaplan, R. (1984). Wilderness Perception and Psychological Benefits: An Analysis of a Continuing Program. *Leisure Sciences,* 6(3): pp. 271–290.

Kaplan, S. and Talbot, J. (1983). Psychological Benefits of a Wilderness Experience. In I. Altman and J. Wohlwill (eds.). *Behavior and the Natural Environment,* pp. 163–204. New York: Plenum.

Katz, R. and Kolb, D. (1968). Outward Bound and Education for Personal Growth. In F. Kelly and D. Baer (eds.). *Outward Bound Schools as an Alternative to Institutionalization for Adolescent Delinquent Boys.* Boston: Fandel Press.

Kelly, F. (1974). Outward Bound and Delinquency: A Ten Year Experience. In *Major Papers Presented at the Conference on Experiential Education. Estes Park, CO., October.* Denver: Colorado Outward Bound.

Kelly, F. and Baer, D. (1968). *Outward Bound: An Alternative to Institutionalization for Adolescent Delinquent Boys.* Boston, MA: Fandel Press.

———. (1969). Jesness Inventory and Self-Concept Measures for Delinquents before and after Participation in Outward Bound. *Psychological Reports,* 25: pp. 719–724.

———. (1971). Physical Challenges as a Treatment for Delinquency. *Crime and Delinquency,* 17: pp. 437–445.

Kelly, J. (1982). *Leisure.* Englewood Cliffs, NJ: Prentice-Hall.

———. (1985). *Recreation Business.* New York: John Wiley and Sons.

———. (1986). Investment Theory: Long-term Benefits: In R. Lucas (Comp.). *Proceedings—National Wilderness Research Conference: Current Research,* pp. 393–397. Fort Collins, CO: General Technical Report INT-212. Ogden, UT: Intermountain Research Station.

Kephant, H. (1917). *Camping and Woodcraft.* New York: MacMillan.

Kerlinger, F. (1973). *Foundations of Behavior Research.* New York: Holt, Rinehart and Winston.

Keyes, R. (1985). *Changing It.* Boston: Little, Brown, and Company.

Klausner, S. (ed.). (1968). *Why Men Take Chances.* New York: Anchor Books.

Kleinman, G. (1984). The Attractive Enemy. Paper presented at Chautauqua Lecture Series. Chautauqua, NY.

Knapp, C. (1986). The Science and Art of Processing Outdoor Experiences. *The Outdoor Communicator,* 16(1): pp. 13–17.

Knopf, R. and Lime, D. (1984). *A Recreation Manager's Guide to Understanding River Use and Users.* USDA Forest Service General Technical Report WO-38.

——— and Schreyer, R. (1985). The Problem of Bias in Recreation Resource Decision-Making. In D. Dustin (ed.). *The Management of Human Behavior in Outdoor Recreation Settings,* pp. 23–27. San Diego, CA: San Diego State University's Institute for Leisure Behavior.

Knudson, D. (1980). *Outdoor Recreation.* New York: MacMillan.

Kraft, R. (1985). Towards a Theory of Experiential Learning. In R. Kraft (ed.). *The Theory of Experiential Education,* pp. 4–35. Boulder, CO: Association of Experiential Education.

Lacy, P. (ed.). (1978). *Great Adventures that Changed the World.* Pleasantville, NY: Readers Digest Association, Inc.

Lambert, M. (1978). Reported Self-Concept and Self-Acutalizing Value Changes as a Function of Academic Classes with Wilderness Experience. *Perceptual and Motor Skills,* 46: pp. 1035–1040.

LaPage, W. (1983). Recreation Resource Management for Visitor Satisfaction. In S. Lieber and D. Fesenmaier (eds.). *Recreation Planning and Management.* State College, PA: Venture Publishing Company.

Leonard, R.; Wexler, A.; Siri, W.; and Bower, D. (1956). *Belaying the Leader.* San Francisco: Sierra Club.

Levinson, D. (1978). *The Seasons of a Man's Life.* New York: Alfred A. Knopf.

Levitt, E. (1980). *The Psychology of Anxiety.* Hillsdale, NJ: Lawrence Erlbaum Associates.

Lierheimer, A. (1970). Changing the Palace Guard. *Phi Delta Kappan,* pp. 20–25.

Lowenstein, D. (1975). *Wilderness Adventure Programs: An Activity Profile.* ERIC Report ED 127 102.

Manning, R. (1986). *Studies in Outdoor Recreation.* Corvallis, OR: Oregon State University.

Market Opinion Research. (1986). *Participation in Outdoor Recreation Among American Adults and the Motivations Which Drive Participation.* New York: National Geographical Society.

Marsh, H.; Richards, G.; and Barnes, J. (1986). Multidimensional Self-Concepts: The Effect of Participation in an Outward Bound Program. *Journal of Personality and Social Psychology,* 50(1): pp. 195–204.

Maslow, A. (1943). A Theory of Human Motivation. *Psychological Review,* 50: pp. 370–396.

———. (1962). *Toward a Psychology of Being.* Princeton, NJ: D. Van Nostrand.

Mason, J. (1978). *Uncertain Outposts: The Future of Camping and the Challenge of Its Past.* Bradford Woods, Martinsville, ID: American Camping Association.

Mattews, B. (1976). *Adventure Education and Self-Concept: An Annotated Bibliography with Appendix.* ERIC Report ED 160 287.

McAvoy, L. (1978). Outdoor Leadership Training. *Journal of Physical Education, Recreation and Dance,* 4: pp. 18–19.

———. (1987). The Experiential Components of a High Adventure Program. In J. Meier, T. Morash, and G. Welton (eds.). *High Adventure Outdoor Pursuits,* pp. 200–210. Columbus, OH: Publishing Horizons.

McBride, D. (1984). *The Behaviors of Adolescent Boys in a Residential Treatment Center during High Ropes Course Experience.* Ph.D. Dissertation. The Ohio State University.

McCall, G. and Simmons, J. (eds.). (1969). *Issues in Participant Observation: A Text and Reader.* Reading, MA: Addison-Wesley.

McClellan, G. (1986). The Future of Outdoor Recreation: What the Trends Tell Us. *Parks and Recreation,* 21(5): pp. 45–48, 63.

McDonald, D. (1983). *The Effect of Participation in an Outdoor Experiential Education Program on Self-Concepts.* Ph.D. Dissertation. Oklahoma State University.

McGowan, M. (1986). Self-Efficacy: Operationalizing Challenge Education. *Bradford Papers Annual,* 1: pp. 65–69.

McNamara, E. (1971). *A Comparison of the Learning Behaviors on Eighth and Ninth Grade ESCP Earth Science Students; One Half Experiencing Laboratory Investigations in the Indoor Environment, the Other Half Experiencing Laboratory Investigations in the Outdoor Environment.* Ph.D. Dissertation. The Pennsylvania State University.

Meier, J. (1977). Risk Recreation: Exploration and Implications. Paper presented at the Congress for Recreation and Parks, Las Vegas, NV.

———. (1978). Is the Risk Worth Taking? *Leisure Today,* 49(4): pp. 7–9.

———; Morash, T.; and Welton, G. (1987). *High Adventure Outdoor Pursuits,* 2d ed. Columbus, OH: Publishing Horizons.

Meldrum, K. (1971). Particpation in Outdoor Activities in Selected Countries in Western Europe: Climbing, Canoeing, Caving, and Skiing. *Comparative Education,* 7: pp. 137–142.

Mescon, M.; Albert, M.; and Khedouri, F. (1981). *Management: Individual and Organizational Effectiveness.* Cambridge, MA: Harper and Row.

Metcalfe, J. (1976). *Adventure Programming.* Austin, TX: National Educational Laboratory Publishing, Inc.

Meyer, D. (1979). The Management of Risk. *Journal of Experiential Education,* 2(2): pp. 9–14.

Miner, J. and Boldt, J. (1981). *Outward Bound USA: Learning Through Experience in Adventure-Based Education.* New York: William Morrow and Company.

Mitchell, R. (1983). *Mountain Experience: The Psychology and Sociology of Adventure.* Chicago: University of Chicago.

Morse, W. (1951). An Interdisciplinary Therapeutic Camp. *Journal of Social Issues,* 13(1): pp. 3–14.

Mortlock, C. (1975). *Adventure Education and Outdoor Pursuits.* Keswick, England: Ferguson.

———. (1978). *Adventure Education.* Keswick, England: Ferguson.

———. (1983). *Adventure Education and Outdoor Pursuits.* Keswick, England: Ferguson.

Moses, D. (1968). *Improving Academic Performance.* Provo, UT: Brigham Young University.

——— and Peterson, D. (1970). *Academic Achievement Helps Program.* Provo, UT: Brigham Young University, Academic Office.

Murphy, J. (1981). *Concepts of Leisure,* 2d ed. Englewood Cliffs, NJ: Prentice-Hall.

——— and Howard, D. (1975). *Recreation and Leisure Services: A Humanistic Perspective.* Dubuque, IA: William C. Brown.

Nash, R. (1967). *Wilderness and the American Mind.* New Haven, CT: Yale University Press.

Nelson, N. and Martin, W. (1976). *Project BACSTOP Evaluation Report, 1974*-1975. ERIC Report ED 198 992.

Newton, A. (1968). *Travel and Travelers of the Middle Ages.* London: Barnes and Noble.

Nold, J. (1978). Profiles in Adventure. Denver: Colorado Outward Bound School. Staff Development Paper, 21 pages.

Noyce, W. (1958). *The Springs of Adventure.* New York: The World Publishing Company.

Nurenberg, S. (1985). Psychological Development of Borderline Adolescents in Wilderness Therapy. *Dissertation Abstracts International,* 46(11): 142A.

Nye, R. (1976). The Influence of an Outward Bound Program on the Self-Concept of the Participants. *Dissertation Abstracts International,* 37: 142A.

O'Connor, C. (1971). Study of Personality Needs Involved in the Selection of Specific Leisure Interest Groups. *Dissertation Abstracts International,* 31(11): 5865A.

O'Morrow, G. (1980). *Therapeutic Recreation: A Helping Profession.* Reston VA: Reston Publishing Company.

Orlick, T. (1982). *The Second Cooperative Sports and Games Book.* New York: Pantheon Books.

Parker, T. (1970). *An Approach to Outdoor Activities.* London: Parkam Books Ltd.

Patterson, C. (1972). *Humanistic Education.* Englewood Cliffs, NJ: Prentice-Hall.

Pedhazur, E. (1982). *Multiple Regression in Behavioral Research.* New York: Holt, Rinehart and Winston.

Petrie, A.; Collins, W.; and Solomon, P. (1958). Pain Sensitivity, Sensory Deprivation and Susceptiblity to Satiation. *Science,* 12(1): pp. 45–54.

Petty, M. and Norton, E. (1987). The Dollars and Cents of Outdoor Recreation on the National Forests. *Trends,* 24(3): pp. 40–43.

Petzoldt, P. (1974). *The Wilderness Handbook.* New York: W. W. Norton and Company.

Phipps, M. (1985). Adventure—An Inner Journey to the Self: The Psychology of Adventure Expressed in Jungian Terms. *Adventure Education Journal,* 2(4/5): pp. 11–17.

Pollack, R. (1976). *An Annotated Bibliography of the Literature and Research on Outward Bound and Related Programs.* ERIC Report No. 171 476.

Powell, F. and Verner, J. (1982). Anxiety and Performance Relationships in First Time Parachutists. *Journal of Sport Psychology,* 4: pp. 184–188.

Potts, V. (1974). *Project BACSTOP Evaluation Report, 1973–1974.* Battle Creek, MI: Michigan Department of Education, Battle Creek Public Schools.

President's Commission on Americans Outdoors. (1986). *A Literature Review.* Washington, DC: U.S. Government Printing Office.

———. (1987). *Americans and the Outdoors.* Washington, DC: Superintendent of Documents.

Pride, W. and Ferrell, O. (1985). *Marketing: Basic Concepts and Decisions.* Boston: Houghton Mifflin Company.

Priest, S. (1987). An International Survey of Outdoor Leadership Preparation. *Journal of Experiential Education,* 10(2): pp. 34–39.

Progen, J. (1979). Man, Nature, and Sport. In E. Gerber and M. Nillian (eds.). *Sports and the Body: A Philosophical Symposium,* pp. 237–242. Philadelphia, Lea and Febiger.

Rachman, S. (1974). *The Meanings of Fear.* Baltimore, MD: Penguin Books, Inc.

———. (1978). *Fear and Courage.* San Francisco: W. H. Freeman and Company.

Ratner, S. (1975). Animal's Defenses: Fighting in Predator-Prey Relations. In P. Pliner and J. Alloway (eds.). *Advances in the Study of Communication and Affect; Non-Verbal Communication of Aggression.* New York: Plenum.

Reinharz, S. (1979). *Social Science.* San Francisco: Jossey-Bass.

Resnik, H. and Reuben, H. (1975). *Emergency Psychiatric Care.* Bowie, MA: Charles Press.

Rhoades, J. (1972). *The Problem of Individual Change in Outward Bound: An Application of Change and Transfer Theory.* Ph.D. Dissertation. University of Massachusetts.

Rillo, T. (1984). MegaTrends in Outdoor Education: Past, Present and Future. *Journal of Outdoor Education,* p. 18.

Robb, G. and Ewert, A. (1987). Risk Recreation and Persons with Disabilities. *Therapeutic Recreation Journal.* 2(1): pp. 58–69.

Robbins, S. (1976). *Outdoor Wilderness Survival and Its Psychological and Sociological Effects upon Students in Changing Human Behavior.* Ph.D. Dissertation. Brigham Young University.

Roberts, A. (1988). Wilderness Programs for Juvenile Offenders: A Challenging Alternative. *Juvenile and Family Journal,* 39(1): pp. 1–12.

Roberts, D. (1985). The Growth of Adventure Travel. *1000 Adventures: With Tales of Discovery.* New York: Harmony Books.

Rogers, C. (1961). *On Becoming a Person.* New York: Houghton Mifflin.

Roland, C. and Havens, M. (1981). *An Introduction to Adventure: A Sequential Approach to Challenging Activities with Persons Who Are Disabled.* Loretto, MN: The Vinland National Center.

———. (1983). *Why Have Persons Who Have Disabilities Been Traditionally Excluded from Adventure Programs?* The Deluxe Check Printers Foundation.

——— and Hoyt, J. (1984). Family Adventure Programming. In G. Robb (ed.). *The Bradford Papers,* 4: pp. 19–28. Indiana University Press.

———; Summers, S.; Friedman, M.; Barton, G.; and McCarthy, K. (1987). Creation of an Experiential Challenge Program. *Therapeutic Recreation Journal,* 21(2): pp. 54–63.

Rossman, B. and Ulehla, J. (1977). Psychological Reward Values Associated with Wilderness Use: A Functional Reinforcement Approach. *Environment and Behavior,* 9: pp. 41–66.

Sax, J. (1980). *Mountains without Handrails: Reflections on the National Parks.* Ann Arbor, MI: University of Michigan Press.

Schraer, H. (1954). Survival Education: A Survey of Trends in Survival Education in Certain Public School and Teacher Training Institutions and a Detailed Study of the Elements of Survival Education Found in the Programs of the Boy Scouts and Girl Scouts of America. *Dissertation Abstracts International,* 14: 1966A.

Schreyer, R. and Knopf, R. (1984). The Dynamics of Change in Outdoor Recreation Environments—Some Equity Issues. *Journal of Park and Recreation Administration,* 2(1): pp. 9–19.

——— and Roggenbuck, J. (1978). The Influence of Experience Expectations on Crowding Perceptions and Socio-Psychological Carrying Capacities. *Leisure Sciences,* 4: pp. 373–394.

——— and White, R. (1979). A Conceptual Model of High-Risk Recreation. *Proceedings: First Annual Conference on Recreation Planning and Development.* New York: American Society of Civil Engineers.

———; White, R.; and McCool, S. (1980). Common Attributes Uncommonly Exercised. In J. Meier, T. Morash, and G. Welton (eds.). *High Adventure Outdoor Pursuits,* pp. 24–29. Columbus, OH: Publishing Horizons.

Schroeder, T. and Wiens, M. (1986). The Non-Use of Public Park and Recreation Facilities in Tulsa. *Journal of Park and Recreation Administration,* 4(3): pp. 75–87.

Scorsby, W. (1971). A Survey of the National Outdoor Leadership School, Lander, WY. Masters Thesis. Montclair State College.

Scott, D. (1974). *Big Wall Climbing.* New York: Oxford University Press.

Scott, N. (1974). Toward a Psychology of Wilderness Experience. *Natural Resources Journal,* 14: pp. 231–237.

Searle, M. and Jackson, E. (1985). Recreation Non-Participation and Barriers to Participation: Considerations for the Management of Recreation Delivery Systems. *Journal of Park and Recreation Administration,* 3(2): pp. 23–35.

Sears, G. (1920). *Woodcraft.* New York: Forest and Stream Publishing.

Senosk, M. (1977). An Examination of Outdoor Pursuit Leader Certification and Licensing within the United States in 1976. Masters Thesis. University of Oregon.

Seton, E. (1912). *The Book of Woodcraft.* Garden City, NY: Garden City Publishing Company, Inc.

Severin, T. (1947b). *The Brendan Voyage.* New York: McGraw-Hill.

Seyle, H. (1950). *The Psychology and Pathology of Exposure to Stress.* Montreal, Canada: ACTA Publishers.

Siedentop, D. (1980). *Physical Education: Introductory Analysis.* Dubuque, IA: Wm. C. Brown.

———; Herkowitz, J.; and Rink, J. (1984). *Elementary Physical Education Methods.* Englewood Cliffs, NJ: Prentice-Hall.

Siehl, G. (1985). Federal Trends in Outdoor Recreation Policy. Paper presented at the Outdoor Recreation Trends Symposium II. Myrtle Beach, SC.

Shore, A. (1977). *Outward Bound: A Reference Volume.* Greenwich, CT: Topp Litho.

Shorey, P. (Trans.) (1953). *Plato*—The Republic. Cambridge: Loeb Classical Library, Harvard University Press.

Slawski, C. (1981). *Social Psychological Theories: A Comparative Handbook for Students.* Glenview, IL: Scott, Foresman and Company.

Slovic, P. (1972). Information Processing, Situation Specificity, and the Generality of Risk-Taking Behavior. *Journal of Personality and Social Psychology,* 22: pp. 128–134.

Slusher, H. (1967). *Man, Sport and Existence: A Critical Analysis.* Philadelphia: Lea and Febiger.

Smith, S. and Ng, D. (1982). *Perspectives on the Nature of Leisure Research.* Waterloo, Canada: University of Waterloo Press.

Smith, T. (1982). Self-Concept, Special Populations and Outdoor Therapy. In G. Robb (ed.). *The Bradford Papers,* 2: pp. 1–15.

———. (1985a). Outdoor Therapy: Dangling Ropes and Solid Foundations. In G.

Robb and P. Hamilton (eds.). *The Bradford Papers,* 5: pp. 63–68.

———. (1985b). Issues in Challenge Education. In G. Robb and P. Hamilton (eds.). *Issues in Challenge Education and Adventure Programming.* Martinsville, IN: Bradford Woods, Indiana University Press.

Staley, F. (1979). The Research, Evaluation and Measurement Dragons in Outdoor Education. Paper presented at the National Outdoor Education Association Meeting, Lake Placid, NY.

Stefansson, V. (1950). *Artic Manual.* New York: MacMillan.

Stegner, W. (1961). The Wilderness Idea. In P. Brower (ed.). *America's Living Heritage,* pp. 97–102. San Francisco: The Sierra Club.

Stich, T. (1983). Experiential Therapy for Psychiatric Patients. *Journal of Experiential Education,* 5(3): pp. 23–30.

Stogner, J. (1978). *The Effects of a Wilderness Experience on Self-Concept and Academic Performance.* Ph.D. Dissertation. Blacksburg, VA: Virginia Polytechnic Institute and State University.

———. (1979). The Effects of a Wilderness Experience on Self-Concept and Academic Performance. *Dissertation Abstracts International,* 39: 4704A.

Stowell, S. (1967). *On Top of the World.* New York: MacMillan.

Stromberg, R. W. (1969). *A History of Western Civilization.* Homewood, IL: The Dorsey Press.

Swiderski, M. (1981). *Outdoor Leadership Competencies Identified by Outdoor Leaders in Five Western Regions.* Ph.D. Dissertation. Eugene, OR: University of Oregon.

Tejada-Flores, L. (1973). *Games Climbers Play.* Englewood Cliffs, NJ: Prentice-Hall.

Templin, G. (n.d.). The Element of Stress. In L. Emerson and G. Golins (eds.). *Workbook on Adventure-Based Education.* Denver, CO: Colorado Outward Bound.

Theobald, W. (1979). *Evaluation of Recreation and Park Programs. New York: John Wiley and Sons.*

Thomas, S. (Comp.) (1986). *Adventure Education: A Bibliography,* rev. ed. Amherst, NY: Institute on Classroom Management and School Discipline at State University of New York at Buffalo.

Tinsley, H. and Johnson, T. (1984). A Preliminary Taxonomy of Leisure Activities. *Journal of Leisure Research,* 16(3): pp. 234–244.

——— and Kass, R. (1979). The Latent Structure of the Need Satisfying Properties of Leisure Activities. *Journal of Leisure Research,* 11(4): pp. 278–291.

Underhill, A. H. (1981). Population Dynamics and Demography. *Journal of Physical Education and Recreation.* 52(8): p. 33.

Vander Wilt, R. and Klocke, R. (1971). Self-Actualization of Females in an Experimental Orientation Program (Experiential Studies Program at Mankato State College, in conjunction with the Minnesota Outward Bound School). *National Association of Women Deans and Counselors Journal,* 34(3): pp. 125–129.

Van Doren, C. (1984). State Park Systems. In M. Clawson and C. Van Doren (eds.). *Statistics on Outdoor Recreation,* pp. 235–244. Washington, DC: Resources for the Future.

———. (1985). Social Trends and Social Indicators: The Private Sector. In *Proceedings: 1985 National Outdoor Recreation Trends Symposium II,* pp. 13–23. Atlanta, GA: National Park Service.

——— and Hodges, L. (1975). *America's Park and Recreation Heritage.* Washington, DC: Government Printing Office.

Van Horne, M.; Szwak, L.; and Randall, S. (1985). Outdoor Recreation Activity Trends—Insights from the 1982-83 Nationwide Recreation Survey. Paper presented at the Outdoor Recreation Trends Symposium II. Myrtle Beach, SC.

Vinton, D. and Farley, E. (eds.). (1979). *Camp Staff Training Series.* Bradford Woods, Martinsville, ID: American Camping Association.

Vogl, R. and Vogl, S. (1974). *Outdoor Education and Its Contributions to Environmental Quality: A Research Analysis.* Austin, TX: National Educational Laboratory Publishers, Inc.

Walsh, V. and Golins, G. (1975). *The Exploration of the Outward Bound Process.* Denver, CO: Colorado Outward Bound.

Webb, E.; Campbell, D.; Schwartz, R.; and Sechrest, L. (1966). *Unobtrusive Measures: Nonreactive Research in the Social Sciences.* Chicago: Rand McNally and Company.

Wenker, K. (1984). *Foundations of Professional Morality.* Colorado Springs, CO: United States Air Force Academy.

West, P. (1981). *Vestiges of a Cage.* Natural Resources Sociology Research Lab, Monograph 1. Ann Arbor, MI: University of Michigan.

Wetmore, R. (1972). *The Influence of Outward Bound School Experience on the Self-Concept of Adolescent Boys.* Ph.D. Dissertation. Boston University.

White, B. (1978). Risk Recreation: Exploration and Implications. Paper delivered at the Congress for Recreation and Parks. Las Vegas, NV.

White, R. (1959). Motivation Reconsidered: The Concept of Competence. *Psychological Review,* 56: pp. 297-333.

Whymper, E. (1871). *Scrambles Amongst the Alps: In the Years 1860-1869.* Reprinted by Ten Speed Press, Berkeley, CA, 1981.

Wilder, R. (1977). *EEI: A Survival Tool. Parks and Recreation,* 12(8): pp. 22-24, 50-51.

Wildland Research Center, University of California. (1962). *Wilderness and Recreation*—A Report on Resources, Values, and Problems. ORRRC Report No. 3. Washington, DC: U.S. Government Printing Office.

Willman, H. and Chun, R. (1973). Homeward Bound: An Alternative to the Institutionalization of Adjudicated Juvenile Offenders. *Federal Probation,* 37(3): pp. 52-58.

Wilson, R. (1981). *Inside Outward Bound.* Charlotte, NC: The East Woods Press.

Wilson, W. (1977). *Social Discontent and the Growth of Wilderness Sport in America: 1965-1974. Quest,* Winter, 27.

Wright, A. (1982). *Therapeutic Potential of the Outward Bound Process: An Evaluation of a Treatment Program for Juvenile Delinquents.* Ph.D. Dissertation. Pennsylvania State University.

Yenser, S. (1972). Personal and Interpersonal Effects of Outdoor Survival. Master's Thesis. Brigham Young University.

Yerkes, R. (1985). High Adventure Recreation in Organized Camping. *Trends,* 22(3): pp. 10-11.

——— and Dodson, J. (1908). The Relation of Strength of Stimulus to Rapidity of Habit-Formation. *Journal of Comparative and Neurological Psychology,* 18: pp. 459-482.

Young, R. (1983). Toward an Understanding of Wilderness Participation. *Leisure Sciences,* 4: pp. 339-357.

——— and Crandall, R. (1984). Wilderness Use of Self-Actualization. *Journal of*

Leisure Research, 16(2): pp. 149–160.

Zook, L. (1986). Outdoor Adventure Programs Build Character Five Ways. *Parks and Recreation,* 21(1): pp. 54–57.

Zuckerman, M. (1971). Dimensions of Sensation-Seeking. *Journal of Consulting and Clinical Psychology,* 36: pp. 45–52.

———. (1979). *Sensation-Seeking: Beyond the Optimal Level of Arousal.* Hillsdale, NJ: Lawrence Erlbaum.

———. (1985). Biological Foundations of the Sensation-Seeking Temperment. In J. Strelau, F. Farley, and A. Gale (eds.). *The Biological Bases of Personality and Behavior,* pp. 97–113. Washington, DC: Hemisphere.

Zweig, P. (1974). *The Adventurer: The Fate of Adventure in the Western World.* New York: Basic Books.

INDEX